The Colonial
Architecture of Salem

PLATE I. — Andrew-Safford Entrance Porch, 13 Washington Square.
Erected 1818.

The Colonial
Architecture of Salem

By

Frank Cousins and Phil M. Riley

DOVER PUBLICATIONS, INC.
Mineola, New York

Bibliographical Note

This Dover edition, first published in 2000, is an unabridged republication of the edition first published by Little, Brown, and Company in 1919.

International Standard Book Number: 0-486-41250-4

Manufactured in the United States of America
Dover Publications, Inc., 31 East 2nd Street, Mineola, N.Y. 11501

Foreword

MUCH has been written about the fine old architecture of Salem. The most noted residences and other edifices have often provided subject material for magazine articles and chapters in volumes devoted to historic homes and Colonial furnishings; writers have described their rambles about the quaint and handsome streets; antiquaries have expatiated on the beautiful wood-carving, ironwork, brasses, furniture and wall papers; architects have exalted the exquisite detail and fine proportions of the doorways and mantels, and hailed Salem as among the greatest storehouses of American antiquities; and the publications of the Essex Institute and other historical and genealogical societies have compiled and presented much interesting data regarding important persons, places and things. This miscellany of subjects has been treated at random, however, and is widely scattered through so many forms of literature as to constitute a voluminous and ill-assorted library in itself.

But Salem architecture is such an important and many-sided subject as to deserve more ambitious and unified treatment, yet strangely enough no attempt has ever been made to gather and present in a single volume in chronological sequence and logical classification, from the viewpoint of the home-builder and the architect, the whole array of Colonial architecture in Salem from its settlement in 1626 to the cessation of Colonial development in 1818, exactly a century ago, and the advent of Greek revival influence shortly afterward.

The hearty welcome and extensive sale accorded "The Wood-Carver of Salem" in 1916, devoted as it was to the work of only one man in a single period between the years 1782 and 1811, has led the authors to undertake this larger task and to present the results of their collaboration in a companion volume. It is believed that the wider scope and broader appeal of the present book will meet a still greater demand that has long existed, for its predecessor merely scratched the surface of Salem building lore.

In terms of the so-called Colonial style, our national building heritage, Salem is the architectural center of New England, and to New England and Virginia we instinctively accord the highest places in our regard as the principal fountains of American culture and development. But the architecture of Virginia implies the great estate; it is neither for the town nor the person of moderate means. Thus in Salem oftener than elsewhere do leading architects and intelligent home-builders find inspiration for modern adaptation. Indeed, this fascinating city has become a synonym for the best in Colonial architecture, especially doorways and chimney pieces. Variety and the opportunity for comparison render Salem architecture unique and especially valuable in that it embraces four dissimilar types developed in as many distinct periods.

First came the primitive, small, gable-roof cabin or cottage, and almost simultaneously the larger peaked-roof or many-gabled houses patterned after English Elizabethan prototypes. Soon, however, the growing custom of enlarging gable-roof houses with a lean-to addition along one side produced a new and distinctive mass and picturesque contour of roof line which was prevalent about the time of the witchcraft delusion of 1692. Early in the eighteenth century came the gambrel-roof type, adapted from the French of Mansard, but with characteristics, in most Salem instances as else-where throughout New England, so unlike similar structures about New York and in the South as to impart decided local color. Following the Revolution, Salem architecture reached the pinnacle of its development in the square three-story house. Until about 1810 most square houses were of wood, but thereafter brick construction increased and in 1818, after which year the architectural decadence began to manifest itself, brick houses prevailed.

The fourth period therefore consists of two divisions so clearly marked by the difference in constructive materials as almost to be designated as separate periods. In none of these four periods do Salem houses aspire to the manorial splendor of the South, but each house type frankly interprets the refinement, the domestic spirit and simple dignity of the people, both in the prosperous period of brick construction and the earlier days when the meager comforts of the wooden cottage sufficed.

Strictly speaking, the first two periods constitute the only truly Colonial houses in Salem, but the custom everywhere is to place in the Colonial category all buildings with Renaissance detail up to the beginning of the so-called Greek revival. This is logical and proper, inasmuch as the structures erected immediately preceding and following the Revolution represent direct developments of their simpler predecessors and hence are very closely related to them. Such a broad interpretation of the meaning of the word Colonial seems especially appropriate with regard to Salem architecture because it did not attain the full measure of its development until after the Revolution.

The word Provincial has been suggested as a more accurate substitute for Colonial, the argument being that little worthy of serious architectural consideration to-day was erected in America before the Provincial period in our history. On this basis those splendid houses built during the first three or four decades of our national life might well be called Federal. But the word matters far less than its meaning, provided the latter be well understood. The term Colonial has long since received the stamp of popular approval and become a familiar byword, while the architecture it designates, very largely because of its very comprehensiveness and varied local color, expresses our national spirit as nearly as we have been able to give it expression. Indeed, it is so inseparably associated with our glorious history, and so inexhaustible in its possibilities for modern adaptation, that there appears to be no prospect that it will be supplanted as the American national style.

So great is the wealth of subject material in Salem that much of genuine merit has of necessity been omitted from these pages. Exigencies of space obliged the choice to be restricted to the best and most typical examples in each period, first preference being given to architectural excellence and second to historic interest. No attempt has been made to tell the complete story of Salem architecture; the aim has been rather to tell the story of Colonial architecture in Salem. The work covers the four periods from 1628 to 1818, aggregating 190 years, and this explains the omission of several prominent public buildings not of Colonial character and erected since the latter date. The omission of a few well-known Colonial houses in what is commonly understood to be the Greater Salem of to-day, such as the Page Tavern in Danvers, for example, is accounted for by the fact that several adjacent communities, once parts of Salem, were not parts of that town at the time the houses in question were erected, Marblehead being set off in 1648, Beverly in 1668, Danvers in 1752, while Peabody was set off from Danvers in 1855.

Mr. Cousins, in gathering and preparing the illustrations, and Mr. Riley, in writing the text, owe much to the generous assistance of Mr. John Robinson, of the Peabody Museum, who offered many helpful suggestions and furnished much of the historical data.

FRANK COUSINS AND PHIL M. RILEY.

APRIL 1, 1919

Contents

[xi]

List of Plates

[xiii]

List of Plates

List of Plates

[xv]

List of Plates

List of Plates

[xvii]

List of Plates

List of Plates

[xix]

List of Plates

List of Plates

[xxi]

List of Plates

[xxii]

List of Plates

The Colonial Architecture of Salem

CHAPTER I

THE GABLE AND PEAKED-ROOF HOUSE

IN Salem, as in most other early settled communities of America, some at least of the first houses were probably log cabins; simple, gable-roof structures a single story or at most a story and a half in height. According to tradition the first dwelling erected on the soil of old Naumkeag by the "planters" under the Sheffield patent in 1626 was for their leader, Roger Conant, but its character is not recorded. Little is definitely known about the pioneer architecture of those days, but its primitive character rendered it virtually without interest to the architect or prospective home-builder of the present time.

Such rustic makeshifts were of short duration, however. When Governor John Endecott arrived in 1628, as the representative of the Dorchester Company, he brought with him skilled men of all trades, and the work of the builders among them continued along the general lines of their previous training. It was inevitable that aggressive men of the resolution necessary to venture the dangers and hardships of the new world should soon aspire to replace former comforts in the freer atmosphere of their new surroundings. Being home-loving British people who had emigrated for no lack of love for their native land, but merely to wring a livelihood from New England lands and waters unmolested by the obnoxious acts of the king, it was natural that their early architecture should have been patterned after that of the mother country, for in England more than in any other land have the ideals of what a home and home life implies been realized.

And such was indeed the case, though the translation to wood, the most plentiful and easily obtainable building material, so altered characteristic appearance as almost to conceal the origin and virtually to create new house types. We are thus reminded that as early as the sixteenth century wood ceased to be a building material of moderate cost in England. The more pretentious manor houses, churches and public buildings, were being erected of quarried stone; Flemish brickwork had influenced the last phase of Gothic in England, and most ordinary buildings were still of half-timber work filled in between with rubble masonry or plaster on oak laths.

Salem began its architectural history during the transition period in England from Early to Classic

Renaissance, so that two influences were almost simultaneous in American building. That one really preceded the other, however, and was of short duration seems to be proved conclusively by the scarcity of examples extant as compared with the abundance of houses of every later type. The first Salem houses of note, therefore, were patterned after the Elizabethan and Jacobean types developed during the periods 1558–1603 and 1603–1625, when some of the Tudor characteristics of Perpendicular, the last phase of English Gothic, were combined with classic orders and ornament considerably modified and subordinately used. The English classic, or so-called Georgian, was adopted a few years afterward, and, as will appear in later chapters, took unto itself American characteristics no less distinctive than those adapted from earlier sources.

Thus the transplanting of the rambling Elizabethan dwelling and its construction entirely of wood gave us the little less picturesque many-gabled houses of Salem which have been immortalized by Nathaniel Hawthorne in "The House of the Seven Gables." Many, probably most of these quaint houses were not originally built in their final condition, but like their British prototypes represented the result of successive additions to meet the needs of growing families and other requirements. The beginning was usually a simple gable-roof structure, such as the Robert Prince farmhouse in Danvers, and the Becket cottage in Salem proper, from which wings and second-story gables were thrown out as occasion demanded.

Aside from their historic associations these two houses are in several respects of unique architectural interest. Their roofs may never have been covered with thatch, yet the pitch is sufficiently steep to have made thatch shed water. Although both houses were built during the period when thatch was much used in Salem, many contemporary shingled roofs perpetuated the thatch tradition through equal steepness of pitch. It is a matter of record, however, that until 1660 most Salem dwellings were mere cottages having roofs of thatch, cut on the Beverly shore of the harbor, and catted wooden chimneys composed of sticks with ends laid over one another at right angles and plastered with clay. Fires were the inevitable sequence of the employment of such combustible materials, and in 1631 Governor Dudley wrote the following regarding the formal fire order:

"For the prevention whereof in our new towne, intended this somer to bee builded, wee haue ordered that noe man there shall build his chimney with wood, nor cover his house with thatch, which was readily assented vnto, for that diverse other howses haue beene burned since our arrivall (the fire allwaies begininge in the woodden chimneys) and some wigwams, which haue taken fire in the roofs covered with thatch or boughs."

PLATE II. — Sarah Prince Osburn House, Danvers. Erected about 1656; Retire Becket House, 5 Becket Street. Erected soon after 1655.

PLATE III. — Deliverance Parkman House.   From an Old Sketch in
the Essex Institute; Governor Bradstreet Mansion.
From a Painting at the Essex Institute.

The Gable and Peaked-Roof House

This scare soon passed, and on December 20, 1636, the governor's order was revoked at the instance of the townspeople. However, it had served in a measure to curb the tendency of the time and to encourage more substantial building, despite the fact that the use of thatch continued for half a century, especially for outbuildings. On the better houses, erected after 1660, shingles were used as a roof covering, and occasionally tiles, which were made in Salem as early as 1629. Bricks began to be used for the chimneys, and sometimes were also laid upon their narrow sides between the timbers and joists, plastered with clay inside and out, and covered externally with clapboards, at first more accurately termed clayboards, since their mission was to protect the clay from being washed away by heavy rains.

The Danvers farmhouse previously referred to was built by Robert Prince about 1656, on what is now Maple Street, about one mile northwest of Danvers Square. As seen at the left, the house formerly had an overhang, but in the course of subsequent repairs this has been nearly obliterated.

After Prince's death his widow, Sarah, continued to live in it, and later married Alexander Osburn. Osburn came from Ireland and was one of the so-called Redemptioners; that is, one who procured his passage to America by selling his services for a stipulated time. It appears that Sarah Prince bought Osburn's time of the man he was serving, hired him to work on her own farm, and eventually married him. In 1692, bedridden and of unbalanced mind, Sarah Prince Osburn was one of the three original victims of the witchcraft delusion, and died in Boston jail while awaiting trial. The house remained in the possession of the descendants of Robert Prince until the opening of the nineteenth century, and is now the farmhouse attached to St. John's Normal College, a Catholic institution.

The house at Number 11 Becket Street appeals strongly to the imagination as having been for six generations the home of the Beckets, a family of shipwrights who played an important part in the up-building of Salem's merchant marine. Among the famous vessels built by Retire Becket, the foremost designer of the family, and who occupied the house for many years, were the merchant ships *Active, Recovery, Margaret, Mount Vernon,* and the fourth *America,* the latter being converted into a privateer in 1812; the brigantine *Becket* and *Cleopatra's Barge,* Captain George Crowninshield's pleasure yacht.

Architecturally this house interests the student not only because of its steep-pitched roof, suggestive of thatch, but because of the overhang of the second story, a frequent characteristic of Salem's seventeenth-century dwellings. This jutting of the upper story of early Colonial houses a foot or two beyond the lower has sometimes been said to have provided gun apertures, after the manner of a blockhouse, for fighting hostile Indians. It is improbable, however, that this construction was ever so used in Salem, for the Indians of the locality were friendly. The idea is of much earlier origin, and as it was characteristic of the Elizabethan house, its manifestations in America, like the many steep-pitched shingled roofs, were for the most part mere persistence of British traditions. The overhang of some of the fifteenth and sixteenth century houses of England is said to have been sufficient to provide shelter from the rain before the introduction of umbrellas; but this was probably incidental to the more essential protection they afforded against the disintegration of the customary plastered walls of the time. Thus developed the characteristic penthouse roof at the second-floor level of the ledge-stone houses of Germantown and eastern Pennsylvania the walls of which at first were laid up in clay.

Lime for making more permanent mortar was far from plentiful for many years after America was first settled. For a time the rooms were plastered with clay mixed with straw, and no attempt was made to conceal the hewn beams of the ceiling. Later, in more expensive houses, a lime made of shells was used and mixed with cattle hair, sand and chalk. We read that one of the commissions of Thomas Graves, who came to Salem in 1629, consisted in "fynding out sorts of lime stone and materials for building." In 1663, referring to the builders of Salem, John Josselyn wrote of the absence of stone that would "run to lime, of which they have great want." Not many years later, however, an abundant supply was found in Pennsylvania, and supplies were brought to Salem by ship, not only for plastering but for whitewashing the plastered walls occasionally, as was the custom until the advent of wall papers about the middle of the eighteenth century or later. However, the fact that in 1724 it was "ordered that muscles shall not be used for making lime or any thing else, except for food and bait to catch fish" indicates that shell lime was still in use at the time.

According to the records, in April, 1655, John Becket, a shipwright and the head of the family, bought of Samuel Archer, a Salem carpenter, "one dwelling house and three acres of land behind it, be it more or less, for the sum of sixteen pounds." The dwelling referred to may not have been the present Becket house, but that the latter was erected about this time or a few years later is indicated by its seventeenth-century character. A complete model of the house, made by Daniel C. Becket, Retire Becket's nephew, now reposes in the Essex Institute, and indicates to what extent the original structure has been altered.

In the days when this old house commanded a view of the harbor and the distant Marblehead shore, it was nearly double its present length. In 1850, an undivided half of the estate being sold to Stephen

C. Phillips, the building was literally cut in half, the front portion remaining on the original site and the rear being converted into a barn which stands somewhat back from its original location. Thus the inclosed entrance porch, formerly at the center of the front, is now at the rear end, while the present large outbuilding is of more recent origin. The huge chimney was removed and a third story provided by raising the roof several feet, but the overhang was retained. In 1857 the front portion of the house also passed out of the Becket family, and in 1916 the house was purchased for preservation by Miss Caroline O. Emmerton, the guiding influence of the House of the Seven Gables Settlement Association, and will be completely restored.

Among the earliest seventeenth-century many-gabled structures of which we have any accurate knowledge was the so-called Governor Bradstreet house which, until taken down in 1753, occupied the present site of the museum building of the Essex Institute at Number 136 Essex Street. The house was built by Emanuel Downing the barrister, probably in 1638, the year he settled in Salem, and, as shown by an old painting preserved in the Essex Institute, was a typical Elizabethan house, constructed of wood. One notices at once the characteristic doorway with fanciful, latticed, flanking towers reminiscent of feudal days, the diamond-paned casement windows, and the large ornamental-topped chimney stacks and finials at the peak of each gable.

Emanuel Downing married Governor John Winthrop's daughter, Lucy, and it was for their son, Sir George Downing, the English soldier and diplomatist, that Downing Street, London, now a synonym for the official residence of the Prime Minister, was named. Later, Downing College, Cambridge, England, was named for Sir George's grandson, the third baronet. Emanuel Downing's daughter, Ann, married Captain Joseph Gardner, the "Fighting Joe" of King Philip's War, and it was from this very house that he set forth to the "Great Swamp Fight" in 1675, where he met his death. His widow married Simon Bradstreet, the last Colonial governor of Massachusetts under the first charter, who occupied the house in his old age and died there March 27, 1697, at the age of ninety-four. After her death in 1713 the old mansion was used for a time as a tavern under the "Sign of the Globe", and later it was for several years the home estate of the Bowditch family, of which Nathaniel Bowditch the mathematician was the most eminent member.

On this site, in a handsome three-story square mansion designed by Samuel McIntire in 1790 for Congressman Nathan Read, William Hickling Prescott, the historian known throughout the world for his "Conquest of Mexico", "Conquest of Peru" and other historical works, was born May 4, 1796. In

PLATE IV. — The House of the Seven Gables. Erected about 1669. Restored in 1909.

PLATE V. — Parlor of the House of the Seven Gables, showing Buffet; Stairway of the House of the Seven Gables.

1799 the house became the residence of Captain Joseph Peabody, a wealthy merchant prominent in the Calcutta trade, and in 1856, after the death of his widow, it was razed to make way the following year for the erection of the building now occupied by the museum of the Essex Institute.

In Nathaniel Hawthorne's day several many-gabled houses were still standing, but aside from that immortalized by him in "The House of the Seven Gables" none remains but the remodeled Pickering house. Notable among those that have been taken down were the Deliverance Parkman house, erected about 1673 and razed in 1835, which stood on the northeast corner of Essex and North streets; the Philip English house on the corner of Essex and English streets, erected in 1685 and razed in 1833; and the Lewis Hunt house on the northwest corner of Washington and Lynde streets, erected about 1698 and razed in 1863. The two former are shown by sketches preserved at the Essex Institute, while the latter remained long enough to be permanently recorded by photography.

All were drawn upon largely by Hawthorne in his writings. The Deliverance Parkman house was referred to by him in his "Notes" as the one "wherein one of the ancestors of the present occupants used to practice alchemy", and is brought into the story of "Peter Goldthwaite's Treasure", first published in "The Token" of 1838 and reprinted in

"Twice Told Tales." He described it as "one of those rusty, moss-grown, many-peaked wooden houses which are scattered about the streets of our elder towns, with a beetle-browed second story projecting over the foundation, as if it frowned at the novelty around it." The similarity of this story to considerably elaborated portions of "The House of the Seven Gables" is obvious, and indicates that the house of this romantic name was not an existing dwelling accurately described, but represented a composite of several many-gabled houses of Salem together with generous additions from Hawthorne's vivid imagination.

Although no single homestead actually comprised the giant elm tree, the shop, Clifford's chamber, the arched window and the secret closet behind the portrait, the old house at Number 54 Turner Street known as "The House of the Seven Gables" was so intimately associated with the story of that name, and, in fact, with Hawthorne's whole literary career, as to have justified the appellation. Like many quaint dwellings of the period, it was gradually enlarged, the oldest part probably being that seen in the right-hand portion of the accompanying illustration, which shows the restored house as it stands to-day. The lean-to, however, while it is typical and enhances the general picturesqueness, is of recent origin. Indoors, also, successive alterations were made, and the elaborate woodwork of the parlor is of later date than the house. Somewhat before 1891 the big, old-fashioned chimney-stack in the original part of the house was removed, and from it was taken a fireback dated 1669, probably the date of erection.

For many years this house was occupied by the Ingersoll family, relatives of the Hawthornes. Nathaniel Hawthorne was a frequent visitor and received much of his literary inspiration there. In those days the house boasted only four or five gables, but Hawthorne's cousin, Miss Susan Ingersoll, is said to have told him that it formerly had seven and to have shown him beams and mortises in the attic to prove the statement. Upon coming down the winding stairs, so the story goes, Hawthorne remarked abstractedly, "House of Seven Gables — that sounds well", and as the novel of that name appeared soon afterward the incident is thought to have determined his choice of a title. That he had the romance well in hand before naming it is indicated by a letter to an old friend not long before the date of publication, in which he wrote:

"I am beginning to puzzle myself for a title for the book. The scene of it is in one of the old projecting-storied houses familiar to me in Salem. . . . I think of such titles as 'The House of Seven Gables,' there being that number of gable ends to the old shanty; or 'Seven Gabled House,' or simply, 'The Seven Gables.'"

The inspiration for that delightful collection of children's stories called "Grandfather's Chair" is also said to have resulted from a suggestion by Miss Ingersoll. During one of his visits, Hawthorne complained dejectedly that he had written himself out, whereupon Miss Ingersoll remarked, pointing to an old armchair long in the family, "Nat, why don't you write about this old chair? There must be many stories connected with it." This chair may still be seen in its accustomed place in the old house.

The episode of the picture of the dead judge seen through the window, which every reader of "The House of the Seven Gables" will recall, was apparently developed from another visit to the Turner Street house. One day an adopted son of Miss Ingersoll fell asleep in his chair in the south parlor where he could be seen through an entryway by any passer-by who happened to look in at the low window. Hawthorne, approaching the house, startled by his friend's motionless attitude and confused by the half shadow and cross lights, awoke him, exclaiming, "Good Heavens, Horace, I thought you were dead." The window in question is supposed to have been the lookout occupied by the toll gatherer of the Marblehead ferry which left the foot of Turner Street two centuries ago.

It was Horace Ingersoll who told Hawthorne the story of the Acadian lovers, as recounted in the first volume of his "Notes." This story was the

PLATE VI. — Philip English House. Erected in 1685. Razed 1833; Lewis Hunt House. Erected about 1698. Razed 1863.

PLATE VII. — The Pickering House, 18 Broad Street. Erected 1660. Remodeled 1841 ; Rebecca Nurse House, Tapleyville. Erected about 1636.

basis of Longfellow's classic "Evangeline", and an account of the connection of the novelist and his friend with the poem is to be found in the second volume of the "Life of Longfellow" by Samuel Longfellow.

Through the generosity and active encouragement of Miss Caroline O. Emmerton in 1909, this interesting old house of so many pleasant associations was restored throughout to practically its former character and entirety, and made the center of a philanthropic neighborhood settlement. As in earlier days its many-paned windows now look out upon the harbor, for the seaman's "Bethel" which for many years stood in front of it has been removed to the rear and altered for settlement needs. To this estate also was brought the quaint "Old Bakery", formerly at Number 23 Washington Street, and likewise completely restored. Indeed, visitors find this group of buildings one of the most interesting attractions of Salem.

Joseph Everett Chandler, the architect in charge, is to be congratulated upon the success of his work, for it perpetuates a picturesque and disappearing type of our early architecture and is delightfully characteristic, even though perhaps conforming more nearly to the description of Hawthorne's fancy than the original house ever did. Mr. Chandler found the mortised beams shown to Hawthorne, and the two missing gables were added accordingly. He also discovered that the original overhang of the southern gable, with second-story posts extending below the supporting girt and terminating in turned drops, had been boarded down to conceal it, and this false structure was promptly removed. Hawthorne also detailed minutely a rough-cast ornament under the eaves that was probably never a feature of this house. Rather it appears to have been an accurate description of an ornament which was taken from the Colonel William Browne mansion, afterward the Sun Tavern, when William Gray, Jr., one of Salem's greatest merchants, razed it to make way for his own more modern residence. Hawthorne had doubtless noticed this in the Essex Historical Society collection, and it may still be seen to-day in the Essex Institute.

The Pickering house at Number 18 Broad Street, frequently said to be the oldest dwelling now remaining in Salem proper, stands on land granted to John Pickering, one of the first settlers, in 1637, and has ever since been owned and occupied by his lineal descendants. It was erected in 1660, as shown by the date on the fireback, now preserved at the Essex Institute, and which was cast by Elisha Jenks of Saugus, the first iron founder in the colonies. The several gables and steep front pitch of the roof suggest the thatched Elizabethan house, while the broader, flatter pitch of the rear indicates a subsequent lean-to addition. Unfortunately the house lost much of its former interest and charm as a result of extensive alterations in 1841, when the fanciful wood trim and flamboyant fence of the Victorian period were added.

Colonel Timothy Pickering, soldier, statesman and the most illustrious member of his family, was born in this house in 1745. From the first armed resistance to British tyranny at the North Bridge two months before Paul Revere's immortal ride until after the surrender by Cornwallis he was conspicuous in the Continental army. He fought in the battles of Germantown and Brandywine, and as a colonel and adjutant-general served his country well. Later, he was elected a representative and senator, and at different times held the portfolios of Postmaster-general, Secretary of War and Secretary of State in Washington's cabinet. His son was John Pickering, LL.D., the Greek lexicographer and famous linguist, who lived for many years in the house at Number 18 Chestnut Street which Nathaniel Hawthorne occupied for about sixteen months in 1846–1847.

CHAPTER II

THE LEAN-TO HOUSE

WITH the passing of thatch, roofs were somewhat less steeply pitched, and with the waning of Elizabethan influences in design, newer conceptions gradually supplanted the rambling, many-gabled dwellings of former years. Builders sought to enlarge the ground floor rather than garret space, and frequently accomplished this in Salem and neighboring colonies by placing a lean-to or shed with a single-pitched roof against one wall of the larger gable-roof structure. Many existing houses were enlarged in this manner and in erecting new dwellings the lean-to was frequently built as one with the main house. While the lean-to was joined to the house in several ways and positions, it was oftenest formed by a downward continuation of the back side of the main roof at the same pitch, with the result that this snug cottage of angular contour and long sweep of roof line has become a strikingly characteristic type of the early domestic architecture of New England.

Picturesque in mass and outline, its façade relieved by an inclosed porch of later date with gable roof and small oval side windows, the Rea-Putnam-

PLATE VIII. — Rea-Putnam-Fowler House, Danvers. Erected before 1692; Maria Goodhue House, North Street, Danvers. Erected 1690. Burned 1899.

PLATE IX. — John Ward House, formerly at 36 St. Peter Street. Erected 1684. Restored 1912.

Fowler house in Danvers is perhaps the most attractive and best-preserved example extant. It is supposed to have been built and occupied by Daniel Rea, the original immigrant of that name, who came to Salem from Plymouth in 1632 and later was granted the tract of land on which the house stands. His daughter Bethia's husband was Captain Thomas Lothrop, who, with many of his men, "the flower of Essex", was massacred September 18, 1675, in the fight with King Philip and his Indian warriors. In 1692 this house was owned by Daniel Rea, a grandson of the first Daniel, and many years afterward came into the possession of Captain Edmund Putnam, who led his company of "minute men" in that memorable opening fight of the Revolution on April 19, 1775. It was later occupied by Honorable Elias Putnam and more recently for many years by Augustus Fowler.

Another house of generally similar character, though presenting interesting variations in fenestration and having the front entrance to one side of the center, after the frequent manner of the time, is the Bishop-Nurse house located in Tapleyville, which attained historic interest as the home of Rebecca Nurse, one of the martyrs of the witchcraft delusion of 1692. It was built and occupied by Townsend Bishop upon a grant of three hundred acres made to him January 11, 1636. Later it passed through the hands of Henry Chickering to

Governor John Endecott, as part of his thousand-acre estate, of which "Orchard Farm" and the "Governor's Plain" were parts. From the governor the place passed into the possession of his son, John Endecott, Jr., and on his death to his wife Elizabeth. She afterward married Reverend James Allen of the First Church, Boston, and he eventually deeded it to Francis Nurse, whose wife Rebecca was hanged as a witch July 19, 1692, by order of the judges and contrary to the verdict of the jury. A woman of exemplary character, she bore the ordeal of her trial nobly and as her chief defense uttered the heroic statement, "I can say before my Eternal Father I am innocent, and God will clear my innocency."

Two other houses of almost identical lean-to arrangement deserve a record here, although space does not permit the illustration of both. Before its destruction by fire in 1899, the so-called Maria Goodhue house, a shingled structure on North Street, Danvers, interested students of architecture by reason of the unusual plaster coving under the front eaves and the large, nicely worked chimney stack of Tudor origin. Benjamin Putnam, grandson of John Putnam, the patriarch of the Putnam family, holder of many civil and military offices and a deacon of the First Church, built it in 1690.

Numbers 27 and 29 Daniels Street, the early childhood home of Honorable Nathaniel Silsbee, United States senator from 1826 to 1835, presents an exceptional example of the large three-story lean-to, with foreshortened upper windows, after the manner of the square mansions of a later day.

Coming as these lean-to cottages did, simultaneously with the last of the Elizabethan houses, it was natural that they should in some instances continue certain features of their predecessors, such as the overhanging second story, usually confined to one or two opposite sides rather than circling the entire structure. The transitional character of such buildings is best shown by the old John Ward house. In the accompanying illustration it is seen as it stood for many years on the original site at Number 38 St. Peter Street where it had been built in 1684 by John Ward. For a time a bakery business was conducted there, the lean-to providing the shop. This house must originally have rested on the ground, the brick cellar wall seen in the photograph probably having been put under because of a change of grade in the street and court on which it stood. Brickwork did not become a feature of Salem architecture until the eighteenth century, the first brick house having been built there in 1700 and later taken down. It will be noticed that the lean-to takes a flatter pitch than the roof of the main house, which is steep enough to have been thatched, and this difference in a continuous roof suggests the probability of a subsequent addition.

The John Ward house now stands in the garden at the rear of the Essex Institute among old-fashioned flowers that are only names to many, and has been restored as nearly as possible to its presumable pristine appearance. Mortises and boarding were found for peaked windows in the front of the roof, indicating that the structure had at an early date been remodeled to conform to the prevailing mode. These peaked windows antedated the dormer, and their reconstruction with diamond-paned, leaded, casement sashes throughout the main house has resulted in an enhanced air of Puritan quaintness. The front door is of primitive batten construction with wide, vertical boards on the outside and horizontal boards inside nailed to them. It has an old English lock with ponderous key. Every detail of the restoration was carefully worked out in comparison with the large and varied collection of antiques in the museum of the Essex Institute, and the resources of the Institute were also drawn upon generously to furnish the house throughout in an appropriate manner, with the result that visitors find it a veritable treasure house of relics of bygone days.

Downstairs there are two main rooms, and a kitchen to the right of a small entry and well-designed winding stairway. Above, there are two chambers. The attic is unfinished and contains many interesting old "castaways." Summer beams cross the ceilings, carrying the lighter floor joists, about five inches in diameter and hewn nearly square in section. The lean-to includes an apothecary shop modeled upon

PLATE X. — The Old Bakery, formerly at 25 Washington Street.
Erected 1683; Detail of Old Bakery Overhang.

PLATE XI. — The Narbonne House, 71 Essex Street. Erected before 1671; Rear of the Narbonne House.

that of Doctor William Webb and containing goods
owned by him and two contemporaries, a Salem
"cent shop" where young folks might buy books,
cookies, candies and the like, and a weave room, all
fully furnished in the period of 1830.

Like the original houses of this and the earlier
period the restored John Ward house is not painted,
either inside or out, and the clapboarding long since
took on the weather-beaten effect of age. Red was
the first color used for house painting in America, perhaps because of the prevalence of brickwork for the
better buildings in England, whence the paint was
imported. It is doubtful whether white or yellow
was the next to follow. These three are the accepted
colors for Colonial architecture.

Unique among the overhangs on Salem buildings,
the Old Bakery attracts notice chiefly because of the
heavy oaken supporting girders or summer beams,
with their chamfered edges and ends carved to the
form of simple ornamental brackets. Here, indeed,
one sees embellishment of genuine sincerity, added
not for itself but to improve the appearance of
structural necessities. The oaken corner posts are
shouldered, the spaces between the studding are
filled with bricks laid up in clay, and laths split from
the log were found in the plastering of the attic stairway. This building, erected in 1683 by Benjamin
Hooper, was originally a one-room cottage with the
overhang extending along its entire front, the large

chimney then having been at the eastern end. Like the John Ward house it probably rested on the ground originally, the high brick foundation having been put under it at the time the grade of Washington Street was lowered. For many years it stood as shown by the accompanying illustration at Number 23 Washington Street, until in 1911, at the instance of Miss Caroline O. Emmerton, it was moved to the garden of "The House of the Seven Gables" and thoroughly restored.

The two-story wooden building seen beyond it at the left was erected in 1784 by the town of Salem for the Centre Grammar School, and there in 1840 the late Honorable Joseph Hodges Choate, the eminent lawyer and diplomat, who served as United States ambassador to Great Britain from 1899 to 1905, went to school, Abner Brooks being master.

Often a lean-to roof joined the main house several inches below the gable roof, suggesting the curb of the gambrel roof, except that the pitch of the two was usually identical, any difference being a flatter lower slope as opposed to the steeper slope of the gambrel type. The lateral division of the building thus formed recalls church architecture to a degree, the lean-to having the same relation to the main house, in respect to exterior appearance, that an aisle has to the nave. An especially interesting case in point is presented by the Narbonne house, Number 71 Essex Street, erected before 1671. The steeply pitched roof, the large chimney stack and the many-paned windows are all characteristic of the period, while the Dutch door in the lean-to was formerly the entrance to another "cent shop", a Salem institution of a century ago which inspired a bit of vivid description in Hawthorne's "House of the Seven Gables."

A study of the rear of this house will prove as interesting as of the front. The original structure boasted only one room to each floor besides the shop in the lean-to. When more rooms were needed the gambrel roof had come into fashion and was chosen for the addition, the lean-to being extended and its single-pitch roof being run up to the curb of the gambrel to form one of those curious combinations of which only a few remain in Essex County.

The lower front room is probably the best preserved interior of this period in Salem. Accompanying photographs show clearly the hand-hewn framing along the floor and ceiling, the chamfered corner posts and exposed summer beams across the ceiling. The two-panel door with its wrought-iron latch, the three-part window shutters with six-pointed star openings and strap hinges, the simple mantel, paneling and corner buffet of later date, all have a quaint appeal no less than the many antiques of worth among the furnishings. As one stands in this ancient, low-studded room, fancy wanders back to the time of its building and readily pictures it before its walls had been papered or its floor had known other coverings than light blue sand from the beaches of Gloucester and Ipswich scattered upon it in circular and spotted patterns in lieu of rugs, following the customary Monday scouring. We are thus reminded that such was the policy of the governors under the first charter, Endecott and Bradstreet, to exclude "luxuries" for the most part, that not until after this charter was annulled in 1686 did the refinements, as distinguished from the meager necessities, of home life find much encouragement. The door at the second landing leading to the attic still has its old latch string, probably the only remaining example of this primitive fixture in Salem.

Several old houses still standing illustrate the frequent though unattractive custom of extending the lean-to far enough beyond one end of the main house to permit a side door facing front and opening into the rear part of the dwelling. While this arrangement known as a "jut-by" furnished a little additional room, though no obvious advantage over a door in the end of the lean-to like that of the Rea-Putnam-Fowler house, it was gained at the expense of angular, almost ugly severity. The George Jacobs house, Danversport, still standing in the fields east of Gardner's Hill, shows this and also the strange occasional location of the front door well to one side of the center with pairs of windows widely spaced on one side and near together on the other. It was probably built by Richard Waters early in the

PLATE XII. — Front Room of the Narbonne House; Mantel and China Closet, Narbonne House.

PLATE XIII. — George Jacobs House, Danversport. Erected before 1658; Judge Samuel Holton House, Danvers. Erected about 1650.

seventeenth century and in 1658 was conveyed to George Jacobs, Sr. From this house the aged man, over eighty years old, was taken away and jailed, tried for witchcraft, condemned, and finally executed on Gallows Hill, August 19, 1692, in the presence of Reverend Cotton Mather, minister of the Old North Church, Boston. A painting by Matterson depicting the trial of George Jacobs may be seen in the picture gallery of the Essex Institute. His words, "Well, burn me or hang me, I will stand in the truth of Christ," indicated that he was a good and brave man who suffered an awful injustice at the hands of his accusers.

One of the most picturesque dwellings of this period, with a side door in a "jut-by" lean-to, is the Goodale house in Peabody. Isaac Goodale erected this farmhouse on the one hundred acres of land conveyed to him in 1667–1668 by his father, Robert Goodale or Goodell, a husbandman, from the 480 acres the latter had acquired by purchase prior to 1653 and including two grants of twenty acres each from the Town of Salem in or before 1636 and in 1638–1639. Eight generations of Goodales, all yeomen from the second to the sixth generations inclusive, have occupied this old house, and not until 1915 did it pass out of the family, when Jacob Oscar Goodale sold it to Charles R. Stackpole, of Nahant.

Much like the foregoing, the John Walcott house near by in Danvers has a "jut-by" lean-to considerably less steeply pitched, the side entrance being elaborated by a pedimental doorhead. In 1700 this house and the farm on which it stands belonged to John Walcott, and in 1715 it was the homestead of Zachariah Goodale, of Salem, yeoman. Until 1889 it was owned by members of the Goodale and Pope families, having been sold in 1753 by David Goodale, Zachariah's son, to Nathaniel Pope, of Danvers, yeoman. The place is now owned by Miss Caroline O. Looney, of Salem, who has expended a large sum of money in improvements upon the house.

Another house of similar lean-to construction, not shown here, was the so-called Clark house, Summer Street, Danvers. This, too, was built early in the seventeenth century, and while the front entrance porch is centered there are two windows to each floor on one side of it and only one on the other side — another expression of the custom of that period to let exterior appearance frankly express interior arrangement. During the anxious days of 1692 this was the home of Joseph Putnam, another grandson of the first John Putnam and the father of that hero of the Revolution, General Israel Putnam. Courageous and outspoken, he did not hesitate to denounce the witchcraft delusion as such in no uncertain terms, nor to let it be known that he and his family were constantly armed and could be arrested only at the peril of life. Had enough other men as frankly asserted and as energetically maintained their convictions it is doubtful if any executions for witchcraft would ever have occurred either in Salem or Boston.

Rarely was a lean-to placed across the gable end of the main building as in the case of the Judge Samuel Holten house, erected about 1650 by Benjamin Holten at the corner of Center and Holten streets, Danvers Center, and this interesting though unattractive arrangement, wherever found, was usually a subsequent addition. In fact, the sagged portion of the main house at the left gives the impression that the whole of it as it now stands was not erected at one time, but that two constructions of similar character are represented. Colonial houses with two front doors, even though occupied by only one family, are by no means unusual, but this inclosed porch with its double doors is peculiar, and the large twenty-paned windows exceptional. As the birthplace and home of Judge Holten this old house claims more than passing attention, for this ardent patriot was one of the most noted men of Essex County and has a public record to his credit equaled by few Americans.

Born in 1738, he became a physician by profession, having studied medicine with Doctor Jonathan Prince and practiced in both Danvers and Gloucester. He was a delegate to the Colonial Convention in 1768; five years in the Continental Congress, at times acting as president; a member of the Constitutional Convention; two years a congressman; five years a senator; eight years a representative to the General Court; twelve years a councillor; twice Presidential elector; thirty-two years a judge of the Court of Common Pleas, half of the time presiding; thirty-five years Judge of the Court of General Sessions; fifteen years Chief Justice; nineteen years Judge of the Probate Court for Essex County, and twenty-four years Town Treasurer.

When the gambrel roof came into vogue in the eighteenth century the lean-to was not altogether discontinued and several gambrel lean-to houses with a long rear roof line sloping from the curb downward still remain in Salem. At Number 374 Essex Street the house erected before 1773, with its simple, well-proportioned dormers, tall chimneys and English chimney pots, is a good example. It was, at the time of his death, the residence of Doctor Henry Wheatland, founder of the Essex County Natural History Society, which in 1848 by union with the Essex Historical Society was merged into the Essex Institute. As indicated by its Greek revival character, the entrance porch is of much later date than the house.

Other notable dwellings of similar character include the John Waters house, Number 5 Mason Street; the Jesse Putnam house, Maple Street, Danvers, erected before 1750 by Deacon Joseph Putnam; the birthplace of Senator Benjamin Good-

PLATE XIV. — Isaac Goodale House, Peabody. Erected about 1667-8; John Walcott House, Danvers. Erected before 1700.

PLATE XV. — John Waters House, 5 Mason Street.   Erected 1800;
Wheatland House, 374 Essex Street.   Erected before 1773.

hue, erected about 1736 by his father, Benjamin
Goodhue, Sr., at Number 70 Boston Street; and the
Babbidge-Crowninshield-Bowker house, in the rear of
Number 46 Essex Street, erected before 1700. This
latter house was the birthplace of Captain George
Crowninshield, Honorable Jacob Crowninshield and
Honorable Benjamin W. Crowninshield, three
brothers who rank among Salem's greatest historic
figures, and of whom more will be recorded elsewhere
in these pages. Under its roof also was organized
the Second or East Church, made famous by the long
pastorate of Doctor William Bentley, the historian,
patriot, radical and scholar.

The accompanying photograph shows the western
end of the house as it formerly stood directly upon
the street, the eastern end beyond the front door
having been cut off some fifty years ago and moved
to Grant Street. The western end was recently
removed to the rear of the lot and a modern building
erected on its former site.

The Jeffrey Lang house, Number 371 Essex Street,
erected in 1740, instances an uncommon lean-to
addition with its rafters springing from the eaves
rather than the curb of the gambrel, the rear portion
of the roof therefore being in three distinct planes.
At the time of its purchase and demolition several
years ago by the late Daniel Low, whose estate
adjoined it on the left, this was one of the oldest
gambrel-roof structures in Salem and the huge main

chimney, the absence of dormers, the high, narrow, eighteen-paned original windows and the pedimental doorway with its heavy paneled wood door, iron thumb latch and narrow top-light, all speak eloquently of those early days. Jeffrey Lang was a goldsmith, and like most tradesmen of the time had his shop in the corner of his house in an addition at the extreme left, probably made soon after the house was first erected. More recently, probably just before 1850, the opposite corner room was remodeled as a variety store and continued as such until 1889. Wider windows were presumably put into the room above as part of the alterations at the time this second store was installed. Benjamin J. Lang, the noted organist, pianist and conductor, is a descendant of Jeffrey Lang.

Without exception these primitive seventeenth-century dwellings of the early settlers, whether having clustered gables or introducing the long, sloping, lean-to roof, reflect the simplicity and frugality of Puritan life and character. They indicate that imperative necessities were supplied in the frankest, most direct way, with but scant attempts at embellishment either within or without. Several of the interiors now contain eighteenth-century woodwork, and in consequence have lost much of their former appearance. The exterior wood trim, however, including corner and verge boards, door and window casings, still remains as severely plain

PLATE XVI. — Babbidge House, 46 Essex Street. Erected before 1700; Jeffrey Lang House, 371 Essex Street. Erected 1740.

PLATE XVII. — Senator Benjamin Goodhue House, 403 Essex Street. Erected about 1780; Clark-Morgan House, 358 Essex Street.

as ever, and so by contrast serves to emphasize the elaboration of decorative detail which accompanied the advent of the gambrel-roof house and which likewise characterized all the Colonial architecture which followed.

CHAPTER III

THE GAMBREL-ROOF HOUSE

THE year of the witchcraft delusion in Salem marked the end of Colonial times in Massachusetts. In 1686 the first charter was annulled, and in 1692, after a stormy six years politically, William III granted to the Province of Massachusetts a second charter, under which the governor and lieutenant-governor were appointed by the Crown and all laws were sent to England for royal approval. Provincial times covered the period from 1692 to the days of the Revolution. During these years the gambrel-roof house was the prevailing style, at first small and very simple, but toward the middle of the eighteenth century being developed into perhaps the largest, handsomest and most distinctive type of American residence.

The gambrel roof represents an evolution of the seventeenth-century Mansard roof, designed by the distinguished French architect, François Mansard, or Mansart, 1598–1666, which was extensively adopted in France and other European countries. Mansard's roof was devised to make attics available for rooms in consequence of a municipal law limiting the height of front walls in Paris, the idea being to keep all construction within a semi-circle about the ends of the lower tie-beam and struck from a point midway of its length. It is best described as a hipped curb roof having on all sides two slopes unequally inclined, the lower slope being steeper than the upper, hence the terms "French curb" and "French hip" by which it was frequently designated. From a structural standpoint it has an advantage over the ordinary gable roof in that the outward thrust upon the supporting walls is less, the load coming almost vertically upon them.

Mansard roofs as such never achieved great favor in America, although attaining a certain vogue as very unsatisfactorily interpreted during the so-called Victorian period of the nineteenth century. Nevertheless, many of our northern early-settled communities have a few more pleasing eighteenth-century examples. The best in Salem, the residence of Honorable Benjamin Goodhue, the first United States senator from Essex County, was burned in the great fire of 1914. Benjamin Goodhue was born in 1748 at Number 70 Boston Street in the same house where Doctor Henry Wheatland, the founder of the Essex Institute, was born in 1812. He was a friend of Washington, served as senator from 1796 to 1800 and was one of the commission that framed the first revenue laws of the country. The Clark-Morgan house at Number 368 Essex Street presents somewhat the same appearance from the street, but in reality consists of two old gambrel-roof structures and a modern flat-roof building butted together to form a U-shaped ground plan. In this house half a century ago the Morgan sisters kept a Dame school such as was so well described by Eleanor Putnam in her book "Old Salem."

In the heart of Paris, Mansard roofs were frequently employed on houses built in solid blocks where the double slope occurred only at the front and rear. The rebuilding of houses on adjoining lots occasionally exposed the cross section of this roof type, and while the French apparently gave it little thought, American builders who saw it were impressed with its strikingly pleasing outline. Appreciating the value of Mansard construction in providing extra rooms at small cost without recourse to an additional story for the building proper, they also realized that this flat gable arrangement gave all its advantages at less expense for labor than was involved by the hipped curb on all four sides, then customary in the case of single, detached houses, — its name being derived from the resemblance of each side of the gable contour to the gambrel or hock of a horse.

No recognized rule was followed for the proportion or pitch, but it was perceived that unless the roof as a whole were adapted to the general size, height and character of the house, ungainliness might result. Local color in the gambrel roof, therefore, lies in its shape as seen from the end. In Salem, and elsewhere throughout New England, the two slopes were usually of about equal width and medium pitch, as distinguished from the flatter pitches and wider lower slope of the New York and New Jersey Dutch roofs, and the steeper pitches and wider upper slope of the Maryland roofs. Numerous variants of the gambrel roof occur wherever found, and several in Salem show Dutch influence, notably the Ropes' Memorial, which will be considered more fully later. Mrs. Cook's house at Number 1 Cambridge Street about opposite the Ropes' Memorial presents a fine example of modern carpenter work executed about fifteen years ago, when the former hipped roof was replaced by the present perfect gambrel.

While peaked roof and lean-to houses were the typical dwellings of witchcraft times, the house that tradition has most intimately identified with the delusion is now a gambrel-roof structure. This so-called Witch House at Number 310 Essex Street, corner of North Street, received its name by reason of the fact that in it lived Jonathan Corwin, one of the judges of the witchcraft court, and here he is said to have held some of the preliminary examinations of the accused. The history of this ancient dwelling is obscure and a difference of opinion exists among those who have investigated the matter carefully. Authoritative sources of information are lacking to establish definitely its date of erection and the continuity of its subsequent record. That it has undergone alterations and additions since first built which have changed its exterior appearance is certain, and that it did not at first have a gambrel roof is highly probable.

The overhanging second story indicates the seventeenth-century origin of the present structure. This architectural feature long antedated the gambrel roof, with which it is very rarely found. The disparity of periods alone would tend to indicate the gambrel roof as a subsequent alteration were it not for the more conclusive evidence to this effect presented by the large front chimney. Whether this house was built about 1671, as some antiquaries claim, or at an earlier date, the fact is well established that in 1675 Jonathan Corwin, one of the witch-craft judges, bought it of Captain Richard Davenport, who, from 1645 to 1665, was commander of the fort on Castle Island in Boston harbor. That it was in a primitive or unfinished condition at the time is indicated by the work Corwin immediately contracted with Daniel Andrews to do for its improvement. This contract, now preserved among the Corwin papers at the Essex Institute, is an in-

PLATE XVIII. — Diman House, 8 Hardy Street; The Witch House, corner of Essex and North Streets, as it appeared in 1856.

PLATE XIX. — General Israel Putnam's Birthplace, Maple Street, Danvers.   Erected 1641 ; Thomas Ruck House, 8 Mill Street. Erected before 1651.

teresting contemporary document little less verbose
than builder's contracts of to-day. It reads as
follows :

Articles and Covenants made, agreed upon, and
confirmed between Mr. Jonathan Corwin, of Salem,
merchant, and Daniel Andrews of Salem, of the
other part, concerning a parcell of worke as fol-
loweth, viz. : Imprimis the said parcell of worke
is to be bestowed in filling, plaistering and finishing
a certain dwelling house bought by the said owner
of Capt. Nath'll Davenport of Boston, and is situ-
ate in Salem aforesaid, towards the west end of
the towne betweene the houses of Rich. Sibley to
the west and Deliverance Parkman on the east ;
and is to be performed to these following directions, viz.

1. The said Daniel Andrews is to dig and build
a cellar as large as the easterly room of said house
will afford (and in the said room according to the
breadthe and lengthe of it) not exceeding six foot
in height ; and to underpin the porch and the
remaining part of the house not exceeding three
foot in height ; also to underpin the kitchen on the
north side of the house, not exceeding one foot ;
the said kitchen being 20 foot long and 18 foot wide ;
and to make steps with stones into the cellar in two
places belonging to the cellar, together with stone
steps up into the porch. 2. For the chimneys he
is to take down the chimneys which are now standing,
and to take and make up of the bricks that are now
in the chimneys and the stones that are in the leanto
cellar that now is, and to rebuild the said chimneys
with five fireplaces, viz., two below and two in the
chambers and one in the garret ; also to build one
chimney in the kitchen, with ovens and a furnace, not
exceeding five feet above the top of the house. 3. He
is to set the jambs of the two chamber chimneys

and of the easternmost room below with Dutch tiles, the said owner finding the tiles; also to lay all the hearths belonging to the said house and to point the cellar and underpinning of sd. house and so much of the three hearths as are to be laid with Dutch tiles, the said owner is to find them. 4. As for lathing and plaistering he is to lath and siele the 4 rooms of the house betwixt the joists overhead with a coat of lime & haire upon the clay; also to fill the gable ends of the house with bricks and to plaister them with clay. 5. To lath and plaister partitions of the house with clay and lime, and to fill, lath and plaister them with lime and hair besides; and to siele and lath them overhead with lime; also to fill lath and plaister the kitchen up to the wall plate on every side. 6. The said Daniel Andrews is to find lime, bricks, clay, stone, haire, together with labourers and workmen to help him, and generally all materials for the effecting and carrying out of the aforesaide worke, excepte laths and nailes. 7. The whole work before mentioned is to be done, finished and performed att or before the last day of August next following, provided that said Daniel or any that work with him, be not lett or hindered for want of the carpenter worke. 8. Lastly in consideration of all the aforesaid worke, so finished and accomplished as is aforesaid, the aforesaid owner is to pay or cause to be paid unto to the said workeman, the summe of fifty pounds in money current in New England, to be paid at or before the finishing of the said worke. And for the true performance of the premises we bind ourselves each to other, our heyers, executors, and administrators, firmly by these presents, as witnesse our hands, this nineteenth day of February, Anno Domini, 1674–5.

JONATHAN CORWIN.

DANIEL ANDREWS.

The Gambrel-Roof House

Doubtless the principal chimney specified in Section 2 of the contract is the one already referred to. Not only is it elaborately stacked like those almost exclusively associated with the earliest peaked-roof houses in Salem, but the present roof exposes several inches of the plastered chimney below the brick corbeling. It is very doubtful if a chimney built to special order with the idea of improvement would have been so constructed as to fail to bring about a proper meeting of the exposed brickwork of the chimney shaft with the roof as it existed at the time. Rather, it is more likely that at some later time in the eighteenth century the former gable roof was arbitrarily remodeled to the prevailing gambrel mode regardless of the appearance of the chimney. There is a tradition that this alteration took place in 1746.

This house continued in the possession of the descendants of Jonathan Corwin until sold to Doctor G. P. Farrington in 1856. The interior and chimney remain much the same as in 1692, but the exterior is now defaced by a modern drug store nearly half the width of the original house and extending from it to the sidewalk in front. From this store one passes into the house through an arch in the great chimney which is about eight by twelve feet at the first floor.

Architecturally the house at Number 8 Hardy Street, now remodeled beyond recognition, is of interest chiefly as the only example of the gambrel-gable overhang remaining in Salem at the time the accompanying photograph was made. Like many of the early houses it stood end to the street, yet the gambrel extending directly along the street did not conform to the customary arrangement. The cornice was perhaps the oldest in Salem and the wide spacing of the dentils recalls the fact that the primitive cornice was simply an overhang with the ends of the rafters showing. One notices the fenestartion immediately, not only because of the quaint sashes with twenty-four small panes to each window, but on account of the peculiar spacing of the windows without attempt at symmetry or balance. The effect seems to express something of the ingenuous and stubborn character of those sturdy people who braved the perils of a virgin land for the pursuit of religious freedom and personal liberty. Possibly this thought arises from the fact that this old house was the home of Reverend James Diman, pastor of the Second or East Church, from 1737 until 1788, and the predecessor of Reverend William Bentley, the historian, whose diary has established so many interesting facts in the history of Salem.

In its U-shaped arrangement with wings of unequal length and virtually three gambrel-roof dwellings in one, the Ruck house, Number 8 Mill Street, has few if any parallels in American architecture.

The Gambrel-Roof House

The oldest part, at the northwest corner where the large chimney stands, was built by Thomas Ruck and dates back to before 1651. Each of the several subsequent additions, however, has preserved the high, narrow proportions of the original structure characteristic of many seventeenth-century buildings. In 1751 the old part was bought by Joseph McIntire, a joiner and the father of Samuel McIntire, the famous architect of Salem, of whom much more in another chapter. It was during the occupancy of the elder McIntire that he built the house next door at the corner of Mill and Norman streets where Samuel was born on January 16, 1757.

When Joseph McIntire moved into his new home in 1754 he sold the old part of the Ruck house to Samuel Bacon, owner of the new part, and during the latter's ownership Richard Cranch, a watchmaker and local justice, occupied it in 1766 and 1767. Cranch and John Adams, afterwards second President of the United States, married sisters, and so it happened that, as a young lawyer riding the eastern circuit, Adams more than once stopped in the house. In his journal under date of November 3, 1766, he wrote that "Cranch is now in a good situation for business, near the Court House . . . his house, fronting on the wharves, the harbor and the shipping, has a fine prospect before it."

After Cranch moved to Boston in 1767 John Singleton Copley, the celebrated English artist, became a tenant of the house while painting portraits of leading Salem citizens. To it he brought his infant son, afterwards Baron Lyndhurst, Lord Chancellor of England. Being in sympathy with the crown, however, the family left America in 1774.

At Number 27 Union Street stands a cottage almost devoid of architectural appeal; a structure too nearly square to possess charm of proportion and now still further defaced by an inappropriate modern door and windows, although inside it has been changed but little. Its claim to notice lies in the fact that on the patriotic day of July 4, 1804, Nathaniel Hawthorne, the famous American novelist, was born in the northwest, or left-hand chamber of the second story. The house was built in 1680 by one of the several Salem men who have borne the name of Benjamin Pickman and in 1772 came into the possession of Hawthorne's grandfather.

Another gambrel-roof cottage in which Hawthorne lived from 1828 to 1832 has only slight architectural value. It was originally built for Hawthorne's mother by her brother on land adjoining the present Manning homestead, but was afterward sold and moved across the street where it now stands numbered 26 Dearborn Street. The upward lift of the roof at the eaves shows the influence of Dutch work in New York and New Jersey, while the high position of the dormers just beneath the curb characterizes frequent New Eng-

PLATE XX. — Nathaniel Hawthorne's Birthplace, 21 Union Street. Erected 1680; Hawthorne's Home from 1828 to 1832.

PLATE XXI.— Eighteenth Century Addition to the Putnam House; The room in which General Israel Putnam was born.

land practice. Although simple and attractive in itself, the pedimental inclosed entrance porch, with blind-shaded side lights, is on too heavy a scale to accord with the house.

Located at Number 431 Maple Street, near the Newburyport Turnpike in Danvers, is the birthplace of General Israel Putnam, one of the most prominent Revolutionary leaders. It has a peculiar interest for the student of architecture in that it combines gable and gambrel roofs and has the uncommon lean-to across the gable end of the original main house, the eighteenth-century gambrel-roof addition being across the other end. The older part of the house was built by General Putnam's grandfather, Lieutenant Thomas Putnam, probably soon after the grant of the fifty acres of land on which it stands had been made to him in 1641. Thomas was the son of the immigrant John, one of the Puttenham family from Aston Abbots, Bucks County, England. After the death of Thomas and his wife this ancient house came into the possession of Joseph, the father of the general. Here many a Putnam has come into the world and lived, and in a small room over the inclosed porch on the side, General Israel Putnam was born January 7, 1718. This low-studded room with its whitewashed summer beams, batten doors, primitive fireplace, quaint wall paper, faded old prints and antique furniture still retains the atmosphere of bygone days. The eighteenth-century gambrel-roof addition, beyond the monster willow planted by a Putnam slave, was erected by Colonel David Putnam, son of Joseph and a brother of Israel. Exteriorly it differs from the early type of New England gambrel-roof structure without dormers only in its inclosed entrance porch with almost flat balustraded roof, and this porch was probably a later addition. Within, the rooms are spacious and have great fireplaces as indicated by the sturdy chimney.

Here General Putnam lived until his marriage shortly after which, in 1740, he moved to Connecticut, where he was living at the outbreak of the Revolution. Upon receiving news of the fighting at Lexington and Concord he left his plough in the furrow and hastened to Cambridge, where he was made a major-general by Washington after the latter took command of the army. The tale of how "Old Put" galloped down the stone steps is still told in Connecticut, and his distinguished career throughout the war was little less spectacular. But the Putnams of Massachusetts served their country quite as gallantly if less conspicuously. Seventy-five Putnams, more men than from any other family, responded to the call on April 19, 1775, and it is believed that this family also gave more men to the Union Army in the Civil War than did any other.

While, as already recounted, many of the first

gambrel-roof houses came into being as additions to existing gable-roof and lean-to structures, and were for the most part without dormers and devoid of architectural embellishment either of doorway or exterior trim, toward the middle of the eighteenth century there began to be built original residences more pretentious than had been the average hitherto. Merchant shipowners and sea captains were accumulating fortunes made in trade with the West Indies, England, France, Holland, Spain and Portugal, large families were the rule, and a more generous scale of living called for town houses of ample proportions, with numerous rooms. The influence of Georgian architecture in the mother country was beginning to be felt, and it is known that in those days the New England carpenter-builders had for ready reference little books of measured drawings with excellent details. "The Country Builder's Assistant" by Asher Benjamin was such a volume. These builder's assistants and similar publications are the real explanation of the many charming old Colonial buildings with their excellent details, and may rightly be regarded as the fountain head of Colonial design.

The Lindall-Barnard-Andrews house, Number 393 Essex Street, erected in 1747, typifies these spacious gambrel-roof houses with ranging windows, well-proportioned pedimental doorways and roofs pierced by three dormers and two or three great brick chimneys. Built by Timothy Lindall, a man prominent in the political life of Salem and Speaker of the House of Deputies in 1720 and 1721, this comfortable old dwelling was in Revolutionary times the home of the Reverend Thomas Barnard, pastor of the old North Church, who averted bloodshed during the first armed resistance to British tyranny on Sunday, February 26, 1775. Dismissing his congregation in response to the urgent summons of a messenger, he hastened to the North Bridge in the rôle of peacemaker, and finally succeeded in persuading the townspeople to lower the draw and permit the British troops to cross in their fruitless search for cannon, which, meantime, had been transferred to a new hiding place.

The Orne-Ropes house, Number 318 Essex Street, erected in 1719 and now known as the Ropes' Memorial, presents in several respects the most effective Provincial residence in Salem. It was occupied by the Ropes family for several generations and contains a splendid collection of furniture, family portraits, Nanking china and Russian glass accumulated by its various owners. In 1768 it came into the possession of Honorable Nathaniel Ropes, Judge of the Probate and Superior courts, and was thereafter occupied by a Nathaniel Ropes until the death of the fifth Nathaniel in 1893. Judge Ropes was a loyalist and his death on March 18,

1774, was probably hastened by the attack of a mob of patriots while he lay ill there the previous day.

Under the wills of Mary Pickman Ropes and Eliza Orne Ropes, the last owners, the Ropes' Memorial was established in 1912 with an incorporated board of trustees. An ample maintenance fund insures the perpetuation of the house and a beautiful formal garden in the rear, both of which are open to visitors at frequent stated times from May to December, thus affording an exceptional opportunity to view a typical home of a prosperous family in the early years of the nineteenth century.

Architecturally the house reflects Dutch influence in the outline of its gambrel roof; and the balustrade about its upper slopes, after the manner of the decked roofs of a later period, at once draws attention to a picturesque feature of many of the later gambrel-roof houses intended to provide ornamentation of a refined character. This, like the beautiful recessed Ionic doorway, dating about 1805, was doubtless of more recent date than the house, although of exceptional simplicity as contrasted with the balustrade on the roof of "The Lindens", for instance. The accompanying photograph shows the house as it originally stood close to the sidewalk. In 1894, however, it was moved back many feet and the beautiful fence and carved gateposts illustrated in the chapter on entrances and doorways were erected. A large L was constructed in the rear and other changes were made.

Occasionally the rear half of a gambrel-roof house was extended several feet beyond the front half, as had often been the earlier lean-to, forming a "jut-by" to provide a side door facing front.

The Derby-Ward house, Number 27 Herbert Street, erected in 1738, is an instance that well exemplifies the first and plainer type of large gambrel-roof residences that were built by ship owners and sea captains with the proceeds of their venturous sea voyages. The eighteen-paned windows and the simple boxed cornice are characteristic of the time, and one notes the returns on the gable ends, which had not been employed previous to about this date. The double verge board, a plain narrow strip at the outside upper edge of the board proper, was the forerunner of the moldings of later years. Early cornices had no gutters and the flagstones laid in the ground below were provided to catch and distribute the drip. The pedimental, inclosed entrance porch, with its pilaster corner treatment and oval side lights, may have been added at a later date. As in many other houses of the time a large chimney rose through the ridge eight or ten feet from each end, so placed as to locate fireplaces midway of inside lengthwise walls of the house in rooms each side of the central hall.

This house was erected in 1738 by Richard Derby,

PLATE XXII. — Lindall-Barnard-Andrews House, 393 Essex Street.
Erected 1747; Derby-Ward House, birthplace of Elias Hasket
Derby. Corner of Herbert and Derby Streets. Erected 1738.

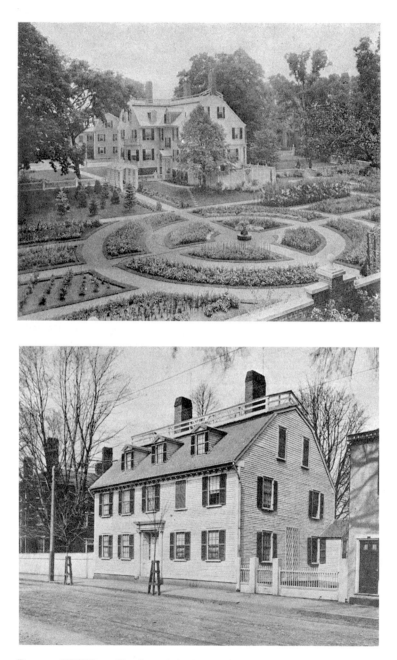

PLATE XXIII.—Garden of the Ropes Memorial, 318 Essex Street. Laid Out 1913; Ropes Memorial, 318 Essex Street. Erected 1719.

a prosperous sea captain and shipowner, delegate
to the Provincial Congress, and the father of Elias
Hasket Derby, Salem's greatest merchant, who was
born here in 1739. Richard Derby owned part of
the cannon sought by Colonel Leslie's troops during
the first armed resistance to British tyranny at the
North Bridge on February 26, 1775, two months
before Paul Revere's immortal ride; and he it was
who, when importuned to use his influence to have
them given up, boldly replied to Leslie's messenger :
"If he can find them, he may take them." Nor
were they taken, for the Reverend Thomas Barnard
intervened, preventing a serious clash as already
recounted, and General Gage later reported to his
government that he had been misled and that the
guns did not exist. This old house was afterwards
sold by the Derbys, became the residence of Miles
Ward, a prominent citizen, and was occupied by
members of his family as late as 1837.

During Nathaniel Hawthorne's residence near by
in the house at Numbers 10½ and 12 Herbert Street
he was on very friendly terms with the family of
a relative then occupying the Derby-Ward house,
and frequently he ate and slept there in one of the
spacious chambers reserved for him. In this room
and in a little summer house among the lilacs and
syringas, shaded by an old apple tree of the garden,
he wrote some of his earliest stories.

Another gambrel-roof residence built by Richard

Derby in 1761 at Number 168 Derby Street, and said by Felt in his "Annals of Salem" to have been intended for Derby's son, Elias Hasket Derby, who had been married at about that time, is the oldest brick house now standing in Salem. The first brick house of which there is any record, erected in 1700, was mentioned in 1707 as having been built for Benjamin Marston by George Cabot, a Boston mason, at the corner of Crombie and Essex streets. It had freestone capitals on its front corners and was considered "an elegant edifice for its day", but after occupying it for a time Marston's wife persuaded him to have it pulled down because she supposed it was damp and injurious to health, a circumstance which for several years created a strong prejudice in Salem against brick construction.

Except for the gambrel roof, which never found favor in England, the Derby house is distinctly of Georgian character. One notes first of all the classic doorway with wood detail worked out in the spirit of carved marble, but the window frames, the closely spaced molded dentils of the box cornice and the dormers with gable and segmental roofs interspersed, all denote the same influence in design. The belief that a more even distribution of heat from fireplaces was effected by locating them on outside walls led to the adoption in large houses such as this of four chimneys in pairs at each end where they became part of the structural walls, their outer sides being flush with them. This picturesque gable construction soon became a distinctive feature of the brick Provincial house. A feature of Georgian brickwork, too, is seen in the projecting band at the level of the second floor, which, corresponding with the water table or projecting underpinning, served to emphasize the stories.

Not only is the Lindall-Gibbs-Osgood house, Number 314 Essex street, erected in 1773, an especially excellent example of the gambrel-roof house of wood with single large chimneys symmetrically placed toward each end, but in its doorways it presents a particularly successful instance of adaptation from the Richard Derby house. The doorway has the same pedimental head and fluted pilasters and the same rustication of the jambs. It differs, however, in being a recessed entrance, and as it is narrower, with a single door, — then being used for the most part, — the pediment is properly more steeply pitched.

Brick and stone were little used in New England as building materials until about the dawn of the nineteenth century. Few bricks were imported except in the South. Clay was plentiful in the North, and even though the product at first was crude, it answered. Corner boards in the spirit of marble quoins were frequently employed with clapboarded walls, however, to give a more substantial appearance. The Cabot-Endicott-Low house, Number 365 Essex Street, is a notable case in point. Erected in 1748 by Joseph Cabot after the design of an English architect, who is also said to have been the architect of the Benjamin Pickman house, the "King" Hooper house at Marblehead and the Hooper-Collins house, now known as "The Lindens", at Danvers, it remains to-day one of the finest Provincial residences in New England, although the doorway is of recent origin. Five closely spaced dormers pierce the roof and light the upper-floor rooms so that three stories are available in virtually a two-story house. As was frequently the case, the gable-roof dormers were symmetrically placed with the central dormer having a segmental rather than triangular pediment. Hipped and lean-to dormers, seen elsewhere, never won favor in Salem. Here again the paired chimneys at the ends of the house, in this instance within the wooden walls, become conspicuous features of the roof line. The verge boards, the curb or coaming retaining the upper slope of the roof, and the gutter are all molded, and the door and window trim throughout shows Georgian influence.

This handsome mansion, noted for its fine interior woodwork, was for many years the home of Joseph S. Cabot, mayor of Salem from 1845 to 1848 inclusive. Later it was for thirty years the residence of Honorable William Crowninshield Endicott, a justice of the Massachusetts Supreme Court from

PLATE XXIV. — Richard Derby House, 168 Derby Street. Erected 1761; Gambrel Gable and Chimneys, Richard Derby House.

PLATE XXV. — Cabot-Endicott-Low House, 365 Essex Street. Erected 1748; Lindall-Gibbs-Osgood House, 314 Essex Street. Erected 1773.

1873 to 1882, and Secretary of War in President Cleveland's cabinet from 1885 to 1889. Here he entertained that eminent English statesman, the Right Honorable Joseph Chamberlain, who married his daughter, Mary, in 1888; also General William T. Sherman in 1890. More recently, until his death, the house has been owned and occupied by Daniel Low, a silversmith of national reputation. The garden has continued to be one of the most beautiful in Salem.

The introduction of quoined corners to wood houses led in a few instances to the adoption as the wall covering of the façade of siding worked with beveled edges and vertical scorings, the latter being so placed as to simulate the bonding of cut stone, as in the case of the Hooper-Collins house, at the end of Collins Street, Danvers. Suitable painting lent realism to the effect, the siding proper being gray, while the quoins and keyed lintels were white in the spirit of marble and the bond scorings also, to approximate the appearance of mortar joints. An additional elaboration of a refined character is provided by the pitched gable, with its oval-topped window, in the lower slope of the roof, the whole being supported by two well-proportioned and nicely executed engaged columns of Corinthian order; also by an ornamental balustrade with handsomely turned balusters and newels surrounding the upper slope of the roof. The gable takes the place of a central dormer, often more elaborate than the others. Of the two dormers each side of it those with broken segmental pediments have properly been made the inner pair.

Few Provincial houses in New England contain so much splendid interior woodwork in as good a state of preservation. The hall and stairway, illustrated and described in Chapter IX, evidently inspired the architect of the Jeremiah Lee mansion in Marblehead, erected in 1768, for the general scheme is identical, though on a larger scale and with variations in detail here and there.

This beautiful country residence, which bears a strong resemblance to the John Hancock mansion which formerly stood on Beacon Street, Boston, near the State House, was erected in 1754 by Robert Hooper, a wealthy Marblehead merchant commonly called "King" Hooper because of his Tory proclivities. Strictly speaking this house finds no logical place in a Salem book, as Danvers was set off from Salem in 1752, but its resemblances to and close association with two prominent Salem houses already mentioned seem to permit this single digression into the architecture of Greater Salem. In 1774 General Thomas Gage occupied this house as a summer residence just after he had been appointed Military Governor of the Province of Massachusetts by the King. In the field opposite during this time were encamped two companies of Colonel Leslie's sixty-fourth British regiment which figured in the North Bridge episode of February 26, 1775, already detailed. More recently, as the home of Francis Peabody, a warm personal friend of the late J. Pierpont Morgan, the estate has been known as "The Lindens." It is a singular fact that John Endecott, the first English governor under the Colonial charter, and Thomas Gage, the last English governor under the Provincial charter, should both have resided in Danvers, and that Endecott once owned the land upon which both residences were situated.

The Benjamin Pickman house, in the rear of Number 165 Essex Street, erected in 1743, was of very similar character. Although still standing it has been partly concealed by stores in front of it. The interior has also been despoiled of its beautiful woodwork characteristic of pre-Revolutionary tendencies and of especial interest because of the carved and gilded codfish on each stair end, indicating the source of the owner's wealth. One of these carved fishes may be seen in the museum of the Essex Institute, however, and the arch with fluted columns between that room and the picture gallery was taken from the Pickman house. About 1800 Samuel McIntire added a unique inclosed porch with hand-carved detail which still remains, although an inappropriate modern door has been substituted for the original.

Several distinguished men were entertained here, notably Governor Pownall on October 22, 1757; Count Castiglioni on June 23, 1784, and Alexander Hamilton on June 20, 1800.

Among the other gambrel-roof houses still standing and of interest, either for architectural merit or historic association, may be mentioned the Hodges-Webb-Meek house, Number 81 Essex Street, erected before 1802; the Derby mansion, Number 140 Lafayette Street; the Eden-Brown house, corner of Broad and Summer streets, erected in 1762; the John Crowninshield house, Essex Street, opposite Union Street, in which the Reverend William Bentley, the historian, lived at one time; the house in which Nathaniel Bowditch, the eminent mathematician, was born March 26, 1773, in Kimball Court to which it was moved from Brown Street; the house of Lieutenant Benjamin West, erected in 1753 at the corner of North and Lynde streets, its original owner being the only Salem man killed at the battle of Bunker Hill; the Lindall-Gibbs-Osgood house, Number 314 Essex Street, erected in 1773, where Benjamin Thompson, afterward Count Rumford, commander-in-chief of the Bavarian army, lived as a boy and made some of his early experiments. Rumford ovens, invented by this eminent scientist and author, are to be found in several of the larger old mansions of Salem, a few of them even now finding occasional use.

PLATE XXVI. — Benjamin Pickman Mansion as it looked prior to 1850. Erected 1750. From an Old Lithograph; "The Lindens," Collins Street, Danvers. Erected 1754.

PLATE XXVII. — Pickman-Derby-Brookhouse Estate, 70 Washington Street. Erected 1764. Razed 1915; Stearns House, 384 Essex Street. Erected 1776.

CHAPTER IV

THE SQUARE THREE-STORY WOOD HOUSE

WITH the entrance of Massachusetts into statehood in 1780, the year previous to the British defeat at Yorktown, which practically ended the Revolutionary War, another change occurred in the domestic architecture of Salem. During the early years of the Commonwealth the square three-story wood house with its foreshortened third story became the prevailing Salem residence. At first of wood with clapboarded walls, or occasionally with rusticated boarding to simulate cut stone, and later of brick with granite trim, this type of Salem town house persisted until shortly after 1818, at about which time the spirit of the Greek Revival supplanted Colonial building traditions, and houses began to resemble the temples of ancient Hellas.

Nothing quite like these substantial square mansions occurs in American domestic architecture outside of New England, and nowhere in such number and perfection as in Salem, for they exhibit the ablest skill of our early native wood-carvers in its very flower. Strictly speaking they are only remotely Colonial, but reflect the broad outlook, the optimistic spirit and the excellent taste of the early years of the republic.

Devoid of that picturesqueness of mass and outline which had given distinction to the peaked-roof lean-to and gambrel-roof houses of earlier times, these post-Revolutionary mansions nevertheless surpassed them all in refinement of ornamental detail. They possessed a certain appealing architectural stateliness, and as large town houses on sites necessarily somewhat restricted in area they were eminently practical. Square, boxlike structures, as a whole monotonous by reason of their broad, high façades, low-pitched, inconspicuous hip roofs and many ranging windows, they were notable for the elegance of their interior woodwork rather than general outward appearance, and in this respect attained the pinnacle of achievement in the woodworkers' art of Salem. Here and there, however, the remarkable craftsmanship of the time asserted itself upon the exterior, and occasionally genuine distinction and even rare beauty were imparted to these unprepossessing structures through the agency of entrance porches and gateways, door and window heads, pilasters and quoined corner treatments, balustraded belvederes and deck roofs.

For the most part these mansions were built by merchants or ship captains, since they or their families felt the need of an elevated place from which to watch for the return of the latest "venture." The belvedere was but a modification of the cupola, that feature so common to the early architecture of New England seacoast towns, while the deck roof, surrounded by a balustrade along the eaves of the entire main house, followed the adoption of very flat hip roofs and the better appreciation of the balustrade as an architectural embellishment.

Probably the best example of the cupola in Salem still exists, although the Pickman-Derby-Brookhouse mansion at Number 70 Washington Street, on the roof of which it originally stood, was razed in 1915 to make way for the new Masonic Temple referred to at length in Chapter XII. This house was built in 1764, for Benjamin Pickman, Jr., a wealthy merchant, replacing the large wooden house of the Reverend Nicholas Noyes, pastor of the First Church at the time of the witchcraft delusion and very rabid in the witch trials of 1692. Later it became the residence of Elias Hasket Derby, who occupied it during the best years of his life until, in 1799 and shortly before his death, he moved into his eighty-thousand-dollar mansion designed by McIntire and to which further reference is made in Chapter XI. John Rogers the sculptor was born in this house, October 30, 1829. Although the house was of brick, McIntire added a front of rusticated boarding, heavy Ionic corner pilasters, the balustrade of the roof, the cupola and the stable, all of wood, during Derby's occupancy. When the buildings were razed in 1915, the cupola was moved to the garden of the Essex Institute, where it may now be seen. Its sculptured eagle is an exact copy of the original, hand carved by McIntire and now preserved at the Brookhouse estate in Marblehead. On the arched ceiling of the cupola a fresco by Corné depicted the several vessels of the Derby fleet, and in the blind of one of the windows a hole was left through which a telescope could be pointed to watch for ships. The festooned drapery on the stable was transferred by Mr. John Robinson, director of the Peabody Museum, to the stable adjoining his residence at Number 18 Summer Street.

While the houses of this period are commonly referred to as being square, three-story structures, fully as many were of oblong shape, some with a long, others with a short side fronting on the street. As a rule an L at the rear, or rarely a wing at the side, provided the service rooms. Hipped roofs, with or without a surrounding belvedere, prevailed, yet there is here and there to be seen a house having a broad, low-pitched gable roof above a third story, with foreshortened windows and otherwise conforming to the early Federal type of Salem. Like the Stearns house, at Number 384 Essex Street, erected in 1776, most of such houses were built during the Revolution and represent a transitional stage rather than a distinct type; they were the forerunners of the hip roof.

PLATE XXVIII. — Hosmer-Townsend-Waters House and Boardman House, 80 and 82 Washington Square East.   Erected
1795 and 1785 respectively; Simon Forrester House,
Derby Street.   Erected before 1800.

PLATE XXIX. — Captain Edward Allen House, 125 Derby Street.
Erected 1780; Briggs-Whipple House, 38 Forrester Street.
Erected about 1800.

The Square Three-Story Wood House

Exteriorly the Stearns house is notable chiefly for the handsome Doric porch added by McIntire in 1785, and which is referred to in detail in Chapter VI. This was the residence of Major, afterward Colonel Joseph Sprague, who was related by marriage to the Stearns family, members of which have occupied the house and have kept it in good order since Colonel Sprague's death in 1808.

Colonel Sprague, then a major, participated conspicuously in the first armed resistance to British tyranny at the North Bridge on Sunday, February 26, 1775, when Colonel Leslie's British troops were foiled in their search for cannon, which leading men in Salem had in hiding.

The house at the corner of Derby Street and Hodges Court, erected before 1800 by Simon Forrester, a wealthy sea captain, retains many details of the Provincial period, although generally Federal in its characteristics. One remarks at once the absolutely symmetrical arrangement of the façade and the location of two chimneys at each end of the house, as was the case in so many gambrel-roof dwellings. More steeply pitched than many hip-roof constructions, the roof of the Forrester house boasts neither belvedere nor balustrade. The quoined corners of the clapboarded walls recall the more pretentious wooden gambrel-roof mansions. The paneling of the door was evidently inspired by that of the Richard Derby house, but the Doric porch is typical of the Federal period, although exceptional in its square columns.

A rare example of the square — nearly cubical — dwelling with its hip roof rising to a single great chimney in the exact center is to be seen in the Hosmer-Townsend-Waters house, Number 80 Washington Square, designed for Captain Joseph Hosmer by McIntire in 1795. It contains much fine interior woodwork and is famous for its wistaria-clad, inclosed side porch referred to again in Chapter VI. This house was long the home of Henry FitzGilbert Waters, author of "John Harvard and His Ancestry", "An Examination into the English Ancestry of George Washington" and many papers devoted to the genealogy of prominent Salem families. Mr. Waters is said to have had the best private collection of rare Colonial furniture in New England.

To the left in the accompanying photograph is to be seen the Boardman house at Number 82 Washington Square East, with its handsome inclosed porch and gateway, to which further reference is made in Chapter VI. By the beauty of its proportions and detail this house attracted the attention of George Washington when visiting Salem in 1789. It was then new, having been erected in 1785, and was offered for Washington's use. Captain Boardman stood in the front doorway when Washington passed by on his way to breakfast with his old friend George

The Square Three-Story Wood House

Cabot at Beverly and overheard Washington's query, "How do you build such handsome houses?"

The Captain Edward Allen house, Number 125 Derby Street, erected in 1780, is an example of an oblong house with a single great chimney centrally located. Otherwise the structure greatly resembles the Simon Forrester house, except for the different sash arrangement of the foreshortened third-story windows and the broader inclosed porch.

Two more houses on corner sites, with attractive though simple Colonial fences, and resembling the Hosmer-Townsend-Waters house more or less nearly, are of interest not so much for individual architectural merit as for their frank simplicity and appearance of substantial comfort. Each forms a typical picture redolent of the spirit of early Federal days in Salem. Both have interesting doorways, which are alluded to in Chapter VI.

The Briggs-Whipple house, Number 38 Forrester Street, erected before 1800, was the home of Enos Briggs, one of the principal master shipbuilders of Massachusetts. Briggs came to Salem in 1790, previous to which he had followed his occupation on the North River in Plymouth County. After superintending the erection of two ships at the head of Derby wharf, he launched one of them sideways as a matter of novelty which drew a great crowd. This was on May 3, 1791, and on the eighteenth of the same month he launched the *Grand Turk*, a ship of

564 tons, the second of that name owned by Elias Hasket Derby and said to have been the largest ship intended for merchant service ever built in Salem. Briggs then established his own yard in South Salem near Stage Point. There he continued in business until 1817, two years previous to his death, building fifty-one vessels aggregating 11,500 tons, including the famous frigate *Essex*.

The George M. Whipple house at Number 2 Andover Street, erected in 1804, interests the student of architecture chiefly for the unusual location of the front doorway to one side of the center. Such an arrangement in seventeenth-century houses is by no means infrequent, but in the square houses of this period is rarely seen. The inclosed porch and Palladian window above are modern.

Until about 1902, when it was razed, there stood at Number 376 Essex Street the handsome residence of Aaron Waite, of Pierce and Waite, a firm of prosperous merchants and shipowners. Waite's partner, Jerathmel Pierce, in 1782 erected, after plans by McIntire, the so-called Nichols house at Number 80 Federal Street, now commonly spoken of as the finest old wooden house in New England. The Aaron Waite house was erected in 1789–1790 and has been accredited to Daniel Bancroft, the architect and builder who constructed the court-house of 1785 designed by McIntire.

The photograph shows well a characteristic estate

PLATE XXX. — Aaron Waite House, 376 Essex Street. Erected 1789-1790; George M. Whipple House, 2 Andover Street. Erected 1804.

PLATE XXXI. — Timothy Orne House, 266 Essex Street. Erected 1761; Peabody-Rantoul House, 19 Chestnut Street. Erected 1810.

of the time, a square main house standing directly on the street, with stately gateposts and picket fence at each side of the lot to accommodate a stable at the rear adjoining the L of the house, the stable door being architecturally treated, and the side door of the house also serving as a carriage entrance. As in the case of the Boardman house, the hip roof rises to a balustraded belvedere, and one notices the growing custom of locating chimneys only where needed without regard for exterior appearance.

While quoined corners were still frequently employed with clapboarded walls, rusticated boarding to simulate cut stone, which had enjoyed a certain vogue during Provincial times, rarely found favor with those who built square three-story houses. The Timothy Orne house at Number 266 Essex Street, however, was erected in 1761 while Provincial influences were at their height, and although in general design and arrangement the house was rather ahead of its time, in finish it was not unlike several gambrel-roof structures of Essex County. The two large chimney stacks symmetrically located are characteristic of the earlier period, and the deck roof with its slender ornamental palings and posts differs from most arrangements on hip-roofed houses in that the balustrade is placed neither near the ridge nor the eaves, but about midway between them.

Timothy Orne was one of the leading merchants of Salem just before the Revolution. His leanings at times seemed to favor the Crown, and Felt in his "Annals of Salem" relates that an old letter, dated November 18, 1775, tells how Orne was taken in the evening from a house in School Street and threatened with being tarred and feathered for some expression not sufficiently anti-royal, but was released by the Committee of Safety.

Deck roofs such as that of the Orne house and other dwellings in Salem undoubtedly induced Mr. William G. Rantoul, the eminent Boston architect, to embellish his residence at Number 19 Chestnut Street in the course of alterations about 1905, by adding a balustrade, located, however, at the eaves as on the Pierce-Johonnot-Nichols house. Both posts and palings accord with older Salem work, yet possess a certain individuality, particularly the palings which, unlike most others, comprise two pleasing patterns in alternation. New and attractive window frames with architrave casings of typically Salem pattern were added at the same time, while the Doric porch and door with glass lights in the two upper panels were copied from that of the Goss-Osgood house at Number 15 Chestnut Street. Of broad street frontage but no great depth, this is one of the many three-story wood houses of this period that are oblong rather than square and depend on a two-story L in the rear for several rooms. It was erected in 1810 by the Reverend Charles Cleveland, great-uncle of President Cleveland, and deputy collector of the port of Salem from 1789 to 1802, who lived to within a few days of a complete century.

A house of virtually the same general character, though lacking the decked roof and pleasing fenestration of the Rantoul residence, is the birthplace of General Frederick W. Lander at Number 5 Barton Square, erected about 1800. Here the third-story windows are smaller and the intended effect of foreshortening was not achieved, the high-studded rooms with windows of normal height on the two lower floors leaving too broad, unbroken wall spaces. The six-pane upper windows do not possess the pleasing scale of the more common nine-paned foreshortened windows. The side entrance and veranda are of more recent date than the house proper.

A brave officer with an enviable record in the government service, both before and during the Civil War, General Lander was one of Salem's most honored men. Being a civil engineer by profession he was employed by the government to report on the feasibility of a transcontinental railway to the Pacific Coast, and he later constructed the great overland wagon road which made the construction of the railway possible. Prospecting in those pioneer days was fraught with many dangers, and on one surveying expedition, undertaken at his own expense, he was the only member of the party to return alive. At the outbreak of the Civil War in 1861 he was in Texas on a secret mission for the government, but escaped with great difficulty with important advices. He was thereupon made a brigadier-general and soon afterward assigned to a command on the upper Potomac. In the battle of Ball's Bluff on October 21, 1861, he was shot in the leg. The wound had not healed when he reported for duty to General Hancock in January, 1862, and his death followed early in March, being announced in a special order by General McClellan. His body was brought to Salem where it lay in state at the City Hall and was buried with honors unequaled since the funeral of Captain Lawrence and Lieutenant Ludlow of the *Chesapeake* who were killed in the memorable engagement with the *Shannon* in 1813 off the port of Salem.

Occasionally where an ample site permitted, a wing extended to one side of the main house along the street, instead of an L projecting from the rear, and thus by greatly elongating the oblong arrangement reduced in a measure the apparent height of a three-story structure. A notable example was the Crowninshield-Devereux-Waters house at Number 74 Washington Square East, as it appeared prior to 1892 and as shown by the accompanying illustration. A hip-roofed dwelling, three stories high and of the utmost simplicity, the elliptical porch over the front doorway with its heavy Tuscan columns and the inclosed porch of the three-story wing afford the only architectural embellishments, aside from the necessary windows, to break the great expanse of the

PLATE XXXII. — Cook-Oliver House, 142 Federal Street. Erected 1804; Crowninshield-Devereux-Waters House, 72 Washington Square East. Erected 1805.

PLATE XXXIII. — Birthplace of General Frederick W. Lander, 5 Barton Square. Erected about 1800; Home of Samuel McIntire, 31 Summer Street. Erected 1780.

façade. The fence with its small square posts, light molded rails and base, and unique jig-sawed member between each five square pickets, is of simple grace and provides an effective foil for the severity of the house itself.

The house was erected in 1805, after plans by Samuel McIntire, for Clifford Crowninshield, a merchant who accumulated considerable wealth by many daring ventures at sea. It is interesting to recall that the *Minerva*, owned by him and Nathaniel West, was the first Salem vessel to circumnavigate the globe. After Mr. Crowninshield's death in 1809, his wife having died and there being no children, the house was occupied by Captain James Devereux, who had married Mr. Crowninshield's sister Sarah in 1792. It was Captain Devereux who commanded the ship *Franklin* of Boston, the first American vessel to trade with Japan, half a century before commercial intercourse was opened between the island empire of the Far East and the United States. His ship was also among the first to engage in the Mocha trade, the records showing that in 1808 the *Franklin* brought from there a cargo of 532,365 pounds of coffee, consigned to Joseph Peabody, on which a duty of $26,618.25 was paid. In 1846 Captain Devereux died and the house was occupied by Captain William Dean Waters, whose wife Abigail was a daughter of Captain Devereux. On the death of Captain Waters in 1880 it was inherited by his son William

Crowninshield Waters, who sold it in 1892. Up to that time the structure had remained unchanged, but the new owner, Zina Goodell, changed the main part of it from an oblong house with three rooms on each floor to a square house with four rooms on each floor by moving the wing around to the rear and about doubling the depth of the building.

Residences arranged like the Crowninshield-Devereux house as it was originally built, but standing end to the street on a deep lot of narrow street frontage, the service wing extending straight back from the rear end of the main house, were frequently erected, and many still remain. Although of quaint simplicity yet only slight architectural pretension, none of these holds more of interest than the modest gable-roof house at Number 31 Summer Street which was the home of Samuel McIntire, the eminent architect and wood-carver, whose life and work have been so completely detailed and illustrated in a previous book by the present authors entitled "The Wood-Carver of Salem."

Of a family of carvers, joiners and housewrights, whose skill descended through several generations, McIntire stands forth as the genius among them. In his father's shop he learned the trade of carpenter and joiner, and, as the result of persistent application with his tools and of cultivating his inherent sense of design through diligent study of the classic masters, he not only became probably the most highly skilled American wood-carver of his time, but the most eminent architect of the city most widely known for the rare beauty of its Colonial residences and public buildings.

For thirty years, until his death in 1811, Salem architecture was dominated by this man whose name in the annals of New England building ranks second only to that of Charles Bulfinch, architect of the Massachusetts State House. During that period most of the finer residences and several public edifices were designed by him. Working at a time when virtually all the large houses in New England were being built three stories high and square or oblong, he naturally followed the tendency of the time, but obtained considerable individuality by variation of the floor plan, particularly by alteration of the relation between the main houses and the L, where the latter existed. And what the style lacked in picturesqueness of line and mass he supplied in variety of embellishment, as seen in the beautiful detail of his doorways, porches, windows, cornices, deck roofs, belvederes and occasional pilaster treatment of the façade. He was also especially successful in cleverly foreshortening the third story, with nearly square windows to reduce the apparent total height of the structure, the effect being due to nice proportions carefully determined.

That McIntire's achievements are incomparably

more pleasing than similar contemporaneous work elsewhere in America is due to his skill with tools, inherent good taste, keen sense of proportion and native ingenuity. Unlike many American builders who took their inspiration chiefly if not wholly from Georgian work, McIntire, like Jones, Wren, Gibbons, and the brothers Adam, went back to original sources and adapted directly from the Greek and Roman classics, with modifications and innovations of his own, the result being that his designs are more chaste, original and imaginative. His detail, in its freedom, refinement, lightness and graceful dignity, presents a more domestic, personal, direct and altogether charming interpretation of Renaissance motives and therefore more useful suggestions for present-day work. Indeed, his doorways, chimney pieces and other wood trim have furnished the inspiration for more of the best modern Colonial houses than has the work of any other early American architect, and a consideration of these sources brings his name frequently into the pages that follow.

Many of McIntire's plans and a few of his tools are preserved at the Essex Institute, and an examination of the incomplete character of the former and the crudity of the latter redoubles one's admiration for the nicety of the work he accomplished with their aid. In 1793 McIntire entered a design for the national capitol at Washington in the first architectural competition ever held in America. His plans, preserved by the Maryland Historical Society, compare favorably with the other submitted plans, and had he lived .it is likely that, after the death of William Thornton in 1827, he would have been associated with B. H. Latrobe and Charles Bulfinch in the modification and construction of the design chosen.

After he had become established in his career McIntire bought the modest house at Number 31 Summer Street which had been erected in 1780, and in the yard at the rear located his shop, where much of the wood finish and fine carving for houses designed by him was prepared. During his brief career he was too busy to build himself a house such as he might have desired, and it is not known to what extent he improved the Summer Street house, if at all. Although of the utmost simplicity, the mantels and other wood trim resemble his work and possess a certain pleasing distinction. The front room on the third floor was his music room, and the coved ceiling under the gable roof was probably his own idea. Here he had his best furniture, an organ and other musical instruments on which he was an accomplished performer, and here he spent his leisure hours and entertained his friends.

Turning now to specific examples of McIntire's genius as an architect, the Cook-Oliver house, Number 142 Federal Street, compares favorably with anything in Salem. A stately mansion, standing in the shade of giant trees, its beautiful entrance porch, fence and gateposts at once attract the eye. As recounted in Chapters VI and XI they were hand-tooled by McIntire, together with much of the interior finish, for the Elias Hasket Derby mansion formerly on the site of the Market House, and were removed to their present location soon after 1804, previous to the complete razing of the Derby mansion in 1815. The house at Number 142 Federal Street was built after plans by McIntire and under his direction for Captain Samuel Cook, a master mariner. Although erected in 1804, the house was from eight to eleven years in the building because of unsuccessful voyages which rendered the expense of faster work a burden. The need for economy perhaps accounts for the use of much woodwork from the Derby mansion. However that may be, its employment transformed what had been planned as an ordinary house into one of exceptional charm and distinction and preserved some of McIntire's most notable personal handicraft.

In more recent years this house was occupied until his death in 1885 by Captain Cook's son-in-law, General Henry Kemble Oliver, the famous composer and musician, and here he wrote the music for "Federal Street" and several other well-known church hymns. General Oliver was at various times one of the early mayors of Lawrence, treasurer of her great cotton mills, Adjutant General and State

PLATE XXXIV. — The house where Hawthorne achieved fame, 14 Mall Street; Paved Courtyard between Pierce-Johonnot-Nichols House and Barn.

PLATE XXXV. — Pierce-Johonnot-Nichols House, 80 Federal Street; One-story Wing, Pierce-Johonnot-Nichols House.

The Square Three-Story Wood House

Treasurer of Massachusetts, and Mayor of Salem in his eightieth year.

Like most residences of the time the Cook-Oliver house is a square structure, three stories high, with a two-story L at the rear jutting by on one side of the main house far enough to permit a side door. The third story of the main house is foreshortened, with almost square, nine-paned windows to reduce the apparent total height and the roof was originally decked with a surrounding balustrade and reached through a scuttle. All walls are clapboarded, except for the flat boarding of the "jut-by" and the eastern wall of the main house, which is of brick, affording, before its neighbor was built, greater protection against the northeast storms off the sea.

Several refined and attractive architectural features relieve the severity of line inevitable in a square building. Most important of these, the porch and doorway are treated in Chapter VI. Windows with molded architrave casings range absolutely on all elevations, the second-story window frames being elaborated by the addition of beautiful hand-carved beads. A heavy cornice with large molded modillions adorns the eaves, and a broad, horizontal belt of vertical-fluted wood finish at the level of the second floor and porch cornice extends across the entire façade and serves to tie the porch to the house as a whole.

Of the many mansions designed by McIntire,

most of which still stand in excellent condition, thanks to Salem thrift and the durability of white pine, the Pierce-Johonnot-Nichols house at Number 80 Federal Street is looked upon as the principal monument to his genius. His masterpiece was probably the Elias Hasket Derby mansion which formerly stood on the site of the present Market House and to which detailed reference is made in Chapter XI. To-day, however, the Pierce-Johonnot-Nichols house is the architectural gem of old Salem, and is commonly spoken of as the finest wooden Colonial house in New England.

While it boasts no important association with historic events in national affairs, the pathos of its romantic memories makes direct appeal to all. Erected in 1782, and its last interior woodwork completed in 1801, it was the pride and joy of Jerathmel Pierce, a wealthy East India merchant. Here were centered all his life interests, for a path led from the inclosed porch directly to the wharf and warehouse on the North River, then a navigable stream, where his ships came laden with spices and fabrics from the Orient. The gradual completion of the house, room by room, and the development of the terraced garden were objects of his daily attention while still in constant touch with his business. In 1826, however, financial adversity deprived him and his son-in-law, George Nichols, of their fortunes, and in consequence the house was sold in 1827 to

George Johonnot, an old friend of both families. Mr. Pierce, then in his eightieth year, could not bear so great a shock; only once after going to live with his son-in-law in the famous old Tontine Block did he look at the mansion which had formerly been his, and shortly afterward he died. During the year 1839 both Mr. and Mrs. Johonnot died, and it was discovered that the house had been willed by them to George Nichols and his wife to be held in trust for their four daughters. Thus the estate came back into the family, and the son-in-law was enabled to pass his declining years in the house where he married his first wife and where his second wife, Betsy Pierce, was born. After relinquishing active management of his business upon the verge of seventy in favor of two of his sons, he devoted himself to the care of the beautiful garden at the back of the house which even to-day retains much of its former charm.

Thus architects, antiquaries, lovers of romance and Colonial art rejoice that in 1917 the house was purchased by the Essex Institute for permanent preservation as a magnificent specimen of the residence of a Salem merchant and ship owner during the period of great commercial prosperity following the Revolution.

As a whole the greater depth, breadth and fore-shortened third story of the Pierce-Johonnot-Nichols house give it a mass much more pleasing than the average square Salem house. Its particular distinction, however, lies in the classic balustrades of the low, decked, hip roof and belvedere, whence arriving ships might be watched for, and the attractive embellishment of the fluted pilaster treatment at the corners, a free use of the Doric order, which does much to mitigate the severity in shape of a square house. The Doric spirit also pervades the entrance porch at the front and the inclosed porch at the side doorway, which in pleasing proportion and delicate detail are the equal of any to be found in New England. The fence and charming urn-topped gateposts framing the doorway vista harmonize well with these porches; the posts, reproductions of the originals, are especially well formed as to proper height and classic outline, the urns being the originals and carved out of solid blocks of wood. The window treatment, both of caps and casings, is one of effective simplicity, and the dark-painted doors with panels well spaced are equipped with quaint brass hardware, including one of the handsomest knockers in Salem. At the rear of the house the stable and various outbuildings range about a brick-paved court and form a picture of remarkable picturesqueness. Whereas the gable ends of the outbuildings are embellished with keyed round arches, the one-story wing of the house on the opposite side of the court consists of a series of broad doors under elliptical fanlights somewhat after the manner of a colonnade. This device, reflecting the

The Square Three-Story Wood House

Adam influence which dominates the treatment of the eastern rooms of the house, presents a motive of exceptional charm for modern adaptation where a glazed sun porch is desired. Indoors McIntire found ample opportunity to display his best efforts as a designer and wood-carver, and much of the splendid woodwork and several magnificent mantels and chimney pieces are treated in succeeding chapters devoted to those subjects.

Houses of every principal period of Salem architecture are more or less directly associated with Nathaniel Hawthorne, and the so-called three-story square type is no exception. At various times Hawthorne occupied five different places of residence in Salem, and many other old dwellings, such as the Grimshawe house, were among his favorite haunts or were described by him in his books.

For about sixteen months in 1846 and 1847, while serving as surveyor of the Port of Salem and Beverly, Hawthorne occupied the house at Number 18 Chestnut Street. Like many others it was oblong rather than square and stood end to the street with a wing projecting from the opposite end. Three stories high and hip roofed, it afforded a comfortable home of the time, yet without special architectural distinction, and was considerably altered during the Victorian decadence, the treatment of the former principal entrance at the side on Botts Court and the addition of the present front entrance with bay windows above being most unfortunate. It was during the early months of Hawthorne's occupancy that his son Julian was born in Boston at the home of his father-in-law, Doctor Nathaniel Peabody. Little of his important literary work was done in the house, yet his remarkably retiring disposition led him to live here in seclusion as much as ever. To avoid callers whom he did not wish to meet, he would steal out of the back door, which opened on the narrow court running between Chestnut and Essex streets, and remain as long as necessary in the house of his friend Doctor Benjamin F. Browne at the other end of the court.

It was in his last Salem residence at Number 14 Mall Street that Hawthorne achieved fame, although this house proved to be not a place of joy as he had anticipated, but rather one of sorrow. Here he lived from the autumn of 1847 until he moved to Lenox in 1850, and in his study on the third floor overlooking the street he wrote "The Scarlet Letter" under the severe pressure of dismissal from office and financial distress, and interrupted by his mother's death in 1849 and his own serious illness. A change in the administration at Washington brought a new appointee as Surveyor of the Port, and to his Mall Street home he came to tell his wife that he had been turned out of office. "Very well," said she, "now you can write your romance." And in response to his query as to what they should live on meantime

PLATE XXXVI. — The "Grimshawe" House, 53 Charter Street.
Erected about 1780; Hawthorne's Residence in 1846 and
1847, 18 Chestnut Street.

PLATE XXXVII. — Gardner-White-Pingree House, 128 Essex
Street. Erected 1810; Dodge-Shreve House, 29 Chestnut
Street. Erected 1817.

she showed him in a bureau drawer the gold she had saved from portions of his salary which he had given her occasionally.

It was in "a chamber over the sitting-room" early in 1850 that James T. Fields, the Boston publisher, found the despondent Hawthorne "hovering near a stove", and induced him to submit his manuscript of "The Scarlet Letter" for a reading. In "Yesterdays With Authors" Fields tells of Hawthorne's great reluctance, repeated refusals and grave fears that the book would be a failure, also of his own enthusiasm as he read this powerful romance, and of its immediate publication and complete success.

The Mall Street house is also oblong and stands end to the street with a wing in the rear. It is three stories high, hip roofed, and like many others its broad, picturesque "front" door opens upon a yard with trees at one side of the lot. Both house and surroundings remain substantially as when Hawthorne left them.

Another end-to-the-street house, though of much broader frontage and having an inclosed entrance porch on the street, is inseparably associated with Hawthorne and his writings. This so-called "Grimshawe" house, erected about 1780 at Number 53 Charter Street, adjoining the Charter Street Burial Ground, was the scene of Hawthorne's courtship and happiest hours, for it was the home of his childhood playmate, Sophia Amelia Peabody, the daughter of Doctor Nathaniel Peabody of Boston, whom he married in the summer of 1842. Externally the "Grimshawe" house has changed but little in form, but an unfortunate fire in 1915 burned out the interior, and the structure was then remodeled as a lodging house, the inclosed porch described in the first chapter of "Dr. Grimshawe's Secret" being removed for preservation to the garden of the Essex Institute.

CHAPTER V

THE SQUARE THREE–STORY BRICK HOUSE

THE common adoption of brick construction for most of the better residences during the first decade of the nineteenth century considerably broadened the scope of the three-story square house. While the general mass, roof lines and ornamental features continued substantially unchanged, except that the Ionic and especially the Corinthian orders replaced the Doric and Tuscan which had prevailed in former years, brickwork contributed numerous desirable characteristics not possessed by clapboarded walls. Foremost among them should be mentioned its permanence and fireproof qualities which are responsible for the preservation of so many of these splendid century-old homes in almost as good condition as when they were erected. But this is by no means all : brickwork clothed these boxlike houses with that delightful warmth of color, that charming texture of the bonding, that enlivening contrast of marble lintels and sills, mortar joints and white-painted wood trim against a red background, and that satisfying appearance of certain comfort and intrinsic worth which wood construction, however honest and attractive, cannot convey.

On a foundation of large cut-granite blocks the brickwork was for the most part laid up in Flemish bond with headers and stretchers in alternation in the same course. The Richard Derby house, erected in 1761, the oldest brick house now standing in Salem, has this bonding, and it was generally employed until about 1816 and 1817 when longitudinal or running bond began to be used, as in the Dodge-Shreve and Silsbee-Mott houses. Very likely in some of these latter houses transverse or tie courses exist, but are concealed, as in the walls of the East India Marine Hall. While making alterations in this building in 1885 it was found that every eighth course consisted of special square bricks eight by eight by two inches, having the outward appearance of stretchers but the strength of headers in the wall. The brickwork of the Pickman-Shreve-Little house is laid up in running bond with every eighth course consisting of ordinary headers to form a transverse tie course.

Several of the many old brick houses still standing in Salem are the work of McIntire, and are alluded to either here or in Chapter XI. Most of them obviously owe much to the influence of his genius. They are scattered through Derby, Essex and Chestnut streets and about Washington Square; the mansions of Chestnut Street, however, are especially

PLATE XXXVIII.—"The Studio," 2 and 4 Chestnut Street. Erected 1826; Mansfield-Bolles House, 8 Chestnut Street. Erected 1810.

PLATE XXXIX. — Peabody-Silsbee House, 360 Essex Street. Erected 1797; Hodges-Peele-West House, 12 Chestnut Street. Erected 1804.

notable. This broad thoroughfare, bordered by giant elms through which stately residences and welcoming doorways are everywhere to be seen, presents a favorite picture of the days of Salem's former greatness that lingers long in the memory of every visitor. Indeed, it has been spoken of as the finest architectural street in America, and who cares to deny it? The accompanying illustration was made from a point in front of Number 10 Chestnut Street, the residence of Philip Little, the artist. This house was erected in 1804, but the gateposts are modern, yet Colonial in spirit.

A few more oblong houses were erected during this final period of Colonial architecture in Salem, now and then one being located end to the street; but generally speaking the nineteenth-century Colonial mansions of brick were very nearly square with service wings at the rear, sometimes centrally located, or again jutting by the main house at one side.

Of the end-to-the-street houses perhaps the Mansfield-Bolles house at Number 8 Chestnut Street best deserves mention here. It is in brick about what Hawthorne's Mall Street residence was in wood. Its chief distinctions lie in its doorway of graceful simplicity and the unusual gambrel-roofed wing of wood at the rear end. Unlike most brick houses of importance in Salem, aside from "The Studio", referred to later in this chapter, its windows boast no lintels, but have molded architrave frames of wood let into the reveals of the brickwork. Built originally as a two-story house, possibly with a gambrel roof, a third story was added about 1825 or 1830 by Deacon John Stone, and the brickwork has since been painted a slate-gray color.

Before its enlargement David Asby kept a shoe store here, and about 1814 the house was occupied by John Thayer. In more recent times it was for many years the residence of the Reverend E. C. Bolles, formerly pastor of the Universalist Church and now the "grand old man" of Tufts College. Although advanced in years and blind, Professor Bolles still holds his chair, and the boys delight to attend his lectures. He it was who in 1886 with William P. Upham and John Robinson made the famous set of witchcraft photographs, the negatives of which are now held by the Essex Institute.

Of the oblong mansions of brick with an L in the rear none is more worthy of detailed attention than the Gardner-White-Pingree house, Number 128 Essex Street, of which Samuel McIntire was the architect in 1810. It was probably McIntire's last important work and may not have been completed before his death. It is considered by many to be his best brick house and contains beautiful interior woodwork. Exteriorly, by the ingenious use of broad, slightly projecting bands of white marble at the second- and third-floor levels McIntire at once relieved the severity of so high a façade and exaggerated the horizontal effect. These bands, together with the sills and keyed flat-arch lintels of the many ranging windows, assist materially in creating a seemingly broader frontage, and so, like the foreshortened third-story windows, tend to reduce the apparent total height. The handsome balustrade of the decked roof, consisting of classic turned balusters between pedestals at regular intervals, also assists to accomplish the same purpose aside from its ornamental value. Instead of increasing the apparent height, it has the very contrary effect, and by locating the solid roof line somewhat below the absolute top of the structure causes the whole mass to look lower. The elliptical porch and doorway, one of the best in Salem, is treated in detail in the following chapter.

Another brick residence designed by McIntire, and one of his best achievements, is the Peabody-Silsbee house at Number 380 Essex Street, erected in 1797. Historically it is of interest as the birthplace alike of the late Francis Peabody, a close personal friend of the late J. Pierpont Morgan, and of S. Endicott Peabody, one of the trustees of George Peabody, the London banker for whom Peabody, Massachusetts, was named. Although a square house with several wings and subsequent additions, this and the Gardner-White-Pingree house have certain characteristics in common, the resemblances being emphasized, perhaps, by the fact that in recent years the brickwork of both houses has been painted a slate-gray color. Except for the foreshortened third-story windows the fenestration is virtually the same, notably the lintels. The balustrades of the decked roofs are also much the same, the more steeply pitched hip roof of the Peabody-Silsbee house, however, being elaborated by a surmounting belvedere of spacious area. Whereas the cornice under the eaves of the Gardner-White-Pingree house conforms fairly closely to the conventional Corinthian order, that of the Peabody-Silsbee house bears the stamp of McIntire's originality. A ball molding, a veritable triumph of hand carving, replaces the usual dentil course, yet gives the same scale, while the under side of the corona is ornamented with square clusters of balls at regular intervals after the manner of the mutules of the Doric order. The Doric porch, with its delicate suggestions of Adam influence, is alluded to at length in the following chapter. As on many old Salem estates a stable in the rear of the grounds is in complete accord with the house, as all outbuildings should be.

Another square, gray-painted brick house of this period that charms the eye by the unaffected simplicity of its façade, with plain marble lintels and the play of light and shadow cast upon it by a great, spreading elm, is the residence of Arthur W. West, Number 12 Chestnut Street, first owned and occupied by Captain Jonathan Hodges. Built originally

Plate XL. — Baldwin-Lyman House, 92 Washington Square
East. Erected 1818; Pickman-Shreve-Little House,
27 Chestnut Street. Erected 1816.

PLATE XLI. — Andrew-Safford House, 13 Washington Square. Erected 1818; Loring-Emmerton House, 328 Essex Street. Erected 1818.

in 1804 for two families, it was converted to a single house by Willard Peele in 1845. At that time the present doorway and probably the porch were added, for both show the influence of the Greek revival in the heavier columns, the detail of the capitals, the oblong transom and the absence of leaded glass in the side lights. The bracket-like modillions of the cornice are also unusual in houses erected as early as 1804. The handsome wrought-iron fence and stair balustrades compare favorably with the best on Chestnut Street, and the stable in the rear, architecturally embellished after the manner of the time, completes a domestic picture that never fails to elicit the admiration of all who see it.

The Baldwin-Lyman house at Number 92 Washington Square East, although erected in 1818, retains several of the characteristics of earlier days, notably the symmetrical arrangement of four tall chimneys in pairs at each end and the ornamental picket fence with architectural gateposts which had proved such an effective feature of the gambrel-roof and square wood houses. The doorway, to which reference is made in the following chapter, reflects the designs of earlier years in the simplicity of its glasswork. Much of the pristine charm of the fenestration has been lost through the substitution of four-paned windows for the original twelve-paned windows which gave such a pleasing scale to the façade.

Palladian windows, which had formerly only

graced stairway landings at the rear of the house, now began to be employed above entrance porches to elaborate the façade and lend added charm to the second-floor hall. In this connection two spacious mansions standing side by side form an interesting comparison. Except for their rear wings the Pickman-Shreve-Little house, Number 27 Chestnut Street, erected in 1816, and the Dodge-Shreve house, next to it at Number 29 Chestnut Street, are substantially the same in mass. Both are square, three stories in height, their hip roofs surmounted by large belvederes with classic balustrades and corner pedestals, and their heavy cornices embellished with modillions, elaborate in their fine-scale detail.

It is in the ornamental details of the façade that these structures differ chiefly, the Pickman-Shreve-Little house being, generally speaking, the simpler of the two. The nicely carved keyed lintels with their central vertical bead of diminishing spheres, perhaps suggested by the lintels of the Mack and Stone houses, are in striking contrast to the more elaborate lintels of the Dodge-Shreve house with a variation of the Grecian fret motive for each floor. These lintels have frequently been copied in modern work.

Both doorways and the Corinthian entrance porches have much in common and represent superlative achievements in the use of this order in Salem architecture. While the balustrade above the Dodge-

Shreve porch enriches it somewhat, and so definitely embraces the Palladian window above it as virtually to render porch and window complements of a single architectural feature, the Pickman-Shreve-Little porch has long held the distinction of being the best hand-carved wood Corinthian porch in America. It is as near perfection in detail and proportion as anything that has yet been achieved in wood. Both entrances are enhanced in charm by delightful wrought-iron hand rails and fences, also leaded glass work of graceful pattern, differing principally in the side lights. As in the case of the porches, so the Palladian window of the Pickman-Shreve-Little house is simpler in detail than that of the Dodge-Shreve house, and unlike the latter has above it a semicircular fanlight in place of the usual Georgian window. Attractive as this is in itself, its use in this location fails to please as does the simpler oblong window. Detailed consideration of these Palladian windows finds a more logical place in the following chapter, because of their intimate relation to the entrance porch and the architectural effect of the doorway as a whole.

At Number 328 Essex Street the Loring-Emmerton house attracts attention as an old mansion of 1818 remodeled and much elaborated in 1886-1887 by the addition of a profusion of Colonial detail adapted from various sources in Salem and elsewhere. The handsome marble window lintels were inspired by those at Number 29 Chestnut Street, and while the Palladian window emanated from the same source, the flattened arch has neither the beauty of line of its higher prototype nor the charm of the character-istic elliptical arch. The Ionic porch and doorway undoubtedly were inspired by those of the Peabody-Silsbee house, a wood balustrade above being substi-tuted for the wrought iron of the older porch. While the door itself is excellent, the leaded glass about it loses much of the beauty of century-old work in its ex-ceedingly fine-scale pattern. At one side of the house an elaborate carriage entrance of obvious modernity exhibits but little of the Colonial spirit. The archi-tectural gateposts, however, have been reproduced after McIntire's best manner and lend an appearance of stately elegance to the carriage entrance.

This mansion was for many years the home of Honorable George Bailey Loring, who was a member of Congress, Commissioner of Agriculture under Presidents Garfield and Arthur, and was appointed Minister to Portugal by President Harrison. On several occasions he entertained President Pierce there. It is now the residence of Miss Caroline O. Emmerton, the philanthropist through whose gener-osity the "House of Seven Gables" and the "Old Bakery" have been preserved, as recounted in the first two chapters of this book.

Among the finest old brick mansions of Salem the Andrew-Safford house at Number 13 Washington

The Square Three-Story Brick House

Square takes a prominent place. It was erected in 1818 by John Andrew, the uncle of John A. Andrew, Civil War Governor of Massachusetts, who was a frequent visitor. At the time of its completion it was regarded as the most costly private residence in New England, and no finer example of the characteristic architecture of its time remains in such an excellent state of preservation. In fact, the whole estate, embracing a stable at the right in harmony with the house and a fine old formal garden at the left, exemplifies as do few others the best that money could provide in Salem a century ago. The house itself is of noble proportions, square and having a service wing centrally located in the rear, the great tall chimneys, five in all, being symmetrically located. Like the Peabody-Silsbee house the hip roof is ornamented by a balustrade about the belvedere and also at the eaves. The balustrade of the belvedere consists of square pedestals and turned balusters of classic outline, whereas a semicircular blind panel in the center of each baluster section elaborates the balustrade at the eaves. Under the eaves the cornice includes heavy modillions and a relatively fine-scale ball molding reminiscent of the Peabody-Silsbee cornice. Like those of the Dodge-Shreve house the nicely carved keyed lintels were perhaps inspired by those of the Mack and Stone houses. At the side entrance a unique and striking effect is created by a portico formed by fluted columns rising the height of all three stories. This and some of the detail of the interior finish show the influence of Greek revival tendencies. An intrusive glass conservatory of recent origin under this columnal veranda mars the former imposing effect of the columns. The ornate Corinthian entrance porch, referred to in detail in the following chapter, is the most elaborate and one of the most admired in Salem, and properly forms the center of interest of this imposing façade. As in the case of several other brick residences, the walls have been painted. Within, the house is notable for its fine wood finish, scenic wall papers and antique furniture, to which further reference will be made in Chapter VIII.

The Silsbee-Mott house, a two-family, semi-detached structure at Number 35 Washington Square and Number 2 Oliver Street West, erected in 1818, interests the student of architecture for its unusual arrangement, made necessary partly by the irregular shape of the site, and partly in conformity with the scheme of building two separate but adjoining houses on a double corner site. The left-hand or Silsbee portion has an L-shaped plan with an entrance on Oliver Street, while the right-hand or Mott portion has an oblong plan with an entrance on Washington Square East, as shown by the accompanying photograph. It will be noticed that this latter entrance, located as it is at the side where this part of the house adjoins the other, lends a pleasing sense of unity and balance to

PLATE XLII. — Mack-and-Stone Houses, 21 and 23 Chestnut Street. Erected 1814-1815; Silsbee-Mott House, 35 Washington Square West. Erected 1818.

PLATE XLIII. — Hoffman-Simpson House, 26 Chestnut Street.
Erected about 1827; Allen-Osgood-Huntington Houses,
31, 33 and 35 Chestnut Street. Erected about 1825.

the entire structure that would not otherwise be the case. In its fenestration, tall chimneys and various details this house conforms to others of the period. The cornice, with its conspicuous ball molding, suggests a modification of that by McIntire on the Peabody-Silsbee house, while the window lintels are like those of the Andrew-Safford mansion. The high, heavy porch, and particularly the high, oblong transom of the doorway, indicate the early Greek revival tendency. Probably the balustrade on the roof of the Mott side of the house, consisting of a section of balusters in alternation with a solid panel, is of relatively recent origin.

The more general use of brick in the construction of dwellings, together with the increased land values as Salem grew, led about this time to the building of many residence blocks of two or more semi-detached houses, with fireproof brick party walls between. These were almost invariably of the three-story square type and usually hip-roofed, with tall prominent chimneys and handsome entrance porches. Of them all the so-called Mack and Stone houses, numbered 21 and 23 Chestnut Street, are perhaps the most attractive. Unlike many other similar structures, the doorways are separate, each having an elliptical porch well designed in the Ionic order and in happy accord with the doorways. The original iron fence and balustrade railings of pleasing pattern remain in excellent condition and greatly enhance the charm of these entrances. One notices, too, the ornamental iron guard along the eaves to prevent the unexpected sliding of snow from the roof. The marble lintels and sills of many ranging windows brighten the broad expanse of brickwork, and the keyed lintel is the more welcome for its nicely executed carving, especially the central vertical bead of diminishing spheres. As indicated by the four-paned sashes on one side and the twelve-paned sashes on the other side, the house is not divided into equal halves, one house having its hall at the side, the other house its hall in the center, with corresponding differences in floor plan.

The four-paned sashes are doubtless of much later date than the house. In the rear the structure presents an interesting appearance because of its "swell fronts" or semicircular terminations the width of the rear corner rooms.

This double house was built by Henry and John Pickering, about 1814–1815, and first occupied by them on its completion. Henry Pickering was a man of literary tastes and the author of "The Ruins of Pæstum" and other poems. His house, Number 21, was afterward occupied for a time by George Peabody, a merchant prominent in the Russian trade, who afterward resided at Number 29 Washington Square, now the quarters of the Salem Club. John Pickering, LL.D., the Greek lexicographer, famous linguist, and city solicitor of Boston at the time of his death, was a son of Colonel Timothy Pickering, and for several years lived across the way at Number 18 Chestnut Street, which, as already recounted, was also the residence of Nathaniel Hawthorne in 1846.

The year 1818 witnessed the final development of the last type of house which, in the broadest possible interpretation of the term, can be regarded as belonging to the Colonial architecture of Salem. After that date the spirit of the Greek revival, which dominated New England building for two or three decades after about 1825, began to assert itself. Houses somewhat Colonial in feeling were occasionally built, it is true, but less frequently. Manifesting no pronounced development, however, they rather echoed, and sometimes combined somewhat indiscriminately, the features of former periods and so lack the distinction of the older residences, although often not unpleasing to the eye nor lacking in the substantial comfort of brick construction. When the Victorian decadence swept the country with its clumsy fantastic forms and wealth of gingerbread work, Colonial building ceased in Salem as it did elsewhere, and not until 1918, a century after its development ended, did the Colonial style again come into favor to any considerable extent. What the great fire of 1914 meant to Salem from an architectural standpoint, however, forms the subject of the final chapter of this volume.

The Colonial Architecture of Salem

It seems fitting to conclude the present chapter with a few representative examples showing how completely the three-story brick houses erected after 1818, aside from those of the Greek revival, owe their inspiration to earlier house types already considered in previous chapters. The Hoffman-Simpson house, for instance, at Number 26 Chestnut Street, with its tall chimneys and hip roof unadorned by balustrade or belvedere, recalls several others near by in general mass. The entrance porch was evidently inspired by that of the Peabody-Silsbee house, yet lacks the elaboration of fine detail of its prototype. The same is true of the cornice with its ball molding from the same source. The leaded glass of the elliptical fanlight and side lights recalls that of the Andrew-Safford doorway. A new and pleasing note, however, is sounded by the simple and effective carved marble lintels, while the side porch and particularly the bay window above the front porch lend an appearance of harmonious modernity.

This house, now the residence of Doctor James E. Simpson, was built about 1827 by Humphrey Devereux, who died there in 1828. It was for many years occupied by Captain Charles Hoffman, a prosperous merchant and a great lover of flowers. His garden and greenhouses, Felt states in his "Annals of Salem", were among the best in Salem, and so they have been maintained to this day, for

PLATE XLIV.—Chestnut Street showing Philip Little Doorway at No. 10. Erected 1804; Gardner and Thompson Houses, 38 and 40 Chestnut Street. Erected about 1846.

PLATE XLV. — Weir House Doorway, 6 Downing Street. Erected 1763. Burned 1914; Thomas Poynton Doorway, Formerly at 7 Brown Street Court. Erected 1750.

The Square Three-Story Brick House

Mrs. Simpson is likewise a great lover of flowers and devotes much time to them. The Dutchman's Pipe in the garden is now seventy-seven years old.

Large gable-roofed houses, not greatly unlike the Stearns house of Revolutionary times, though of brick and with higher stories, were often built and lent themselves readily to the growing demand for semi-detached blocks for occupancy by two or more families. A three-family block of this sort with handsome heavy Ionic porches embraces the so-called Allen-Osgood-Huntington houses, numbered 31, 33 and 35 Chestnut Street respectively. The block was erected about 1825 by Pickering Dodge and finished by John Fiske Allen, who occupied Number 31 for several years and there, in 1853, for the first time in New England, grew and brought to flower in his greenhouse the *Victoria regia*, the great water lily of the Amazon, from seed obtained of Caleb Cope, of Philadelphia. The following season Mr. Allen enlarged his greenhouse and tank and obtained more seed from England, including that of the *Amaryllis*, *Nelumbium* and other tropical species of lilies which thrived and formed a rare collection much admired by many visitors. Mr. Allen published the results of his observations on the *Victoria regia* in a beautiful folio volume, finely illustrated by W. Sharpe from specimens grown in Salem. In 1843 he erected graperies on Dean Street which were soon greatly extended to inclose about three hundred varieties of grapes, also peaches, cherries and other fruits. Mr. Allen's hybrid grape was an interesting feature of his career. He disputed the honors of early hybridization with Rogers. John Fiske Allen is mentioned by Felt as one of Salem's foremost horticulturists. Previous to Mr. Allen's occupancy the house was for a time the home of Nathaniel Silsbee, United States senator from 1826 to 1835.

Among the early occupants of Number 33 was Captain Charles M. Endicott, of the ship *Friendship*, and an experience from his adventurous life merits recounting here as characteristic of the exploits in which the seafaring men of Salem often risked their lives in opening up new lines of trade in the East. On February 7, 1831, while the *Friendship* lay at Qualah Battoo she was attacked by Malays in a native pepper boat. The first mate, Charles Knight, and two seamen were killed, while several others escaped, although badly wounded. Once in possession of the ship the assailants plundered her of every movable article and endeavored to run her ashore, but without success. Captain Endicott, the second mate and four men were ashore weighing pepper at the time, and, perceiving that the ship had been captured, managed to get away in their boat. Rowing twenty-five miles to Muckie they obtained the ready assistance of three American vessels which set sail at once. The following morning a message was sent to the Rajah demanding the return of the *Friendship*, and this being refused, the Americans began an attack which was answered by the harbor forts and the Malays on the ship. The Americans, however, manned their boats, boarded the *Friendship* and soon had full possession of her with what pepper had been put into her hold. A year later the harbor was visited by the United States frigate *Potomac*, and the Malays were "severely chastised" for their attempted piracy.

Reverend Charles W. Upham, mayor of Salem, congressman and author of the standard work on "Salem Witchcraft", was the first occupant of Number 35. In later years it was the residence of Asahel Huntington, mayor of Salem in 1853, county and district attorney, twice a representative to the General Court, president of the Essex Institute and clerk of the courts of Essex County for nineteen years until his death in 1870.

About the end of the first quarter of the nineteenth century there were built in Salem several three-story gable-roof brick houses, with paired brick chimneys at each end after the manner of many gambrel-roof houses of seventy-five years previous. The double house numbered 2 and 4 Chestnut Street, long known as "The Studio", furnishes a case in point and presents a rare instance in Salem of Boston's so-called "east wind" recessed doorway with granite steps running up under an elliptical arch into an outdoor vestibule. It was erected in 1826 by Deacon John Stone, who occupied Number 2, the half on the corner of Summer Street, and in 1827 advertised the other half to let with the privilege of selecting the paper and the chimney piece. For four generations this building has not passed from the ownership of a member of the family in direct descent, Mrs. Richard Wheatland, wife of the present owner, being the great granddaughter of the builder. After 1869 Number 2 was occupied for ten years by John Robinson, director of the Peabody Museum. Later the entire building was rented for studios, among the tenants being Philip Little, Frank W. Benson, Charles Fred Whitney and the schools of Miss Mary Mason Brooks, Miss Mary Stone, Miss Draper and the Kindergarten of the Misses Osgood and Whitney. Both sides have now been thrown into a single house for occupancy as a winter residence by the owner.

Resembling this structure in general character, though more nearly in accord with Salem architecture in its heavy Ionic entrance porch, the double house numbered 38 and 40 Chestnut Street is of much later date. It was erected about 1846 by Nathaniel West, Sr., and Reverend James W. Thompson. The bay window above the entrance to Number 40 is quite modern, as are probably the door and elliptical fanlight, for most houses of the time had oblong transoms above the door like that of Number 38. Colonel Joseph Andrews, mayor of Salem in 1854–1855, was among the occupants of Number 38.

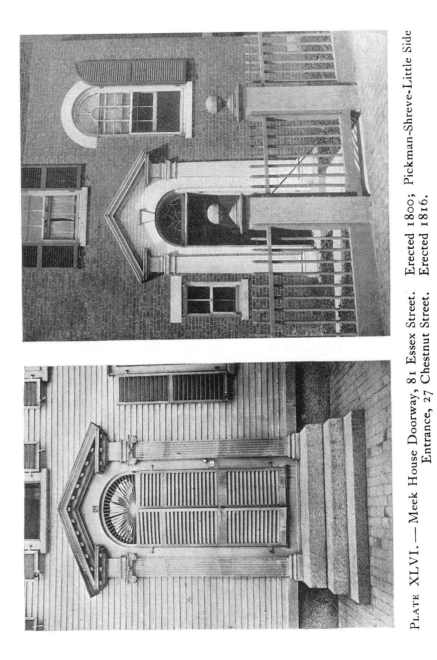

PLATE XLVI. — Meek House Doorway, 81 Essex Street.   Erected 1800;   Pickman-Shreve-Little Side
Entrance, 27 Chestnut Street.   Erected 1816.

PLATE XLVII. — Enclosed Porch at 23 Summer Street. House erected 1745; Pierce-Johonnot-Nichols Doorway and Gateposts, 80 Federal Street. Erected 1782.

CHAPTER VI

DOORWAYS AND PORCHES

ACCORDING to the chroniclers of early days in Salem the first doors constructed there were of the batten type, common ledged doors, consisting of vertical oak planks nailed to horizontal inside battens. Larger and heavier doors were both ledged and braced with oblique battens to prevent any tendency of the door to sag. The upper end of the brace was bird's-mouthed into the under side of the upper horizontal batten near the lock edge of the door, while the lower end was bird's-mouthed into the upper edge of the lower rail near the hanging edge of the door. Such doors were hung with heavy wrought-iron strap hinges and fastened inside with bars of wood or bolts of iron. Some were opened from the outside by means of the primitive latchstring, others by quaint wrought-iron thumb latches. A heavy iron knocker, sometimes taking the form of a ring, completed the equipment.

The front doors of the better houses were deeply recessed and had an ornamental arched weatherboard above, providing a sort of outer vestibule to shelter the waiting guest from the cutting east winds that sweep the streets of New England seaport towns in winter. The sketches of the Deliverance Parkman and Governor Bradstreet houses in Chapter I are typical, and the door of the latter house illustrates the frequent practice of marking with a scratch-awl on the outer side a diamond pattern corresponding in size to the diamond lights of the casements, and then studding the intersections with iron or brass nails.

With the advent of English classic tendencies in American building, soon after Salem was settled, came the square-paned sash and the framed and paneled door. The former had its effect on doors as well as windows, and the photographs of the "House of the Seven Gables" and of the old Hunt house show the insertion of a simple sash in the upper part of early doors. Some of the first framed and paneled doors had panels square, flat and sunken on the back side, but flush with the stiles, rails and muntins on the front side and with a small bead molding outlining the panels. A few of these doors and the beveled sunken panel doors which soon followed had a batten back. Usually made in one piece, the Dutch type, divided into two parts halfway between top and bottom, was sometimes adopted. The photograph of the Narbonne house in Chapter II, however, shows a unique, four-part Dutch door for the Cent Shop. Later, came the molded and raised panels, the most pleasing and popular scheme for Colonial doors, and early in the nineteenth century the molded and flat panels, of which there are also many examples in Salem, several being bolection molded.

Six-panel doors were the rule, as shown by numerous illustrations throughout this book. The panels of the upper pair were square or nearly so, the middle and lower panels usually of identical height, although occasionally greater height was given to the middle pair, as indicated by the sketch of the Philip English house. Four-panel doors, such as that of the Clark-Morgan house, are rare in local Colonial work. For the most part, Salem doors are solid, except that just before the adoption of top lights several instances here and there show the use of plain glass or bull's-eye lights replacing the upper pair of panels, as seen in the "Witch House" and John Ward doorways. The better lighting of entries which resulted from this alteration soon led to the general adoption of a simple horizontal top light or transom above the door proper. The George Jacobs and Sarah Prince Osburn doorways deserve mention as among the best early examples now remaining. As halls of ample size replaced the tiny entries of former years, and the architectural treatment of stairways demanded more light to display them, the former sash area was doubled by employing two simple, vertical side lights like those of the Diman house, instead of the single top light. Eventually both were resorted to and the development of fanlights and the adoption of leaded glass followed as natural consequences of the progress in architectural design, the presence of a few English builders in Salem, and the refining influences of frequent visits to the mother country on the part of many wealthy merchants and sea captains.

For some time knockers and quaint door handles with thumb latches, at first of wrought iron and later of brass, continued to be used on framed panel doors, and many of them still charm the eye, as no modern equivalents have succeeded in doing, by reason of that fine grace of line and quality of finish found only in hand-wrought metals. Each piece is a thing unto itself and possessed of individuality. Heavy draw bolts of iron or brass replaced the earlier bars of wood until toward the end of the eighteenth century great rim locks with keys and brass knobs preceded the modern mortise lock. Glass knobs and bell pulls were not made until during the last period of Salem architecture, but many older houses have since been equipped with them.

While the first Georgian door trim consisted of absolutely flat casings, the simple architrave soon came into frequent use, and presently flat caps, followed by projecting heads, complete entabla-

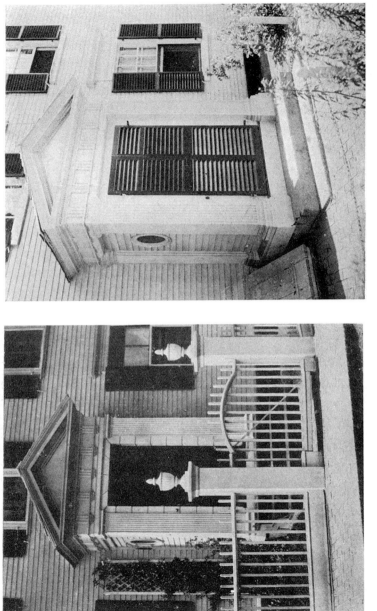

PLATE XLVIII. — Boardman House Enclosed Porch, 82 Washington Square East. Erected 1785; Pierce-Johonnot-Nichols Enclosed Porch, 80 Federal Street. Erected 1782.

PLATE XLIX. — Stearns House Doorway, 384 Essex Street. Erected 1785; Whipple House Enclosed Porch, 2 Andover Street. Erected 1804.

tures and pediments were successfully employed, as shown by illustrations accompanying the first three chapters. Felt, in his "Annals of Salem", states that "the door often had a large porch before it, with a seat on each side for the accommodation of the family and social visitors. In 1655, Edward Wharton had leave to put up an addition of this kind." No examples of such doorways remain in Salem, but the gable-roof inclosed porch forms a part of several old lean-to dwellings, notably the Rebecca Nurse and Rea-Putnam-Fowler houses, and the older part of General Israel Putnam's birthplace, — the earlier ones with square and the Rea-Putnam-Fowler porch with oval sashes in each side wall for the admittance of light. Such porches were the forerunners of the modern vestibule and became a customary feature of country houses exposed to the unobstructed sweep of winter winds as a logical means to keep the interior warmer.

Previous to the gambrel-roof houses of Provincial times few doorways suitable for present-day adaptation were erected. All of the better examples for three-quarters of a century up to 1818, however, will repay careful study. During those years the Salem doorway became, as in all good architecture, the dominant exterior feature, the keynote of the façade. Truly utilitarian in purpose, it lent itself the more readily to elaboration for the sake of decorative effect, and Salem designers, notably

McIntire, did not hesitate to freshen classic motives with new detail, or with classic detail employed in new ways, the work being done with such skill and good taste as to command universal admiration. As the entrance to the home, where a welcome is given and first impressions are received, the best Salem doorways are possessed of strong individuality; each seems to symbolize the house as a whole and to express the personality of its occupants. Happily devised and exceptionally well executed, Salem doorways in the main have given a rare charm and distinction to her remarkable architecture. The number presented here is necessarily limited, yet the principal types and best examples are included with brief references to similar ones not shown.

The Lindall-Barnard-Andrews doorway typifies the entrances of the better Provincial houses of wood and the early manner of utilizing classic detail for embellishment. Pilasters fluted in the Doric manner and supporting a pediment depending entirely on simple planed moldings for its ornamentation provide a frame of great dignity. The dark-painted door with a narrow, horizontal top light above is the original one and an appropriate background for a beautiful brass knocker and door handle. No similar arrangement of molded and raised panels is to be seen in Salem, the long narrow panel being its unique feature. The modern gateposts of the wooden fence, with their peculiar urns, also arrest attention because of their exceptional character. A similar pedimental doorway is to be seen at the childhood home of the late Senator Nathaniel Silsbee, Numbers 27 and 29 Daniels Street.

As the central feature of a brick façade the doorway of the Richard Derby house, Number 168 Derby Street, is properly more elaborate in detail. Jambs and casings with rabbets suggestive of rusticated marble lend greater weight of effect, and the dentils of an Ionic cornice enrich the pediment. The quaint, broad door with molded and raised panels of the utmost simplicity, and also the stone steps are adaptations of Georgian work overseas. Among the few other doors having this panel arrangement may be mentioned those of the Simon Forrester, Boardman and Allan houses. The double blind doors for many years before the manufacture of screen wire served as a partial protection from flies, and are frequent adjuncts of Salem entrances. A recessed doorway of similar character, but having one of Salem's familiar six-panel doors, is that of the Lindall-Gibbs-Osgood house, Number 314 Essex Street.

Of an ornate Georgian character, but much lighter in effect, the famous pineapple doorway of the Thomas Poynton house, Number 7 Brown Street Court, erected in 1750, is a splendid example of the broken arch pediment elaborated with hand-tooled moldings and fluted pilasters. It is one of the few notable narrow doorways of Salem. On a house of wood, with siding rabbeted like the joints of rusticated stonework and painted gray, this doorway is at once striking and beautiful. Unfortunately the door itself is modern, yet were it of the best, the pineapple, emblem of hospitality, would still hold attention. It is hand carved of wood and is said to have been brought from abroad in one of Captain Poynton's own ships. For many years it was kept painted in its natural colors and the blinds above were cut so as to close without marring it. This doorway has been widely copied by architects, and in 1911 was removed to the Essex Institute for better preservation.

Generally speaking the Weir house doorway, Number 6 Downing Street, also erected in 1763, resembled the foregoing, but was simpler in its absence of dentils, pineapple and rustication. The sunken vestibule, the arrangement of the modest sidelights and the two-panel door had no parallel in Salem. This house was destroyed in the great fire of 1914.

To relieve the severity of the horizontal top light, the semicircular fanlight was developed toward the beginning of the nineteenth century and was considerably used thereafter. By breaking the base of a triangular pediment, the semicircle was found to fit into the space thus afforded in the most attractive manner. More light was admitted to the hall

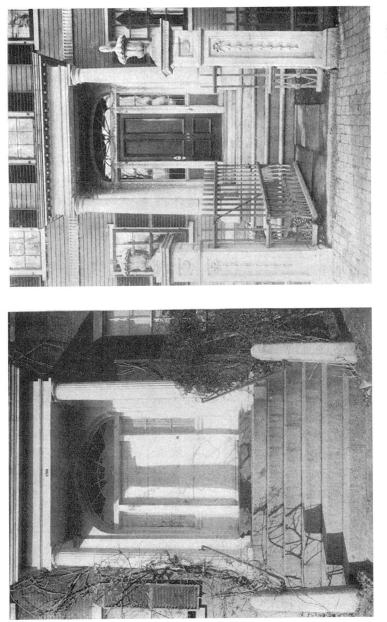

PLATE L. — Entrance Porch, Home for Aged Women, 180 Derby Street. Erected 1810; Cook-Oliver Entrance Porch, 142 Federal Street. Erected 1804.

PLATE LI. — Entrance Porch of the Kimball House, 14 Pickman Street. Erected 1800; Peabody-Silsbee Entrance Porch, 380 Essex Street. Erected 1797.

and the pattern of radiating and variously curved sash bars lent a pleasing grace to the ensemble. The Meek house, Number 81 Essex Street, erected in 1800, has such a doorway in the Ionic order, with fluted pilasters and hand-carved capitals. The cornice differs from the pure type in that widely spaced modillions replace the usual dentils.

Several doorways of this general nature are reminiscent of the high narrow entrances characteristic of much Philadelphia architecture. The White-Lord doorway, Number 31 Washington Square North, erected in 1818, suggests a free composite of the doorway of the famous Morris house in Philadelphia and that of the Perot-Morris house in Germantown where Washington lived in 1793. It has the slender Salem grace and excellence of proportions, however, and the fine-scale, hand-tooled dentils were much used by McIntire and the builders who followed him. The engaged columns are of generally Tuscan order, the entablature Ionic. Whereas the Meek house fanlight had an open blind, this is left uncovered. The simpler, similar side doorway of the Bertram Home for Aged Men at Number 20 Turner Street has all the sturdiness of Philadelphia types.

The pedimental doorhead offered a logical and ready motive with which to embellish the gable-roof inclosed porch, introduced on lean-to houses, but which continued as a feature of many gambrel and square hip-roof houses. Sometimes at the front door, but oftener at the much-used side door, this exterior vestibule helped to insure warm interiors before the days of modern heating systems. In most instances flat or fluted pilasters support a simple Tuscan pediment. The porches of the Hosmer-Townsend-Waters house, Number 80 Washington Square, the Derby-Ward house, Number 27 Herbert Street, and the Briggs-Whipple house, Number 38 Forrester Street, are representative examples. The wider porches of the Grimshawe house, Number 53 Charter Street, and of the Allen house, Number 77 Derby Street, however, have a pair of pilasters each side of the door.

So also has the porch on the house at Number 23 Summer Street, probably added several decades after the house itself was erected in 1745. It is the broadest and most elaborate of the inclosed Doric porches in Salem, its chief distinction lying in the flat-roofed wings each side of the pediment and the slight projection of the latter.

One notices the vertical plain boarding instead of clapboards and that the oval windows have no molded architrave casings, both characteristics of the earlier porches of this type. In company with several other Salem porches the entire structure stands directly upon the sidewalk.

The inclosed porches of the Boardman house, Number 82 Washington Square, and of the Pierce-

Johonnot-Nichols house, Number 80 Federal Street, are also Doric in feeling, the former being a comparatively recent addition admirably made. With the fence and architectural gateposts it forms a striking picture in the best spirit of eighteenth-century Colonial design. The inclosed porch of the Pierce-Johonnot-Nichols house, one of the most admired doorways in Salem, arouses the admiration of all who see it as an eminently successful adaptation of denticulated Doric, with the characteristic repeated triglyph in the frieze and guttæ in the architrave. To relieve the monotony of many rectangular openings, graceful oval sashes admit light to the porch. These, together with the clapboarded side walls in which they are set, lend distinction to this doorway. The dark-painted six-panel door, with simple molded and raised panels, is the original one and an appropriate background for an old glass knob and one of the best brass knockers in Salem. As in earlier days two-part green blinds, hung outside the door, serve as a protection from flies in summer.

The restored flat-roofed, inclosed porch of the Whipple house, Number 2 Andover Street, erected in 1804, typifies the eighteenth-century modification of this sort of entrance. Employment of the ever-charming leaded side lights beside the door rather than oval sashes in the side walls gives it a pleasing breadth and lights it well. Supported by fine-scale reeded pilasters, the entablature is generally Ionic in character, enriched by the balustrade and pedestals above, which form an appropriate setting for the simple Palladian window above. A touch of lightness and grace is lent by the lead work of the side lights in both windows and doorway. The door itself, with molded, raised panels uniquely spaced, and with glass in the two upper spaces, is of the Dutch type, opening in halves, and displays some excellent brass hardware.

A similar doorway of more modest character is to be seen on the newer part of the General Israel Putnam birthplace, while that of the David P. Waters house, Number 14 Cambridge Street, designed by McIntire, has a Corinthian entablature without balustrade and a broad two-part door, three panels wide, often a feature of the houses of 1810 to 1818.

It is a thoughtful host who considers not only his own comfort within the house, but provides shelter from sun and storm before his door for the waiting guest. And so it was that open porches for the front door began to be erected while the inclosed porch for the more frequently used side door continued in favor. For these, also, the pedimental treatment served admirably and many of them remain to-day, for the most part Doric, severest of the orders, yet by reason of their breadth friendly doorways, despite their dignified mien. Of them all

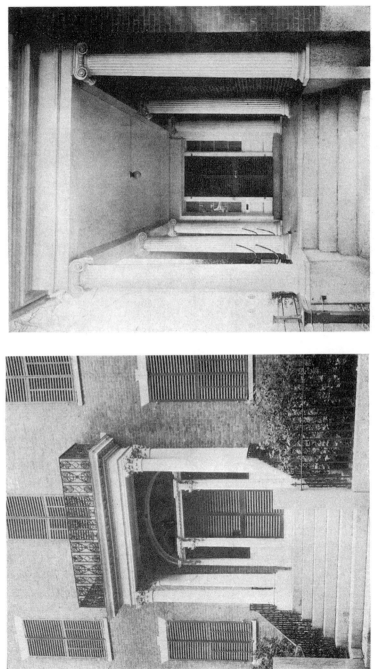

PLATE LII.—Salem Club Entrance Porch, 29 Washington Square. Erected 1818; Veranda of the Saltonstall-Tuckerman House, 41 Chestnut Street. Erected 1812.

PLATE LIII. — Ropes Memorial Doorway and Gateposts, 318 Essex Street. House erected 1719, Fence 1894, Doorway 1807; Double Entrance Porch, 38 and 40 Chestnut Street. Erected about 1846.

no better instance of pleasing proportion and nicely worked detail is to be found in New England than the front porch of the Pierce-Johonnot-Nichols house, Number 80 Federal Street, designed by McIntire. Exercising his admirable originality in adaptation he imparted a measure of individuality to this and other similar porches by combining smooth Tuscan columns set on cubical plinths with a Roman Doric entablature and pediment. Notwithstanding this free use of the orders, it is one of the most admired of Salem doorways, the picket fence and ornamental gateposts, with beautiful hand-carved urns, providing an architectural setting for a vista of rare charm. Above the original eight-panel door, of which there are but few in Salem, a semicircular fanlight under the porch roof admits light to the hall. The quaint brass thumb latch is the original.

Similar porches, some with inappropriate modern doors, are to be seen on the Goss-Osgood house, Number 15 Chestnut Street; the Osgood-Lander house, Number 5 Barton Square; the William G. Rantoul house on Chestnut Street; and the Simon Forrester house on Derby Street, the latter having square columns. The porch of the Stearns house, Number 384 Essex Street, differs in the addition of flat pilasters at each side, which give increased breadth, weight and dignity, and so in modern adaptation render it better suited to public than domestic work, unless the house be one of large size and considerable pretension. This porch was added by McIntire in 1785, the house having been erected in 1776.

As an accompaniment of the later three-story, square houses of post-Revolutionary times, numerous doorways were built between 1800 and 1818 which have contributed more to the fame of Salem architecture than any other single exterior feature. Indeed, the welcoming doorways of Salem have become a figure of speech wherever Colonial architecture is known and appreciated. Doorways usually reflect the character of those for whom they were built; they are the barriers one places between himself and his fellow men and denote his attitude toward them. To the breadth of the door, and particularly to the use of delightful leaded glasswork about it is due the pervading spirit of welcome. Side lights encourage intimacy like hands extended in greeting; moreover, they increase the apparent width of the doorway and foretell a cheerful hall. The wide, handsomely paneled doors, graceful elliptical fanlights and friendly side lights of the Federal period in Salem not only speak eloquently of the gracious hospitality of Salem's merchant princes, but comprise the most beautiful of all so-called Colonial doorway motives. Such entrances possess characteristics of charm and distinction not seen elsewhere, due chiefly to their splendid proportions, refinement of detail and precision of workmanship, while as applied to the square houses of the time their porches relieve in a measure the severity of three-story façades with many ranging windows.

The inviting porch of the Cook-Oliver house, on Federal Street, is notable for the naïve manner in which free use was made of the orders, characteristic of much McIntire work. Its surprising harmony, charm of line and proportion, achieved with such absence of restraint, furnish eloquent tribute to a keen sense of artistic propriety and originality in adaptation. The columns, with their smooth shafts and high, square bases, both at the front and also the engaged columns each side of the doorway, suggest the Tuscan more than the Roman Doric, whereas the entablature seems to be a Corinthian adaptation with flat, plain frieze and modillions supporting the corona. An elliptical fanlight and vertical side lights, all subdivided with exceptional grace, contain the original glass.

This entrance, perhaps better than any other in Salem, demonstrates the fact that gateways and doorways are closely allied when treated in architectural harmony. The gateposts, chaste and beautiful in design, are the work of Samuel McIntire, who hand-tooled them in 1799 to adorn the entrance of the Elias Hasket Derby mansion, where they were first erected.

McIntire's rails and bases were always extremely

simple, with considerable elaboration of the gate-posts, often, as in this instance, four in number in front of the house, with simpler posts for any continuation of the fence and for the wide entrance. These high, square gateposts with shapely urns and surmounting flame motives are the best and most elaborate in Salem. They consist of a base, paneled shaft and entablature, the shaft panels containing beautifully carved, straight-hanging garlands, and the frieze panels containing oval sunburst medallions. The fine-scale cornice includes a vertically fluted belt similar to the much heavier one across the façade of the house at the second-floor level. Another repetition to relate house and fence and to brighten the whole effect is that of the garlands, one of which decorates each vertical surface of the door frame, while a festooned garland stretches across the lintel. These garlands, favorite motives of the brothers Adam, indicate positively their influence upon Salem architecture and account for its delicacy without weakness.

Scarcely less beautiful are the ornamental fence posts erected in 1894 in front of the Ropes' Memorial, on Essex Street, and their arrangement to form an elliptical recess in the fence is unsurpassed, the ramped rails of the fence according excellently with the general scheme. Like the doorway they frame, the gateposts are Ionic in detail, with fluted pilasters, hand-tooled capitals, molded entablature, and

PLATE LIV. — Baldwin-Lyman Entrance Porch, 92 Washington Square East. Erected 1818 ; Pickman-Shreve-Little Entrance Porch, 27 Chestnut Street. Erected 1816.

PLATE LV. — Dodge-Shreve Enclosed Porch, 29 Chestnut Street. Erected 1817; Barstow-West Elliptical Entrance Porch, 25 Chestnut Street. Erected 1810.

solid, carved urns very nearly like those of the Cook-Oliver gateway.

The doorway was built in 1807 during a period of reconstruction. It is of the recessed type often adopted in houses directly on the street, as this was prior to 1894, and has molded jambs, attractively paneled to correspond with the door, and fluted Ionic columns supporting an entablature, with simple modillions under the corona after the Corinthian manner. A unique employment of alternate circles and ovals lends distinction to the leaded glass, and altogether the doorway is one of great dignity and strong appeal. Among other recessed doorways may be mentioned that of the Curwen-Osgood house, Number 312 Essex Street, erected in 1765, and that of the Eden-Brown house, corner of Broad and Summer streets, erected in 1762. The former has composite columns and double modern glazed doors, without top light; the latter an entablature with Adam detail and an elliptical fanlight.

The entrance of the Home for Aged Women, Number 180 Derby Street, is seldom equaled in graceful and chaste appearance. Designed by McIntire in 1810, it resembles none of his other known work, yet displays his ingenuity and good taste in recombining classic detail. The fluted columns convey a general impression of Roman Doric, yet they support a Tuscan entablature and are themselves enriched at the base by the Corinthian double torus. There is an indefinable charm about the broad, flat-paneled doors and the crystal glass knob, while the pattern of the leaded glasswork about it is at once dainty and distinctive. As a whole its excellent proportions and the predominance of white account in large measure for the strong appeal of this doorway.

At Number 14 Pickman Street the Kimball house abuts upon the sidewalk, and a porch, erected by McIntire in 1800, roofs over four granite steps which rise directly from the brick pavement; there is no porch platform proper. Effective simplicity and free use of the orders characterize the design. The hand-carved capitals create a generally Ionic feeling, but jig-sawed Corinthian modillions with sections of fascia molding between replace the customary dentil course of the entablature, and the bases of the smooth columns have the Corinthian double torus, although the square plinth is absent. Molded paneling replaces the usual top light, and the severity of the square-paned side lights is relieved by applied garlands on the door frame, reminiscent of the Cook-Oliver doorway. A well-proportioned, flat-paneled door adds to the pleasing ensemble.

Another much more elaborate instance of the Ionic porch is to be seen on the Peabody-Silsbee house, Number 380 Essex Street, erected in 1797. Despite McIntire's daring innovations it is generally regarded as one of the best doorways in Salem. The fluted columns, with Corinthian acanthus-leaf enrichment of the neck of the capitals below the usual volutes, impart a distinctly Roman aspect to the whole, yet the heavy cubical Tuscan plinths, on which McIntire's columns of whatever order usually rested, were retained, and a strange, though none the less pleasing note has been sounded by the guttæ of the Doric order on the architrave and the mutules under the corona of the cornice. A ball molding, a veritable triumph of hand carving, replaces the customary dentil course, yet gives the same effect of scale. Except for rosettes directly over the columns, the frieze is plain. The wooden door with its delicately molded flat panels and tiny corner ornaments, the artistic leaded fanlights and side lights, the iron fence, stair rail and balustrade over the porch are all distinctive in the extreme and not surpassed by any similar work in Salem. It will be noticed that each of the blind doors has lock and frieze rails and a muntin corresponding to those of the door proper.

Other similar porches, differing somewhat in detail, include that of the Hoffman house, Number 26 Chestnut Street, erected in 1814; that of the Nichols-Shattuck house, Number 37 Chestnut Street, erected in 1812; and that of the Endicott house, Number 259 Essex Street, erected in 1790.

An interesting early use of the Ionic order is seen

in the veranda of the Saltonstall-Tuckerman house, Number 41 Chestnut Street, erected in 1812, where a double row of columns supports the roof along the inner as well as the outer side. Leverett Saltonstall was the first mayor of Salem in 1836, and later a member of Congress.

Of more recent origin, a double entrance porch of the same order is an important feature of the Gardner and Thompson houses, 38 and 40 Chestnut Street, erected about 1846. The entablature, with its prominent dentil course, is truer to the conventional Ionic order than the foregoing, whereas the capitals combine the Ionic and Corinthian feeling, as did many designed by the brothers Adam. The right-hand doorway of Number 38 is the original, the other a modern adaptation.

From 1816 to 1818 the Corinthian order predominated in Salem building, and among the most effective of the more modest applications to the square porch and doorway, the entrance of the Salem Club, Number 29 Washington Square, erected in 1818, deserves especial mention. Cubical plinths beneath the columns and a small ball molding replacing the dentil course of the cornice recall the Peabody-Silsbee porch and indicate McIntire influence. Otherwise the conventional detail of the classic order obtains. The doorway is embellished and closely related to the porch by a fine-scale cornice across the lintel supported by slender colonnettes on the

PLATE LVI. — Gardner-White-Pingree Elliptical Entrance Porch, 128 Essex Street. Erected 1810; Tucker-Rice Elliptical Entrance Porch, Formerly at 129 Essex Street. Erected 1800.

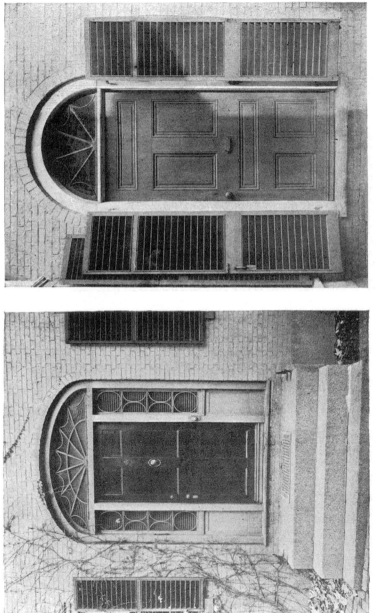

PLATE LVII. — Mansfield-Bolles House Doorway, 8 Chestnut Street. Erected 1810; Abbot House Doorway, 12 Brown Street. Erected 1800.

mullions, and pilasters on the sides of the frame. Distinctive leaded glass work and wrought-iron balustrades of handsome pattern enrich the whole effect,

The entrance porch of the Baldwin-Lyman house. Number 92 Washington Square, and of the White-Lord house, Number 31 Washington Square, both erected in 1818, may be mentioned as of generally similar character, although having wooden surmounting balustrades, smooth columns and no application of the order to the door frame. The beauty of the former is greatly enhanced by the picket fence and handsome architectural gateposts flanking the doorway vista.

By way of comparison the doorway of the Pickman-Shreve-Little house, Number 27 Chestnut Street, erected in 1816, becomes especially interesting. Architects regard it as the best wood, hand-carved Corinthian porch in America and speak in glowing terms of the purity and precision of the detail, and of the effective simplicity of the Palladian window, a feature which served primarily to relieve the severity of a three-story façade with many ranging rectangular windows, yet became virtually a part of the entrance of many houses of this period. The hand-carved columns are conspicuous for precision of workmanship, and the three-piece door is notable for the fact that two pieces form that portion of the door in common use, the third serving merely to widen it upon special occasions.

A delightful wooden balustrade with corner pedestals effects a closer relation between porch and Palladian window in the case of the Dodge-Shreve entrance, Number 29 Chestnut Street, erected in 1817. This window shows considerable elaboration in the use of carved marble keystone and imposts, the beautiful hand-tooled casing about the fanlight and the cornice carried across the lintel of the window. Otherwise the doorway follows the scheme of the Pickman-Shreve-Little entrance closely, the leaded glass work and iron stair rail being a little more intricate in pattern, however. Altogether, this doorway, perhaps, has been more extensively copied than any other in Salem.

Probably the elliptical fanlight suggested the elliptical porch, and certainly the two are very effective when utilized together. The entrance of the Barstow-West house, Number 25 Chestnut Street, erected in 1812, provides an unpretentious and effective example, notable for its chaste simplicity and excellent proportions. A free interpretation of the orders characterizes the detail. The columns are Tuscan, except for the base, which has the Corinthian double torus and a plinth of unconventional height. The entablature is generally Ionic except that jig-sawed modillions replace the customary dentil course. Handsome glasswork of attractive pattern provides a delightful setting for the broad, solid wood door with its six molded flat panels and plain brass knob, key plate and bell pull. Much of the charm of this doorway may properly be attributed to the graceful wrought-iron balustrade, one of the best in Salem.

Reminiscent of this the porch of the Pickering-Mack house, Number 21 Chestnut Street, erected in 1812, is of a more substantial character and has Ionic capitals and a three-piece door.

Such entrances were the forerunners of the more tasteful elliptical porches evolved by McIntire when he realized the possibilities of a slender interpretation of the Corinthian column and entablature. Two excellent instances still remain for comparison as found in the Tucker-Rice porch, now preserved in the Essex Institute garden, erected in 1800, and in the Gardner-White-Pingree porch, Number 128 Essex Street, erected in 1810. The former was removed from the house at Number 129 Essex Street when it was remodeled in 1896 for occupancy by the Father Mathew Total Abstinence Society. The accompanying photograph, however, shows it as it appeared in 1895 when Professor Eleazer B. Homer, of the Massachusetts Institute of Technology summer school, told his class while in Salem that it was the best proportioned porch in the city, although its former beauty of ensemble had been marred by the substitution of inappropriate modern doors and surrounding glasswork.

The Gardner-White-Pingree porch, probably Mc-

Intire's last work, still displays the charming, original leaded glass and three-piece door, but it will be noticed that the columns of this porch are not fluted in the characteristic Corinthian manner. Other differences occur in the entablatures, the moldings of the Tucker-Rice porch being worked to a finer scale, though in this they adhere less closely to precedent. The iron fences and stair rails interest the antiquary as contrasting the wrought iron of the older house with the cast iron of the newer. Whereas the former repeats familiar Florentine motives ever welcome, the latter elicits admiration for the apparent stability, yet light and decorative effect of the square, open-work gateposts. Both porches represent supreme achievement in grace, delicacy and refinement; both detail and proportions are such as to make instant appeal to any seeing eye.

Undoubtedly the most elaborate Corinthian porch in Salem is that of the Andrew-Safford house, Number 13 Washington Square, erected in 1818. It combines the square and elliptical motives and, according to Ross Turner, the artist, is one of the finest specimens of the architecture of the early nineteenth century. Perfect proportion and exquisite workmanship distinguish the fluted Corinthian columns and entablature with its delicate denticulated moldings, while above, the heavy balustrade and Palladian window repeating the motives below provide further effective ornamenta-

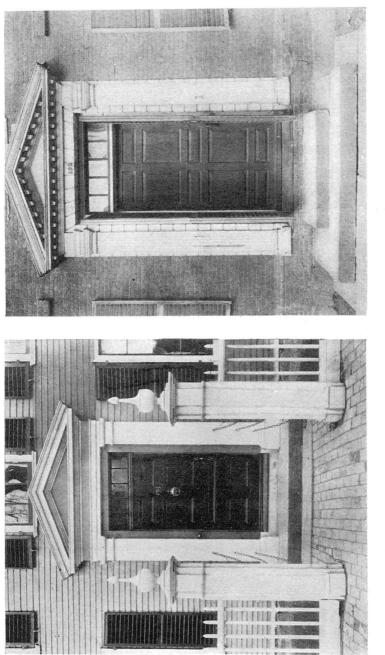

PLATE LVIII. — Lindall-Barnard-Andrews Doorway and Gateposts, 393 Essex Street. Erected 1747; Richard Derby Doorway, 168 Derby Street. Erected 1761.

PLATE LIX. — Nathan C. Osgood Window; Witch House Window.

tion. A unique pattern in the leaded fanlight gives new interest to this ever-welcome motive, but because of the four-paned windows and four-panel door, the pleasing scale of the Dodge-Shreve doorway is lacking. Taken as a whole, however, this doorway is an architectural feature of refined elegance and exceptional pretension.

No review of Salem doorways would be adequate that fails to include some of the unpretentious yet attractive examples which grace the smaller brick houses, and the side entrances of larger structures. Boasting neither porches nor wood trim, other than the frame, they charm the eye with their excellent proportions and beauty of line. Among the more notable of these, its framework set into the arch of a plain brick wall, the doorway of the Mansfield-Bolles house, Number 8 Chestnut Street, erected in 1810, attracts attention through its very simplicity. It is a restful doorway almost devoid of ornamentation except for the leaded side lights and elliptical fanlight. As in the case of many other examples of the period the leaded work is outside the glass and not attached to it in any way, the glass being cut to fit the rectangular or triangular divisions of the sashes. The charm of this entrance lies chiefly in its splendid proportions and the spacing of the six-paneled door with its molded flat panels.

Of still more modest character, the side entrance of the Home for Aged Women, which is at Number

19 Curtis Street, has no leadwork in its square-paned side lights. The four-panel door is of later origin with bolection molded raised panels.

At Number 12 Brown Street the Abbot house, erected in 1800, displays a good instance of a simple doorway with a semicircular fanlight. The arrangement of the molded and raised panels is uniquely pleasing and the double blind doors accord with a favorite Salem precedent. When standing open, as shown by the accompanying photograph, they lend a semblance of greater width to narrow doorways.

CHAPTER VII

WINDOWS AND WINDOW FRAMES

TRADITION says that while oiled paper windows lighted some of the first small cottages of old Naumkeag, glass was employed for the better residences after 1629. It was cut to diamond shape and set in lead lines three to four inches long for use in casement sashes one and one-half to two feet wide and two and one-half to three feet in height. These casements were employed both singly and in pairs, sometimes opening inward but oftener outward. Their stiles and rails were jointed together by halving, dovetailing, or the mortice and tenon, but like all sashes prior to about 1770, including Georgian sliding sashes, were pegged together. Some of the casements had flat corner irons for added strength, and all were hung with quaint wrought-iron strap or L hinges, the latter so designed as to combine the hinge and corner iron in one piece. Such a casement sash from the Buffum house, formerly on Boston Road, and built between 1642 and 1661, is preserved at the Essex Institute. Beside it is to be seen a diamond-shaped sash, such as was often used in the gables of stables and sheds, and containing "bull's-eye" lights, the latter much used in transoms over front doors and sometimes in the top panels of the doors themselves.

Casements continued in favor for about one hundred years, yet meanwhile, about the middle of the seventeenth century, sliding sashes with square panes of glass set in rabbeted wooden sash bars began to be used. These were put together with mortise and tenon joints and even the sash bars were pegged in place with wood. At first the panes of glass were only four by five inches and many in number, but the prevailing size was successively enlarged to five by seven, six by eight, seven by nine, ten by twelve, twelve by fourteen and finally in sizes for four-paned sashes to eighteen by twenty-four, twenty by twenty-eight and even larger. Many of the staid persons of those early days viewed this development with dismay, regarding the tendency as extravagant, particularly during the scarcity of glass in Revolutionary times, and expatiating on the perils of "glass houses."

As the size of the individual panes of glass was increased, their number in each sash was correspondingly decreased. Although numerous variations exist, the custom of having an equal number of panes in both upper and lower sashes predominated. Thus the sketch of the old peaked-roof Philip English house in Chapter I shows windows having fifteen, twelve and ten panes in both upper and lower sashes.

PLATE LX. — Architectural Relics at the Essex Institute.   Casement
Sash from Buffman House, formerly on Boston Road ; Diamond
Sash of later origin with Bull's-eye Lights ; Window Head
from the Elias Hasket Derby Mansion.

PLATE LXI. — Stephen W. Phillips Window, 34 Chestnut Street. Erected about 1810; Narbonne House Window.

Windows and Window Frames

Fifteen appears to be the largest number of panes employed in a sliding sash, and it will be noticed that the restored "House of Seven Gables" includes a window with an upper sash having ten panes and a lower one having fifteen. Many stationary windows in the shops of early days, however, including the quaint bay windows projecting only the width of a single pane of glass, sometimes had as many as fifty lights. All in Salem are now gone, alas! Probably the last was in a building that formerly stood at Endicott and Summer streets.

Twelve-paned upper and lower sashes are found on several old dwellings, notably the "Witch House", the Diman house, the Osgood house, Number 314 Essex Street, and Hawthorne's residence at Number 18 Chestnut Street. The "Witch House" window typifies the others and is well shown by an accompanying detail photograph. Eight-paned upper sashes frequently accompanied twelve-paned lower ones, as instanced by the Hunt house, illustrated in Chapter I, the Samuel Holten house shown in Chapter II and a window in the house of Anne Putnam in Danvers. Anne Putnam, it will be remembered, was one of the "afflicted girls" of 1692. Although only twelve years old at the time, she was largely responsible for the mischief that followed. Before her death she made a confession and was admitted into the church. The reverse arrangement with the larger sash above is rarely found, the John

Ward House being a notable example before its restoration with casement windows by the Essex Institute.

High eighteen-paned windows, nine panes to the sash, had a limited vogue and were employed on both floors of the Jeffrey Lang house. The Narbonne house and the Senator Benjamin Goodhue birthplace, Number 70 Boston Street, illustrate their use in connection with windows having six-paned upper sashes and nine-paned lower ones on the other floor. In the first instance the eighteen-paned windows were on the upper story and in the second instance on the lower story. The detail photograph of the Narbonne window shows it to be one of a relatively few having a top rail as heavy as the bottom rail and both very broad. All early windows had heavier sash bars and muntins than at present.

Fifteen-paned windows with six- and nine-paned sashes were features of the Rea-Putnam-Fowler house, the Maria Goodhue and the Colonel Jesse Putnam houses, all in Danvers. They are to be seen on the restored "House of Seven Gables" and on the lower story of the George Jacobs house, the upper windows, like most of those of the "House of Seven Gables", being twelve-paned with six panes to the sash. Sixteen-paned windows, eight panes to the sash, are very rare. The sketch of the Deliverance Parkman house in Chapter I shows one, but most of the windows in this house appear to have been twelve-paned.

In fact, throughout Salem architecture, the twelve-paned window, six panes to the sash, predominates. It is found in some of the oldest dwellings now standing, such as the Retire Becket and John Pickering houses illustrated in Chapter I, and it runs through every succeeding period up to 1818, and is the one favored in the present Colonial revival. In the earlier houses the upper sash was let into the frame permanently, only the lower sash being movable and sliding upward, but in later years double hung sashes with weights began to be adopted. Large four-paned windows were not employed in Salem architecture until the very latest houses that may be included within the limits of the broadest possible interpretation of the word Colonial were erected. Those of the White-Lord house, Number 31 Washington Square, erected in 1818, may be cited in this connection. The smaller paned windows of several older houses, however, have been replaced by new ones having only four large panes. Invariably such disregard of period not only upsets the scale of the façade, but constitutes an anachronism that renders all semblance of artistic coherence impossible. The windows of Hawthorne's birthplace shown in Chapter III and of the Assembly Hall shown in Chapter XI are cases in point.

Early window casings, like those of the door, were

plain and flat, presently followed by the application of a square band or back molding to the outer edge, and soon afterward casings were almost invariably molded after the manner of an architrave. Indeed, architrave casings have persisted to the present time and are to-day the preferred form in modern Colonial work. At first, top and sides of the frame were cased alike, as indicated by the Ropes' Memorial windows, but about the middle of the eighteenth century more thought began to be given to the exterior decorative possibilities of the window, and heads were placed above the architrave. Simple cornice moldings like those of the Cabot-Endicott-Low house and the Tuttle-Coan house, Number 113 Federal Street, erected about 1800, soon led to more or less elaborate friezes with cornices, which, in conjunction with the architrave casing, formed a complete entablature. The handiwork of skilled carvers employed in the local shipyards, then the most important in America, their hand-tooled moldings and carved friezes obviously owe their origin to the English Georgian. But the English worked mostly in stone; the Americans in wood; and thus the severe and heavy treatment of the former, thanks to the influence of the lighter and more elaborate decorations of ship cabins which the same men were executing, gave way to the graceful and dignified designs which we admire so much to-day. The work is done in a masterly manner, indicating

PLATE LXII. — Hoffman-Simpson Window, 26 Chestnut Street.
Erected 1810.

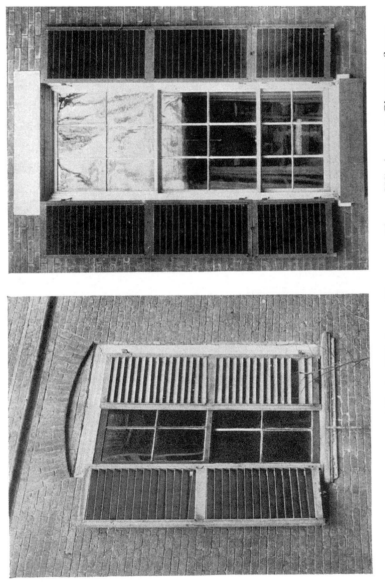

PLATE LXIII. — Richard Derby Window; Thompson House Window, 40 Chestnut Street.

thoughtful adaptation in its delicacy of detail and splendid spacing. When we recall the crude tools of those days our admiration for Yankee ingenuity need know no bounds. We may also marvel at the remarkably perfect condition of this century-old woodwork as it exists in Salem to-day.

Simple and effective, the Pierce-Johonnot-Nichols window heads instance the use of a plain, flat frieze below a molded cornice. The window heads of the Nathan C. Osgood house, Number 15 Chestnut Street, erected about 1810, are much the same except for the four groups of slender, vertical flutings that adorn and lend a touch of greater refinement to the frieze. Of a still more ambitious character the second-story window heads of the Cook-Oliver house are elaborated by hand carving in fine-scale detail with a denticulated cornice supported by a flat pilaster effect, toward each end of the frieze, the latter consisting of a central horizontal band, vertical-fluted, flanked by an oval medallion beside each pilaster. These are believed to be the personal work of Samuel McIntire and upon their design and execution he focused the full measure of his skill, with the result that there are no window heads to equal them in all Salem.

On the Stephen W. Phillips house, Number 34 Chestnut Street, erected in 1800, the window heads consist of entablatures similar to those of the Nathan C. Osgood house further elaborated. Except that the flutings in each group are more numerous and nearer together, the frieze is much the same, but the architrave casings have a molding midway of their width in addition to that along the outer edge. The cornice has the bold projection of the Doric order and the molded mutules of its soffit under the corona. Instead of the conventional guttæ, however, small round holes have been bored into the mutules in double rows to form a rectangular pattern. Just below the customary bed molding a prominent and unconventional, though admittedly beautiful molding suggests a series of tiny Gothic arches and capitals without supporting columns.

Brick walls impose certain limitations with respect to window frames not encountered in houses of wood, although many old brick residences in Salem display interesting examples of attractive treatment. Brick construction does not permit cased frames to have any projections and a lintel or brick arch must replace the ornamental head, often such a pleasing feature of wooden construction. In the earliest brick houses, with square-headed windows only, the openings had either gauged arches or relieving arches of headers with a brick core. The Richard Derby windows, however, with their cased architrave frames and molded wooden sills, are of interest as combining a rough-cut relieving arch of both headers and stretchers with much of the appearance of gauged work.

Windows and Window Frames

Half a century later the adoption of prominent white marble sills and lintels called for simpler treatment of the frame. Architraves were generally omitted and solid molded frames were placed in the reveals of the brick wall. The windows of the house erected by the Reverend James W. Thompson about 1846 at Number 40 Chestnut Street illustrate the construction and the plain broad lintels first used, but arrest attention chiefly as exceptional examples of the high, narrow three-sash window with the lower sash smaller than that above by reason of its square panes. It will be noticed that the blinds are divided so that this lower section of the window, which extended almost to the floor level, may be screened if desirable. Three-sash windows of this character lend themselves well to public buildings and are often seen in modern work, as on the second floor of the Boston City Club.

On the Hoffman-Simpson house, Number 26 Chestnut Street, erected about 1826, the frame boasts only a simple quarter round, the ornamentation of the windows being centered in the delicately cut white marble lintel. Marble was much favored for this purpose because it harmonizes with the white-painted woodwork, brightens the façade and emphasizes the fenestration. The design of this lintel is simple, refined and one of the most effective in Salem. Unlike most blinds of the period these have stiles dropping more than an inch below the bottom rail.

Among the many interesting marble lintels of Salem, those of the Charles Sanders house, Number 43 Chestnut Street, take the shape of a gauged brick arch, with scorings or flutings radiating from an imaginary center below, which further emphasizes this thought. The Pickman-Shreve-Little house, Number 27 Chestnut Street, displays a similar lintel, smooth of surface, however, but elaborated by an ornamental keystone with nicely cut vertical diminishing bead and torus moldings. Remarkably simple and effective, the flat arch lintel with voussoirs and keystone of the Peabody-Silsbee house, Number 380 Essex Street, has no surface ornamentation and depends entirely upon the shape of its parts to form a decorative pattern. Most elaborate of all, the lintels of the Dodge-Shreve house, Number 29 Chestnut Street, attract attention not only for their contour but for the nicely chiseled pattern reminiscent of a well-known Grecian fret.

To reduce their apparent height, three-story houses of both wood and brick were foreshortened with square windows. Single and two-piece sashes were both employed and the number of panes differed considerably. The windows of the Pierce-Johonnot-Nichols house well illustrate the three-pane upper and six-pane lower sash arrangement which was a feature of several of Salem's best houses. Still more common

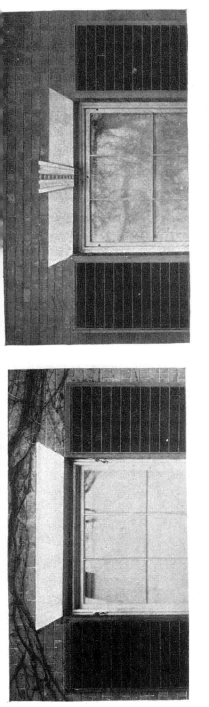

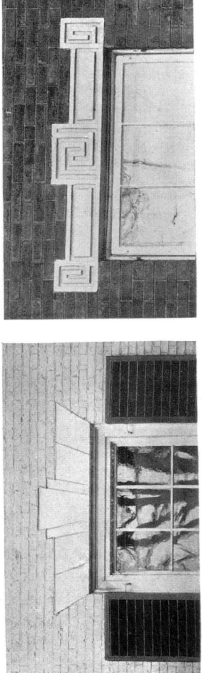

PLATE LXIV. — (From left to right) Charles Sanders Window Head, 43 Chestnut Street; Pickman-Shreve-Little Window Head; Peabody-Silsbee Window Head; Dodge-Shreve Window Head.

PLATE LXV. — Cook-Oliver Window.   Erected 1804 ; Pierce-Johonnot-Nichols Window.

was the double six-pane sash arrangement, exemplified by the Hosmer-Townsend-Waters house, Number 80 Washington Square. The Grimshawe house, Number 53 Charter Street, displays unusual double eight-pane sashes, the Gardner-White-Pingree house, Number 128 Essex Street, equally unusual double three-pane sashes. Solid sashes are to be seen on the birthplace of General Frederick W. Lander, Number 3 Barton Square, and the William G. Rantoul house on Chestnut Street, the former having six and the latter nine panes. Nine-paned solid sashes were also employed on the Briggs-Whipple house, Number 38 Forrester Street, and on the Crowninshield-Devereux-Waters house, Number 72 Washington Square.

The elaborate Palladian windows which became such an important and beautiful accompaniment of square brick houses have already been illustrated and referred to in Chapter V, but this chapter would hardly be complete without including mention of two of the many attractive round-headed windows which lighted the stairway landings of earlier gambrel-roof and square wood houses. The hall window of the Lindall-Gibbs-Osgood house, Number 314 Essex Street, erected in 1773, commends itself for effective simplicity, while that of the Pierce-Johonnot-Nichols house possesses the greater refinement of the keyed arch, the application of blinds and, most important of all, the fanlight motive of the upper sash bars. Such windows not only charm the eye as interior features but relieve the severity of many ranging square-headed windows and provide a center of interest for the rear elevation corresponding to the doorway of the façade that lends grace and distinction to an otherwise nondescript aspect of the house.

PLATE LXVI. — A Chamber in the Cook-Oliver House. Erected
1804; Paneled Wall, Parlor at " The Lindens," Danvers.
Erected 1754.

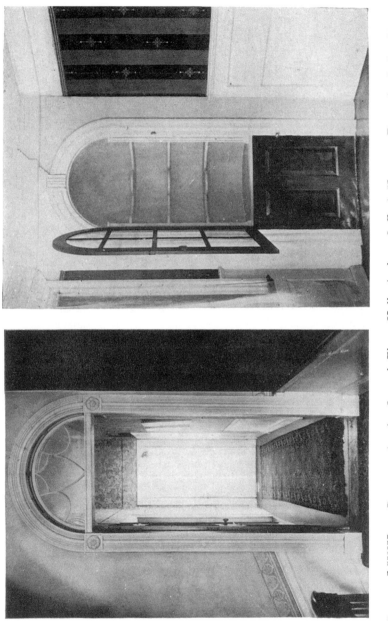

PLATE LXVII. — Doorway in the Second Floor Hall, Andrew-Safford House. Erected 1818; China Closet, Captain Edward Allen House, 125 Derby Street. Erected 1770.

CHAPTER VIII

INTERIOR WOOD FINISH

WHITE–PAINTED interior woodwork, one of the greatest charms of the Colonial house, provides the only architectural background that conveys satisfactorily the sense of mellow warmth and graceful dignity in eighteenth-century furniture of mahogany and other dark woods. It constitutes the setting in which the furniture gems of the room are displayed. Bright and cheerful, chaste and beautiful, it emphasizes the grace of line and richness of color of everything before it, yet seldom forces itself into undue prominence by reason of its color contrast or detail. Indeed this treatment of interiors has stood the test of time and we now appreciate what excellent taste our great-grandfathers manifested in depending upon its subtle influence to display the beauties of their rare pieces of furniture — Chippendale, Heppelwhite, Sheraton and Adam, brought from overseas.

The admirable work of McIntire and others in Salem indicates conclusively that the possibilities of painted white pine and other soft woods are fully as great as those of any hard woods. Effects must be differently achieved, however. The natural grain of the wood is concealed by painting so that broad flat surfaces and simple moldings would become monotonous. Beauty of form must be imparted as a substitute for the beauty of wood grain which is the chief ornamentation of natural wood finish. The motives and detail of exterior ornamentation as found in the several classic orders, such as the entablature, column and pedestal, the round and elliptical arch, moldings, carefully spaced panels and appropriate carving, or its equivalent in applied ornament, were therefore brought to bear upon the interior wood-work in such a manner as to delight the eye yet not to detract unduly from the furnishings of the room. And the charm of much of the resulting woodwork indicates an early realization of the fact that a nice balance between plain surface and decoration is as important as the decoration itself. It was in the design and execution of this woodwork that McIntire and the other skilled wood-carvers excelled; and to the fact that they embraced the best carvers in the country, attracted thither by the local shipyards, then among the largest in America, is attributed the precision of the work and a lightness, grace and ingenuity of adaptation not found in contemporary work elsewhere.

Fireplaces and stairways, the principal architectural features of interiors, were very properly elaborated considerably beyond the somewhat nega-

tive character of background accessories. Being
virtually furnishings as well as parts of the house,
the application of tasteful ornamentation to such
important forms of utility and necessity always
seems amply justified. Indeed, each is a subject in
itself, as indicated by the fact that to-day, as a
century and more ago, stair building and mantel
construction remain independent trades quite apart
from ordinary joinery. For that reason two separate
chapters will be reserved for these important de-
partments of Colonial architecture, the present
chapter being devoted to interior woodwork in
general.

What the interior woodwork of two of the earliest
seventeenth-century houses remaining in Salem now
consists of has already been shown in the first two
chapters of this volume. Passing on, therefore, to
about the middle of the eighteenth century, it is
found that the principal rooms of pretentious
mansions, such as the parlor at "The Lindens",
Danvers, were entirely paneled up on all sides. This
stately room, as was to be expected, since it was the
work of an English architect, was finished in the
typical Georgian manner, with heavy fluted Corinthian pilasters standing on low paneled pedestals
and supporting an elaborate entablature in which a
dentil course, an egg and dart ovolo, a cyma reversa
of leaf pattern and a bead and reel were prominent.
The casings of the large and handsomely paneled

doors repeated the architrave above, while the great rim locks of brass and prominent wrought-iron L hinges are of quaint interest and characteristic of the time. The heavily bolection-molded wall panels please the eye with their variety of shape and size, and one remarks that the chimney piece with its two horizontal panels, the larger above the smaller, has no mantelshelf as was for a time the custom. As in many other houses this wall is treated according to an absolutely symmetrical arrangement, with the fireplace centrally located and a door equidistant at each side. The woodwork, although of white pine, has been painted to simulate the appearance of old mahogany. Altogether this is probably the finest Provincial interior in Greater Salem.

About this time the use of hand-blocked wall paper began to be more general, and a favorite treatment of Colonial interiors, including halls, parlors, dining rooms and even the principal bedrooms of large houses, combined a cornice or often a cornice and frieze, and sometimes a complete entablature and a paneled wainscot or a flat dado with surbase and skirting. The dado was always relatively low as compared with the paneled wainscot. Later the simple skirting only was frequently employed even in the principal rooms of the better houses. Numerous accompanying illustrations show it with the dado, while the interiors of the Richard Derby house, the Captain Edward Allen house and several of the

PLATE LXVIII. — Paneled Wall, Richard Derby House, 168 Derby
Street. Erected 1761; Embrasured Windows and Seats
of the Same Room.

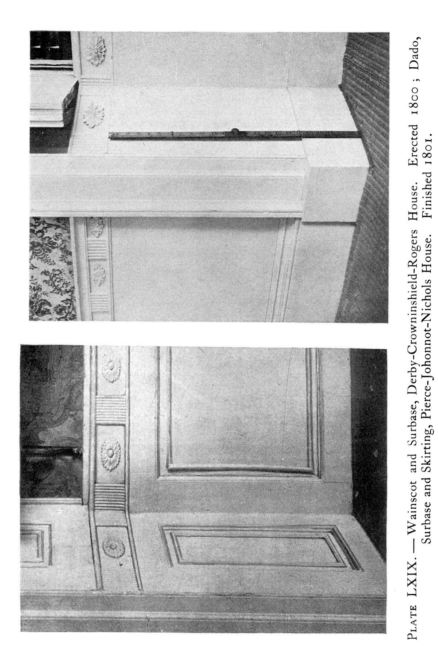

PLATE LXIX. — Wainscot and Surbase, Derby-Crowninshield-Rogers House. Erected 1800 ; Dado, Surbase and Skirting, Pierce-Johonnot-Nichols House. Finished 1801.

halls illustrated in Chapter IX show it with the paneled wainscot. It constituted a pleasing and consistent application of the classic orders to interior walls, the dado, the wall above it and whatever portion of the entablature happened to be employed corresponding to the pedestal, shaft and entablature of the complete order respectively. In a room so treated the dado became virtually a continuous pedestal with a base or skirting and a surbase above the die or plane face of the pedestal. Sometimes this surbase was merely a horizontal molding or group of moldings comprising a fillet with a cyma reversa beneath. Oftener it resembled the upper fascia or the complete architrave of the various orders, as in accompanying illustrations in the Putnam-Hanson, Pitman, Andrew-Safford, Salem Club, Cook-Oliver and Pierce-Johonnot-Nichols houses.

Again the upper fascia was embellished with a characteristic Grecian fret nicely hand-carved, or with vertical reedings or flutings. The latter may be continuous, as in the Cook-Oliver hall; in groups of five to seven or so with sections of plain fascia between them, as in the Crowninshield-Devereux-Waters hall and the east parlor of the Pierce-Johonnot-Nichols house; or still further enriched by an elliptical conventionalized flower medallion, carved or of composition, applied in alternation with the reeded or fluted groups. A handsome surbase of the latter type in connection with a flat dado and molded skirting is to be seen in the east front chamber of the Pierce-Johonnot-Nichols house. The photograph also shows well the detail of the architrave casings of the embrasured windows and the manner in which the shutters fold into pockets at each side. A somewhat similar surbase in connection with a paneled wainscot of later date than those previously mentioned is a feature of one of the chambers of the Derby-Crowninshield-Rogers house, Number 202½ Essex Street. The festoon scheme of the surbase in the hall of the Home for Aged Women exemplifies a pleasing variation from the more common continuous series of vertical flutings.

For the most part the surmounting cornice and frieze of the room was of wood beautifully molded and hand carved, the architrave usually being omitted unless the walls were entirely paneled, as in the parlor of "The Lindens." In a chamber of the Derby-Crowninshield-Rogers house, however, is to be seen a cornice and frieze entirely of plaster work according to designs by McIntire, including familiar classic detail in which the egg and dart molding, scroll and interlacing fillet guilloche are prominent. Such cornices were frequently employed in the houses of the early nineteenth century and thereafter. Later, when chandeliers for candles began to be used in private houses, they were hung from ornamental centerpieces of plaster on the ceiling, the motives usually being circles, festooned garlands and acanthus leaves. Such a centerpiece, with a simple plaster cornice and ornamental treatment of the ceiling at each corner of the room, is a feature of the parlor of the Andrew-Safford house.

The Derby-Crowninshield-Rogers house mentioned above, its street floor converted into stores, is to-day but a mere echo of its former elegance, yet the upper portion still shows that it was an interesting example of the early square town house, with a virtually flat roof. The chambers of the second and third floors still contain much excellent interior finish, particularly mantels such as those mentioned in the following chapter and which are still admired by all who appreciate good architecture, despite the bad treatment to which they have been subjected by tenants.

Shortly after the erection of his house about 1800, after plans by McIntire, it was occupied by Ezekiel Hersey Derby, a son of Elias Hasket Derby, Salem's greatest merchant. Not having the family love of adventures at sea, however, he soon moved to the family estate in South Salem and devoted himself to "horticulture, later exhibiting to his friends, among many other interesting plants and garden effects, the first true specimen of the night-blooming cereus ever shown in Salem and a delightful little pond bordered with bald cypresses, which remained until very recently." His town house then became the last residence in Salem of Honorable Benjamin W. Crowninshield before moving to Boston, and was last occupied as a winter residence by Richard S. Rogers, a wealthy merchant in the foreign trade, whose splendid summer home on a farm in Peabody, also designed by McIntire, is now known as "Oak Hill" and occupied as a summer residence by his son's widow, Mrs. J. C. Rogers.

In most of the better houses during the Provincial period important rooms had paneled wainscots, papered walls and molded cornices like those shown in the Richard Derby house. A fireplace with paneled chimney piece was an important feature of most rooms, and the entire wall including it was often completely paneled up, closely relating the fireplace, doors or windows in a definite architectural scheme. Summer beams were cased and molded like the cornice, and the architrave casings of the windows were brought into engagement with its soffit. Embrasured windows with two-part paneled shutters folding into pockets at each side and seats jutting somewhat into the room were the rule, particularly in brick houses, as in the present instance. The simple and effective mantel appears to be of later date than the bolection molded paneling over the chimney breast, as the lower panel was obviously cut to permit its use.

But the west or Georgian parlor of the Pierce-Johonnot-Nichols house is without question the most notable instance in Salem of this architectural treatment of the fireplace wall of the room with wood paneling throughout. Along Georgian lines and

PLATE LXX. — East Front Chamber, Pierce-Johonnot-Nichols House.
Finished 1801 ; Plaster Cornice and Frieze, Derby-Crowninshield-
Rogers House.   Erected 1800.

PLATE LXXI. — West or Georgian Parlor, Pierce-Johonnot-Nichols House. Erected 1782; Embrasured Windows and Seats of the Same Room.

decidedly substantial in character, it is essentially simple in conception and graceful in form and proportion. A flat dado with molded skirting and surbase, also a heavy cornice, surround the room and serve to combine its several features into a unified whole. First attention properly goes to the chimney piece, and this is fully treated in Chapter X. Its principal moldings are repeated in the cornice and the doorheads. There is the same cymatium and corona, the same ovolo enriched with the exquisitely carved egg and dart motive, used without the customary bead and reel, while beneath in respective order occur the familiar classic dentil course and simple ogee molding. All are executed in a masterly manner, the proportions being well calculated and the precision of the hand tooling remarkably well maintained.

Both the doors and embrasured windows of this room merit careful study, the former for the arrangement of the molded panels, the architrave casings, the striking heads with the returns of the moldings and the contour of the ends of the flat frieze suggesting the cavetto frieze of the Roman Composite and Italian Corinthian orders. Attention is also directed to the delightfully quaint hardware, particularly the brass drop handles used in connection with great rim locks on the opposite side of the door. Were it not otherwise definitely established, the wrought-iron H and L hinges would indicate positively the eighteenth century character of the work. The embrasured windows with built-in seats beneath differ in only minor particulars from those of the Richard Derby house.

About 1800 and thereafter it became the custom to make the fireplace in the principal rooms the center of an absolutely symmetrical arrangement, placing it between two identical windows of an outer wall or doorways of an inner wall. Often, as in the Putnam-Hanson house, Number 94 Boston Street, erected before 1800, one of these doors opened into an adjoining room and the other into a closet. Sometimes, too, a false door was employed merely to preserve the balance. Not only is the mantel of this room, with its applied basket of fruit and flowers on the frieze painted in natural colors, one of simplicity and excellent proportion, but the old scenic wall paper depicting life in the Orient at that time is one of the most interesting and best preserved in Salem. As in many other houses a cast-iron hob grate with classic ornament in the Ionic order now fills the original fireplace opening.

In a room of the Pitman house, erected at Number 4 Boston Street before 1800, and which was destroyed in the great fire of 1914, this symmetrical treatment of the principal wall of the room took the unusual form of two closet-like recesses reached through round headed and keyed arches without doors each side of a projecting chimney piece. Above a mantel of chaste simplicity depending chiefly upon a delightfully proportioned dentil course to give it scale and distinction, the overmantel consists of a great frame the full width of the chimney breast, including an architrave molding enriched with a series of fine-scale vertical reedings. Figured wall paper like that of the rest of the room fills the space within the frame. Quaint andirons such as those seen in the accompanying illustration, representing dwarf human figures, are rarely to be found in Salem or elsewhere.

Two more excellent instances of the symmetrical treatment of the fireplace wall in bedchambers are to be found in the Pierce-Johonnot-Nichols house. The east front chamber, finished in 1801, pleases the eye particularly with its refined and graceful Adam detail to which minute reference is made in Chapter X, while a chamber on the third floor, containing an exceptionally modest mantel, boasting no cornice and having only a skirting about the walls, possesses a quaint charm that is altogether delightful. In both instances clothes closets at each side project several inches into the room, and the chimney piece and mantel respectively occupy the recess between them. It is interesting to notice in the former room that the cymatium of the cornice and the shelf of the mantel are identical, and that the favorite McIntire dentil course, consisting of a double denticulated Grecian fret, is used in both; the vertical reeded ovolo of the cornice, however, being omitted from the mantel. Rare old mahogany furniture and other antiques preserve the atmosphere of the first years of the nineteenth century.

In direct contrast to these recessed mantels may be mentioned the boldly projecting scheme in the dining room of the Cook-Oliver house, also designed by McIntire, and in the chamber above. This construction is of course necessary when the fireplace is located on an outside wall, and while it cuts into the floor area it is by no means without its compensations. Thrusting itself into the room as it does it enables a mantel of modest character to give much of the stately effect of a costly chimney piece, particularly when a mantel mirror or large painting hangs over the chimney breast. As in the present instance an opportunity is often afforded for built-in window seats of great charm.

The refinement of the architrave casings of doorways and windows and the nicely paneled doors are prominent features of these rooms which at once arrest attention. Both have flat dados with molded surbase and skirting, and there is a certain similarity in the mantels, that of the dining room being properly richer in detail than the one above. The cornice, with the double denticulated Grecian fret again, and the frieze, with groups of nine vertical reeds at regular intervals, exemplify McIntire's success in achieving refined and distinctive effects with simple motives. The continuous series of reedings of the architraves and surbase in this room greatly enrich the detail.

PLATE LXXII. — Mantel and Side of Room, Putnam-Hanson House, 94 Boston Street. Erected before 1800; Mantel and Side of Room, Pitman House, 4 Boston Street. Erected Before 1800. Burned 1914.

PLATE LXXIII. — Dining Room, Cook-Oliver House, 142 Federal Street. Erected 1804; Private Dining Room, Salem Club, 29 Washington Square. Erected 1819.

In the chamber above, the repetition of the fine-scale dentil course in both cornice and mantel entablature is most effective; beautiful in its own simplicity as a foil for the horizontal lines of all the other moldings and bringing mantel and cornice into close relation.

A private dining room in the Salem Club is of interest for the extreme simplicity and chaste appearance of its detail, and particularly as showing how an appropriate scenic wall paper can assist a modest mantel to convey the dignity of a chimney piece. This handsome landscape paper is Zuber's "El Dorado", by the Alsatian artists, Ehrmann and Zipelius, and printed from the original blocks.

Toward the end of the eighteenth century Samuel McIntire came completely under the spell of the refined and distinctive elegance of the work of the brothers Adam in England, and until his death in 1811 most of the houses designed by him, especially the interior woodwork, were in the Adam manner. During this period, too, he finished many whole rooms or added new mantels in houses previously erected. For instance, the Pierce-Johonnot-Nichols house was built in 1782, but only the rooms in the western side were finished at that time in the Georgian manner. The whole eastern side is in McIntire's later manner, and the east parlor, done in 1801, has become a veritable Mecca for architects from all sections of the country. America has no contemporaneous example of the Adam influence superior to this room with its symmetrical architectural treatment of the two opposite ends, shown by accompanying photographs. Sixteen and one-half by twenty-six and one-half feet in size and high studded, it possesses the spaciousness necessary to bring out to the full that subtle quality of nice balance between the plain surfaces and delicate ornament to which the Adam manner owes its principal refinement and charm. Indeed, the low, flat dado with its molded surbase embellished with groups of five vertical flutings, the pilaster treatment of the corners with Corinthian capitals and fluted shafts resting on classic pedestals, the elaborate cornice with intricately carved moldings and broad frieze with rosettes and groups of seven vertical reeds in alternation on a flat ground, the embrasured windows with folding paneled shutters and architrave casings, hand tooled much like the surbase, and last, but most important of all, the magnificent chimney piece, constitute an architectural setting of rare beauty which architects and antiquaries rejoice is in a house owned and to be preserved by the Essex Institute.

One of McIntire's favorite motives, ever recurring with minor variations throughout his work in the Adam manner, occupies the string course of the cornice. This double denticulated member or Grecian fret is formed by vertical cross cuttings alternately from top and bottom of a square molding, the fine-scale vertical reeded ovolo beneath giving it just the proper emphasis and serving also to relate the cornice as a whole more closely to the ornamentation of the frieze. Each side of the chimney piece both cornice and frieze project considerably and the soffit is enriched by a guilloche consisting of interlacing circular fillets, large and small circles in alternation, with applied rosettes within the larger circles.

In Chapter X this chimney piece, the handsomest in Salem, is treated at some length. It is fitting here, however, to note the pleasing and logical manner in which both cornice and frieze have been carried about its various projections and made part of it, thus tying it into the entire scheme.

The door trim, like that of others in the house, displays considerable refined embellishment. Flat pilasters beside the architrave casings rise from the skirting to the doorhead, the upper fascia of which consists of a series of hand-tooled reedings. The capitals are formed by a simple use of the acanthus leaf taken from the Corinthian order. Fruit-filled urns, garlands and elliptical medallions of applied work, delicately drawn, ornament the broad frieze and projecting pilasters of the doorhead which, with the architrave casing beneath it, form a complete entablature. It will be noticed that the cornice of the doorhead repeats that of the room, including the reed cross sections between the dentils, but without the tiny holes in each dentil of the main cornice above, which are undoubtedly the marks of a nail set, perhaps purposely left unfilled to add another detail to the pattern. The door itself pleases the eye with its attractive panel arrangement and the flat panels with tiny moldings planted on them about an inch from the edge and replacing the more common beveling. Stiles, muntin and rails are all of the same width except for the broader bottom rail. Brass drop handles such as this accord excellently with Adam detail, and one notices the use of butts instead of the old-fashioned H and L hinges found throughout the west side of this house.

Reverting momentarily to the windows of this room, it will be noticed that unlike the usual two-piece shutters these have three paneled parts on each side hinged together with quaint wrought-iron H hinges. The photograph also shows that the stiles and rails of these shutters are held together by small wooden pins. Various types of shutters were in vogue during different periods in Salem. Exterior solid board shutters came first. On stores they were of the batten type in one piece and held in place by cross-bars of wood or iron, while on houses they were in two parts and hung on strap hinges. For domestic use, however, they were soon brought indoors, the construction being the same, except that openings taking the shape of a star or crescent were often cut through them near the top to admit a little light. Then came the paneled and the folding shutter for

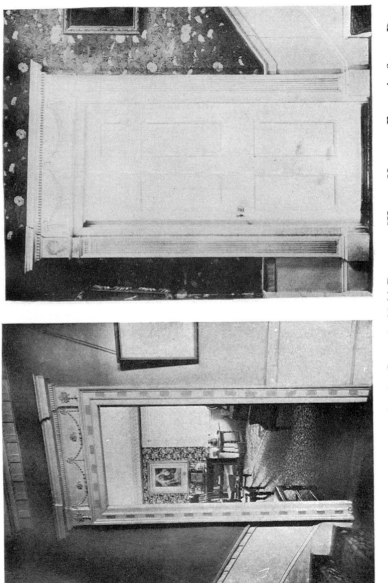

PLATE LXXIV. — Doorway in the Crowninshield-Devereux-Waters House. Erected 1805 ; Doorway in the Cook-Oliver House. Erected 1804. Taken from the old Elias Hasket Derby House.

PLATE LXXV. — East or Adam Parlor, Pierce-Johonnot-Nichols House. Finished 1801; Embrasured Windows of the Same Room.

better appearance and compactness, the openings
sometimes being retained as shown by the photograph of the front room of the Narbonne house in
Chapter II. Another development was a quaint
paneled shutter the full width of the window and
sliding into the wall at one side, there being separate
shutters corresponding to the upper and lower
sashes. They kept out the cold very well, and one
wonders that no one has thought to glaze them for
use in winter as double windows put in place at a
moment's notice without effort.

In several of the best Salem houses erected during
the first decade of the nineteenth century, most of
them by McIntire, the interior doorways have beautiful Adam detail. Those in the hall of the Crowninshield-Devereux-Waters house, Number 72 Washington Square East, combine motives prominent in both
the doorway and window of the east parlor of the
Pierce-Johonnot-Nichols house, already described,
with other new and original detail. There are the
same architrave casings with groups of seven flutings
at frequent intervals on the upper fascia, the same
cymatium and corona, and similar decoration of
the doorhead frieze consisting of dainty applied work
in the form of slender festooned and straight-hanging
garlands with florets between, and ornamental flower
pots with blooming plants on the projecting pilaster-
like portions at each end, supporting a cornice with
corresponding projections and in which a simple

fine-scale dentil course is prominent. No pilasters flank the architrave casings in this instance.

One of McIntire's frequent ingenious innovations replaces the usual cornice and frieze. Below a cyma recta of extreme simplicity a reed, hand-tooled spirally and resembling the twist drills of to-day, though doubtless a modification of the popular rope moldings of the time, occupies the position of the usual fillet. The corona has been omitted, likewise the dentil course, although the spiral reed has much the value of the latter. The narrow frieze with a plain torus below it has its flat surface relieved at intervals with groups of nine vertical reedings corresponding to the groups of seven on the surbase. All executed with the utmost precision, the effect is one of beauty and distinction.

In the hall of the Cook-Oliver house on Federal Street, paneled and fluted pilasters support the ornamental doorhead and serve as casings without architraves, except as a lower fascia bearing a continuous series of fine-scale flutings, and a plain torus faces the jambs. Reedings having virtually the same scale and value adorn the surbase. The projection of the skirting to provide bases for the pilasters is an interesting and effective detail.

Salem has no more exquisite examples of the Adam doorhead and accompanying wood trim than these taken from the Elias Hasket Derby mansion with their gracefully festooned draperies, fruit-filled urns and rosettes. Both the main cornice and that of the doorhead include a prominent denticulated molding, each dentil being nicely hand-tooled with a shallow gouge cutting to give its face the appearance of the letter H. Conforming to the characteristic panel arrangement of the time with small panels above the two sets of larger ones rather than between the latter, as in the east parlor of the Pierce-Johonnot-Nichols house, the doors themselves are excellent, the beveling of the panels and the molding of the stiles and rails manifesting painstaking workmanship. One notices with approval also the brightening effect of the simple brass-mounted glass knob and the brass key plate.

The accompanying plate shows clearly the beautiful old imported wall paper that formerly adorned this hall. It was hand blocked in eighteen-inch squares and consists of pink roses on a background of green leaves, the coloring having softened delightfully with the passing years. Because of its unique character, the pattern apparently having no duplicate in America, the paper of this hall was purchased early in 1916 by the Metropolitan Museum of Art, removed, cleaned and taken to New York to decorate one of the several Colonial rooms that now form one of the important permanent features.

Another notable example of McIntire's versatility in the variation of the detail of his interior wood trim is to be found in the hall of the Home for Aged

Women, Number 180 Derby Street. The doorway shown is, generally speaking, a simplified version of that in the hall of the Cook-Oliver house. Paneled pilasters on projecting bases again support the doorhead, but these pilasters are not fluted. The lower fascia of the jambs bears only a simple torus at the edge and is omitted entirely at the top, while the panels of the door itself are plain and flat. A unique combination of detail adorns the entablature of the doorhead. The architrave across the lintel corresponds to the surbase below, and introduces a rare instance of a continuous series of short vertical flutings so cut as to give a festoon effect which is terminated at each end by the pilaster projections bearing elliptical flower ornaments similar to those in the Cook-Oliver house. No ornament has been applied to the broad frieze, but the cornice is enriched in an unusual manner. A fine-scale rope molding occupies the dentil course, while beneath McIntire's favorite cymatium and corona the soffit is intricately hand-tooled with groups of five flutings in alternation with small sunken panels of diamond shape with scalloped edges. At the ceiling a cornice without frieze is employed. Here the rope molding occurs again, and broad, flat modillions support the corona, somewhat after the Corinthian manner, each modillion having carefully carved upon its under face a sunken, round, flower medallion. A word should be said in passing regarding the spiral newel, indicating

PLATE LXXVI. — Detail of Doorway, Adam Parlor, Pierce-Johonnot-
Nichols House.

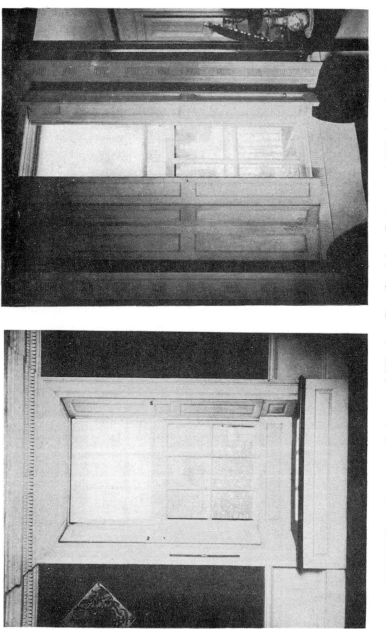

PLATE LXXVII. — Georgian Embrasured Window Detail; Adam Embrasured Window Detail showing Shutters, Pierce-Johonnot-Nichols House.

as it does that when turned balusters are of slender grace this scheme is fully as effective as when plain round or square balusters are used.

In the parlor of the Andrew-Safford house, Number 13 Washington Square, there is a doorway typical of the last period of Colonial architecture in Salem when the Corinthian order was much in favor, but the influence of the decadence that came with the Greek revival had begun to make itself felt. The Corinthian spirit, of course, lies in the typical modillions supporting the corona, nicely hand-carved in classic scroll pattern with the usual acanthus leaf decoration of the under surface. Otherwise the entire treatment is an original creation of its designer, although the customary relation between surbase and doorhead cornice is maintained by the tiny ball moldings. Architects of the present day regard the elaborately molded pilaster casings with their plinths and bull's-eye corner blocks as over-elaborate and rather clumsy. In panel arrangement like that of the foregoing examples, the bolection moldings give this door a considerably different aspect, which is still further emphasized by the dark red-brown painting in the spirit of old mahogany which became a frequent feature of the houses of this period.

It will be noted that all of these six-panel doors with four panels of equal size and two small ones at the top have stiles and muntin of virtually equal width, any variation being slightly wider stiles.

Top and frieze rails are alike and the same width as the muntin, but the bottom rail is somewhat broader and the lock rail the broadest of the four. Moldings are confined to the edge of the panels, with the splayed or beveled panels of earlier years gradually being abandoned in favor of plain, flat surfaces.

Round-headed doorways here and there provided a welcome variation from the customary square-headed types and have been a pleasing feature of Colonial interiors since early times. As framing the glazed doors of china closets they are noticeable in the parlor of the "House of the Seven Gables" shown in Chapter I, and in the front room of the Narbonne house shown in Chapter II. The accompanying example, illustrating the treatment of a corner china closet, is from the Captain Edward Allen house erected in 1770. Nicely molded architrave casings were employed, and the keystone effect carried up through the cornice by a slight projection of the various moldings is most effective. The separation of the upper glazed and lower wood-paneled parts of the dark-painted door is an interesting detail, as are the plastering of the closet to the form of a semi-circular dome-shaped niche, the peculiar shape of the shelves and the small pilasters at each side within the door.

In the second-floor hall of the Andrew-Safford and other contemporary houses the round-headed door-way was utilized to provide an ornamental yet

PLATE LXXVIII. — Plaster Centerpiece, Ceiling of the Andrew-Safford Parlor. Erected 1818; Third-Floor Chamber, Pierce-Johonnot-Nichols House. Erected 1782.

PLATE LXXIX. — Doorway in the Parlor of the Andrew-Safford House. Erected 1818; Doorway in the Home for Aged Women. Erected 1810.

practical fanlight transom over the door between the front and rear part of the hall. Such a transom admitted considerable light from the brighter to the darker side and afforded a degree of privacy whenever desired. The elaborately molded casings and hand-carved corner blocks are characteristic of the latter part of what might be termed the Federal period of Colonial architecture. One notes the effectiveness of the paneled soffit of the arch and the unique sash divisions of the transom with a central light suggestive of the classic urn.

Round-headed openings were employed for landing windows in stair halls, as shown in Chapter IX, and in the central part of the Palladian windows over entrance porches, as shown in Chapter VI, where they became decorative interior features of the front end of second-floor halls.

Elliptical-headed openings, echoing indoors the fanlight of the front doorway, were in most instances reserved for framing the stairway vista at the head or foot of the flight, as mentioned in the following chapter, or for arches between front and back parlors, where they became one of the most charming features of the best Colonial interiors. As in the Andrew-Safford house these elliptical arches between rooms often included a glazed fanlight with graceful sash divisions and sliding doors to separate the rooms if desired. The treatment of this broad doorway through a thick brick partition wall with engaged

Ionic columns at the front and paneling in the reveals and about the soffit of the arch back of the doors has been much admired. Indeed the vista through this arch, the chaste white woodwork and the tasteful mahogany furniture and other appropriate furnishings form a picture of spacious elegance the equal of any in Salem.

PLATE LXXX. — Stairway in the Samuel McIntire House. Erected 1780 ; Stairway in the Pierce-Johonnot-Nichols Side Hall. Erected 1782.

PLATE LXXXXI.—Stairway in the Hosmer-Townsend-Waters House. Erected 1795; Newel and Balustrade, Simon Forrester Stairway. Erected Before 1800.

CHAPTER IX

HALLS AND STAIRWAYS

AS an avenue of approach from the doorway to the fireside the hall ever awakens particular interest. It may properly, and often does, reflect both ways — the welcome of the doorway whatever the degree of its warmth, and the anticipated hospitality of the hearthstone. Its psychological effect cannot be denied. One hall provides only a characterless passage to the rooms beyond, another in its severity forebodes little else than dignified insincerity, whereas the one most to be admired seems to radiate the good cheer of a happy home.

In early Salem houses the halls were mere entries and the stairways purely utilitarian, but with more settled conditions and greater prosperity the hall took its rightful place among the most pleasing rooms of the house. As the stairway affords opportunities for architectural embellishment quite as freely as does the fireplace, so the Colonial hall became a setting for this architectural gem which reached the height of its development during the latter half of the eighteenth century.

At first the hall was regarded almost as a necessary evil, the aim being to devote the least possible amount of space to it. Thus many of the compact English cottage types are to be found with the stairway in the form of a broken flight rising in three short runs with two landings at opposite sides of the hall where right angle turns occur. Such a stairway in the "House of the Seven Gables", probably erected in 1669, was illustrated in Chapter I. Two others of interest are to be seen in the side hall of the Pierce-Johonnot-Nichols house, erected in 1782, and in the little hall at Number 31 Summer Street in the house erected in 1780 where Samuel McIntire lived and died. The two former have the earlier molded close strings, whereas the latter has the open or cut strings showing the step on the stair facing and having jig-sawed scroll brackets beneath the overhanging treads as string ornaments. All three stairways show the customary closet with paneled outer walls and a door under the second landing, but the two latter manifest greater refinement in the spacing of the raised and molded panels and the nicely turned balusters and newels. It will be noticed that the square landing newels are structural uprights, one or both of them extending to the floor, and that both strings and hand rails are mortised and tenoned to them and fastened with wood pins.

In modest halls such as the foregoing, a skirting, sometimes molded, often runs about the walls and

PLATE LXXXII. — Stairway in the Captain Edward Allen House.
Erected 1770.

PLATE LXXXIII. — "Winder" in the David P. Waters House. Erected 1805 ; "Winder" in the Derby-Crowninshield-Rogers House. Erected about 1800.

up the stairway, but in more elaborate houses there
is usually a paneled wainscot notable for good
spacing and pleasing proportions similar to that in
the Captain Edward Allen house, corner of Derby
and Hardy Streets. As a rule the heavy molded
hand rail is of white pine painted in a warm dark
color, although sometimes white painted like the
rest of the woodwork, as in the Simon Forrester and
Cabot-Endicott-Low houses. In the more costly
houses it is occasionally of mahogany. Usually
curving outward to a newel at the bottom, the
rail often sweeps upward in free graceful curves to
the newels of the upper floors, or again swings along
from flight to flight without being broken by newels.
This upward curve of the ramped rail is usually
repeated in the surbase and sometimes in the paneling of the wainscot opposite. Although it had been
the prevailing type in the gambrel-roof mansions
of about 1750, McIntire usually reserved the broken
flight for side halls, as in the Pierce-Johonnot-
Nichols house, yet he employed it in 1795 for the
front hall of the Hosmer-Waters house, Number
80 Washington Square, imparting to it considerable
individuality in arrangement and detail. The exceptionally short first run with ramped rail and dado
followed by a longer straight run with corresponding
balustrade and wall treatment at once arrest attention; likewise the open unutilized space beneath the flight. Rail, balusters and particularly

attractive scroll brackets are of sturdy grace in accord with the newels, which suggest an adaptation of the Roman Doric column. Similar but heavier balusters and newel in the Simon Forrester house, Number 11 Hodges Court, erected before 1800, are found in connection with paneled box stairs which emphasize the broad tread and relatively low rise. In modern adaptation it is better suited to public than private work.

The Captain Edward Allen house contains an elaborated stairway of the cottage type. The hall, being wider, permits more massive construction, especially of the box stairs with paneled ends and sides, and the balustrade, with its twisted balusters and corkscrew newel, which rightly may be considered among the most interesting and spontaneous achievements of the early American builders. Captain Allen was a Scotchman, who came to America as a mariner in 1757 and in 1759 married the sister of the wife of Richard Derby, the father of Elias Hasket Derby.

About the beginning of the nineteenth century the ingenuity of American builders evolved another solution of the short hall problem which came to be known as the full spiral or "winder." Although undoubtedly suggested by the stone stairways of historic round towers and cathedrals in the mother country, it became thoroughly domesticated and harmonized with the lighter treatment of its sur-

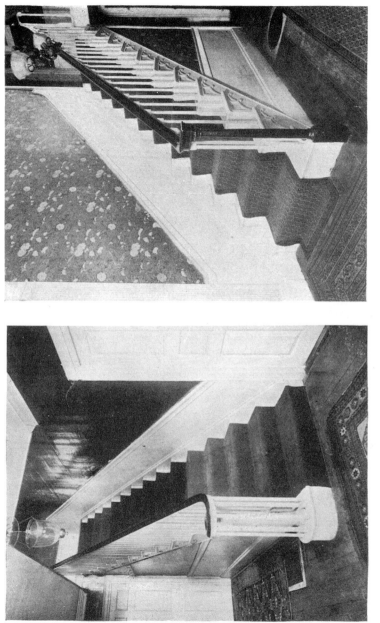

PLATE LXXXIV. — Hall and Stairway, Lindall-Barnard-Andrews House. Erected 1747; Stairway in the Cook-Oliver House. Erected 1804.

PLATE LXXXV. — .Hall and Stairway, " The Lindens."   Erected
1754 ; Stairway Detail, " The Lindens."

roundings. As found in the David P. Waters house, Number 14 Cambridge Street, designed by Samuel McIntire in 1805, its sinuous lines are possessed of a rare grace which should commend itself to prospective home builders desirous of obtaining strong individuality in their present-day small house adaptations. The form of such a stairway is its own ornamentation, hence the simplicity of the molded hand rail and slender square balusters relieved by flat scroll brackets on the string and a hand-tooled rope plaster bead. Could anything be more appropriate than the newel treatment suggesting the volute of the Ionic order, the balustrade winding scroll-fashion about a little round-turned column and the first stair tread taking the outline of the rail above? A paneled wainscot would have been out of place. Instead, as in the Lindall-Barnard-Andrews hall and others of similar character and equally early date, a simple skirting, flat dado and a surbase correspond in total height to that of the balustrade opposite, while hand-blocked paper of interesting design, imported from France or England, covers the wall above.

In the Derby-Crowninshield-Rogers house, on Essex Street, another "winder" at once attracts attention to its generous proportions and broad sweeping curves which lend a stately grandeur, while the dado effect, with molded skirting and surbase displaying a simple Grecian fret, again justifies itself as appropriate in stairways of this sort, aiding materially in the architectural treatment of the room. Both the rope-molded plaster bead and scroll brackets are again employed, the latter of outline form nicely jig-sawed. The slender balusters are turned, however, like the newel, which one might wish were of more distinctive contour. Strangely enough the "winder" never enjoyed the popularity of the straight run and broken flight, whereas wing-flights rising each side from a half-way landing, although they flourished in the South, never gained a foothold in New England.

In the better houses built just prior to the Revolution and immediately following, a hall of generous size took its place among the important interior features. Planned first in the spirit of hospitality, and also "to put the best foot foremost", they were elaborated as much because the presence of the stairway provided opportunities for effective architectural treatment as for any other reason.

Wide halls leading entirely through the center of the house were common, a door at the rear often opening upon a secluded yard or old-fashioned garden, as at "The Lindens", Danvers. In large houses, particularly square ones like the Pickman-Derby-Brookhouse mansion, the hall did not extend the whole way through, and the rear door, if there were one, opened into a back room, while other doors on each side gave access to the more important

PLATE LXXXVI. — Palladian Window, Pierce-Johonnot-Nichols House.   Erected 1782 ; Palladian
Window, " The Lindens."   Erected 1754.

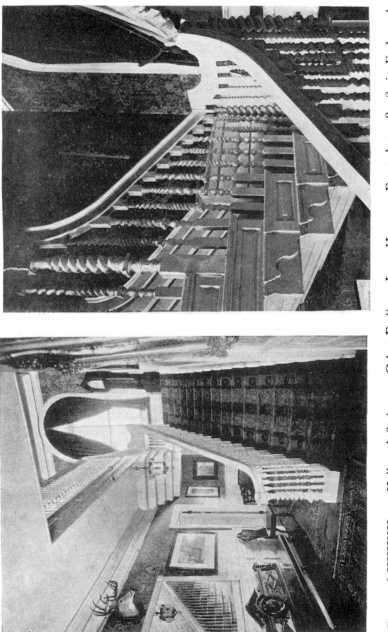

PLATE LXXXVII. — Hall and Stairway, Cabot-Endicott-Low House. Erected 1748; Stair Ends and Landing, Cabot-Endicott-Low House.

rooms. Broken flights of stairs continued, but in long halls a straight run along one wall led to a landing only three or four feet below the second-floor level where the direction of the flight reversed. This arrangement may be seen in several accompanying illustrations, the stairway of the Cook-Oliver house on Federal Street being particularly simple and effective. Delightful in its slender grace, the balustrade consists of a molded rail and simple turned newel and balusters. A flat dado with molded skirting and surbase hand-carved in fine-scale, vertical, reeded motive extends up the flight along the wall, while outline scroll brackets, recalling those of the Derby-Crowninshield-Rogers house, adorn the stair ends. The stairway of the Lindall-Barnard-Andrews house, Number 393 Essex Street, instances a single straight flight in a long hall. The slender grace of the square balusters and turned newel, the attractive scroll brackets and molded surbase, taken as a whole create an unrivaled air of distinction and strong individuality. The newel treatment resembles that of the David P. Waters stairway, already referred to, and both of these stairways are unquestionably among the best simple prototypes for adaptation in a Colonial cottage of the present day. The Waters stairway being a "winder", two types of different arrangement but similar treatment are presented so that a choice can be made to suit the needs in hand.

Two more points are of interest. Economy made it necessary in many houses to forego the luxury of a solid mahogany stair rail and merely to cap a white-painted rail with short thin strips of mahogany as in this instance. A similar treatment of a dark-painted rail may be seen in the Pierce-Johonnot-Nichols house. It will be noticed that the two doors shown in the Lindall-Barnard-Andrews hall differ in their paneling. Whether this was due to the replacement of one of the doors at a later date is not known, but dissimilar doors are frequently found in old houses where often, as in this instance, they do not offend the eye, but rather lend an air of individuality to the house.

As America was a pioneer country in Colonial times a large proportion of the early American fortunes were amassed by merchants, shipowners and sea captains, and it was inevitable that this fact should leave its mark upon the architecture of coast towns, notably Salem, then our most important seaport. Although evidences of this influence may be seen both indoors and out, it is chiefly in the balusters and newels of the stairways that we are reminded of this splendid work, of the men who built it, and of the source of the money which paid for it. They were beautifully turned and often hand-carved in spiral fashion. The handiwork of skilled carvers employed in the local shipyards, then the largest in America, their twisted balusters are obviously based upon the rope moldings and other flamboyant decorations which they were in the habit of making for ship cabins. For this reason their use in the homes of shipowners and sea captains seems the more appropriate. The work was done in a masterly manner and in its refinement of detail indicates Yankee ingenuity and thoughtful designing. At the Essex Institute may be seen a fine old stairway of this character with excellent newels and balusters, many of which were taken from the Hubon house when it was razed to make way in 1906 for the building of Weld Hall, containing offices and work rooms for the Peabody Museum. Many other examples remain in private houses, and in each of the splendid examples shown herewith it will be noticed that there are three designs in the twisted portion of the baluster, one of each standing on every stair, which was broad and not very high. The detail photograph of the stairway at "The Lindens", in Danvers, shows this clearly and also calls attention to the pleasing and clever use of a low, hand-tooled pilaster on the wainscot opposite the newel, also the splendid spacing of the door panels which with their lock rails correspond in level with those of the wainscot.

The wide hall at "The Lindens" extends entirely through the house and opens upon an old-fashioned garden at the rear. On the wall above the paneled wainscot hangs a fine old hand-blocked landscape paper depicting scenes from the adventures of Telemachus. The crowning feature of the hall, however, is the balustrade of the stairway. Balusters, mahogany stair rails and newel are characteristic of this type, but the box stairs, with their paneled ends and decorative brackets, are unique.

As in this instance, when the hall extended through to the rear of the house the stairway was lighted by a Palladian window over the landing that became not only an ornamental feature of the exterior, but the motive for an admirable architectural treatment of the interior wall. At "The Lindens" the deeply recessed, round-headed window, handsomely cased with paneled jambs and soffit, logically accommodates a window seat, and is flanked by heavy fluted pilasters standing on high paneled pedestals and with Corinthian capitals supporting a beautiful cornice with hand-carved, fine-scale denticulated and egg and dart moldings.

In the Pierce-Johonnot-Nichols house, designed by McIntire, a simpler treatment of the Palladian window without seat may be seen. Here the jambs are paneled and the pilaster casings have a sunken panel effect, while the soffit prominently displays a familiar Grecian fret. The sash bar divisions are exceptionally graceful, while the cornice, arch casing and surbase charm the eye with their delicately hand-tooled detail, in which McIntire excelled.

So nearly do the hall and stairway of the Cabot-

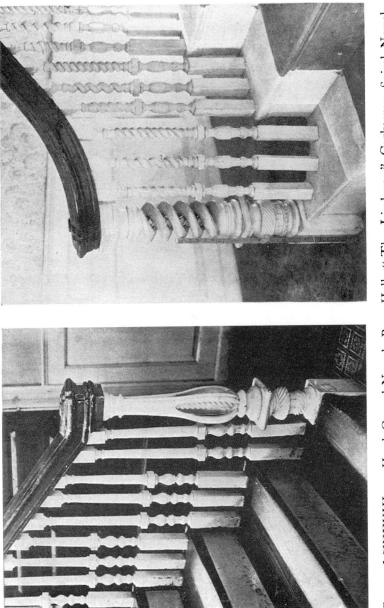

PLATE LXXXVIII. — Hand Carved Newel, Rear Hall, "The Lindens;" Corkscrew Spiral Newel, Richard Derby House. Erected 1761.

PLATE LXXXIX. — Pickman-Derby-Brookhouse Hall and Stairway. Erected 1764. Razed 1915; Stairway in the Babbidge-Crowninshield-Bowker House. Erected 1750. House erected about 1700.

Halls and Stairways

Endicott-Low house on Essex Street resemble those of "The Lindens" that color is lent to the tradition that both of these mansions, together with the Benjamin Pickman house, in the rear of Number 165 Essex Street, and the "King" Hooper house, at Marblehead, were designed by the same English architect. The general arrangement is identical and the paneled wainscot, doors, architrave casings, box stairs, balustrade and newel are virtually the same. Minor differences occur in the cornices, however. In the Cabot-Endicott-Low house the round-headed window, with a seat on the landing, has only simple molded casings without other architectural elaboration and the white-painted newel and hand rail further alter appearances somewhat. Altogether the effect is one of chaste elegance, unexcelled in all Salem. As at "The Lindens" the landing furnishes a convenient place for "the clock on the stairs", immortalized by Longfellow, and in bygone days the opposite corner of the landing was usually occupied by a tip table on which at night stood candles to light guests to their rooms. The panel treatment of the exposed second-floor level accords well with the box stairs, the staggered arrangement of the stiles, reminiscent of the running bond in brickwork, being a logical horizontal continuation of the box-stair effect. The detail photograph shows clearly the three delightful baluster patterns, differing only in their upper portions,

[177]

the handsome twisted landing newels and the sweeping lines of the ramped rails.

Most of the newels accompanying twisted balusters greatly resemble each other, consisting of one corkscrew spiral within another, with small spiral flutings and reedings hand-tooled upon the plain, turned surfaces. Soft pine painted white predominated, as shown by the detail photograph made in the Richard Derby house, erected in 1761, the oldest brick dwelling in Salem.

The back stairway at "The Lindens" combines turned balusters with a unique corkscrew newel, four pierced openings through the thickest portion displaying the much-used spiral spindle within.

Not only were the halls of this period noted for their splendid paneled wainscots, but for similar paneling spaced with the utmost care under the stairs. This charming effect may be seen at its best in the Babbidge-Crowninshield-Bowker house, in the rear of Number 46 Essex Street, erected about 1700; a quaint, twisted wood rod extends from the second-floor level across to the balustrade. Upon this the fire bucket was hung, its position being determined by the central location of the hall and the availability of the bucket to either floor. This stairway is unique in that a short run of three steps to the left of the landing completes the flight; it does not reverse in the conventional manner.

Simple molded panels suffice to ornament the ends

PLATE XC. — Stairway in the Pierce-Johonnot-Nichols House. Erected 1782; Chippendale Balustrade, Pierce-Johonnot-Nichols House.

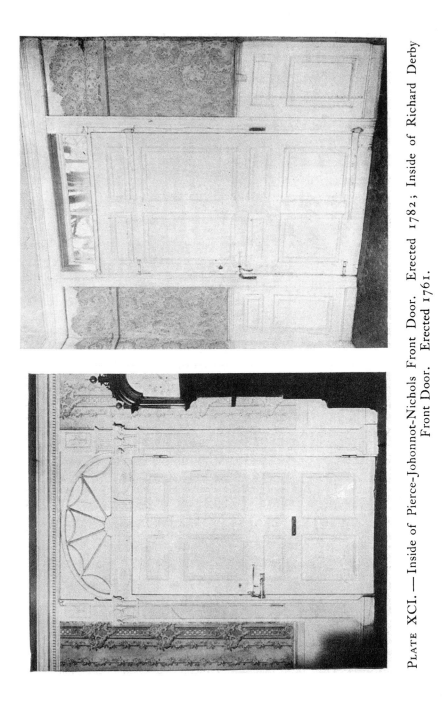

PLATE XCI. — Inside of Pierce-Johonnot-Nichols Front Door. Erected 1782; Inside of Richard Derby Front Door. Erected 1761.

of the box stairs, although flat scroll brackets were usually placed under the overhang of the treads to give an appearance of support.

This house was the birthplace of Benjamin W. Crowninshield and of his brother Jacob, both Congressmen.

In the stairway of the Pickman-Derby-Brook-house mansion, formerly at Number 70 Washington Street, on the site of the new Masonic Temple, this idea of small brackets was carried to the unusual extent of a bracket of solid wood as thick as the width of the stairway. The effect was distinctly pleasing, however, and the scheme worthy of more general application in present-day work. In fact, as shown by the accompanying photograph, this hall presents a notable prototype for modern adaptation in houses where the hall cannot extend through to the rear of the house and so offers no opportunity for a window on the landing.

The latest development of the Colonial stairway in long halls was a curved upper portion of the run instead of a landing. Most of the stairways for several years after 1810 were of this type. Previous to these, however, an attractive transition stage occurred, during which there was a landing three or four steps below the second-floor level, but the rail swung around a curve instead of making square corners with newels. The charm of this effect may be seen in the Pierce-Johonnot-Nichols house, where the stairway is notable chiefly for the balustrade which, as well as the diamond fret along the second-floor level, undoubtedly owes its origin to Chippendale influence. Four slender square balusters alternate with a jig-sawed member very like the well-known chair back to form a scheme at once unique and beautiful. Chippendale's work preceded that of Adam; already occasional examples of his splendid craftsmanship were being brought to America, and it followed naturally that McIntire, the architect of the house, in his search for distinctive motives came as completely under the spell of Chippendale in 1782 as he did later under that of Adam.

After the manner of the time, jig-sawed double-scroll brackets decorate the stair ends, in this instance bearing also three pairs of vertical flutes. The newel recalls that of the Lindall-Barnard-Andrews and Waters stairways. Notable features of the landing include the beautiful Palladian window and the approach from the landing by two semi-circular steps to a door opening upon a chamber at the rear of the house.

At the front end of Colonial halls such as that of the Pierce-Johonnot-Nichols house one sees the interior charm of a typical Colonial front doorway arrangement of the late eighteenth century. The treatment makes an architectural feature of the entire end of the hall, elaborate but in rare good taste. The casings, with their broad, horizontal flutings below the Corinthian capitals, sound an unusual though pleasing note, as do the beaded panels with urn-shaped inserts in applied work each side of the fanlight. The ornamentation of the lintel with festoons and rosettes each side of a vertical, reeded, central panel, however, exemplifies a typical Adam treatment. Other features of interest include a hand-tooled, denticulated molding of the cornice with a reed cross section and dentil in alternation, each dentil having a flute gouged upon it; and the vertical, fluted surface of the dado.

In striking contrast to this, the front door of the Richard Derby house, on Derby Street, with its simple, molded casings, oblong transom and heavy iron strap hinges, forms an interesting comparison.

In many houses of the later period the elliptical arch of the fanlight is echoed elsewhere. To frame the stairway picture, one of the most attractive in the house, it often spans the lower hall at the foot of the stairs, or the upper hall at their head, being supported by flat or fluted pilasters or resting on beautifully carved consoles. Occasionally it frames a vista of the far end of a long hall or determines the shape of a transom to light the rear hall when a door separates it from the front portion, as at the Salem Club, Number 29 Washington Square North. It may also be seen at intersections of hall corridors, as in the Derby-Crowninshield-Rogers house, at

202½ Essex Street. The two arches shown form an interesting comparison, so greatly do they differ in detail. Both are based on the Corinthian order and one has typical Corinthian capitals, whereas the other has festooned Adam drapery replacing the usual acanthus leaf detail. Both are notable for the Grecian fret applied to the soffits of the arches and one has pilasters continuing this fret, whereas the other has sunken panel pilasters with applied straight-hanging garlands. The archivolts also differ, one being merely molded and the other having alternate rosettes and reeded groups applied to its fascia.

Coming now to the long halls with semicircular ends and a curved upper portion of the run instead of a landing, two instances will suffice. In the Hoffman-Simpson house, Number 26 Chestnut Street, erected about 1827, are to be seen the familiar dado with molded surbase and skirting, the scroll-bracket ornamentation of the stair string, the volute newel treatment and balustrade with simple square balusters, dark painted like that of the Pierce-Johonnot-Nichols house. The door casings are deeply molded after the manner of the last period of Colonial architecture in Salem with square plinths and sunken corner blocks. It will be noticed that the rear door takes the curve of the wall and is a splendid piece of joinery trimmed with glass knobs.

PLATE XCII. — Elliptical Arched Doorway in the Salem Club. Erected 1818; Elliptical Arches, Hall of the Derby-Crowninshield-Rogers House. Erected about 1800.

PLATE XCIII. — Hall and Stairway in the Hoffman-Simpson House. Erected about 1827; Hall and Stairway of the Salem Club. Erected 1818.

The similar hall of the Salem Club differs in several details. The round end of the hall occurs only at the head of the stairs where a characteristic niche in the wall provides an appropriate place for statuary or an example of the taxidermist's art, as in this instance. On the lower floor the rear end of the hall is square and the door separating the front and rear halls is elaborated by engaged Ionic columns supporting an elliptical arched transom, with a finely molded archivolt and highly ornamented soffit, in which is set a transom sash of distinctive pattern. The other doorway, like most in the house, has deeply molded casings with flat square plinths and handsomely carved corner blocks; it is surmounted by a head taking the form of a complete entablature with flat frieze and pilaster effect at each end, supporting a fine-scale Corinthian cornice which reflects that of the ceiling above with its nicely ornamented modillions. Like the balustrade with its slender turned balusters the handsome six-panel doors are dark painted. Delicate applied detail adorns the surbase and a beautiful scroll fret gives character to the exposed second-floor level.

CHAPTER X

MANTELS AND CHIMNEY PIECES

NOT until the eighteenth century did the average Salem fireplace include architectural embellishment worthy of emulation to-day. Up to that time a single great fireplace in the living room, which also served as a kitchen, had often sufficed; few houses boasted more than two fireplaces on the lower floor. They were of large dimensions for burning logs of considerable size and length, a long settle — sometimes two settles, one at each side — being provided to seat the entire family conveniently near the only source of heat. The trammel bar and crane with its pothooks were also quaint features, for much of the early cookery was dependent upon the fireplace until brick ovens and finally iron stoves came into general use. These early fireplaces were commonly built of brick though sometimes of stone and often had cast-iron firebacks bearing the owner's initials and the date of erection of the house. Stone flags frequently provided hearths and jambs. In the earlier examples there was no mantel; the great oak beam which supported the masonry over the fireplace opening and called the "mantel-tree" was the only link between the early mantel or hood and the form that followed. Often it projected sufficiently to provide a ledge on which to stand candlesticks and other utensils. Such a kitchen of the olden days has been reconstructed with antiques gathered here and there and forms a notable feature of the Essex Institute museum.

With the coming of more prosperous times a higher standard of living was adopted; larger houses were built and a fireplace for heating purposes became desirable in each of the principal rooms, including chambers. More thought was given to good appearance; the space about the fireplace was paneled, and toward the middle of the eighteenth century the whole side of the room began to be thus treated. About this time, too, the mantel-tree was discontinued, the width of the fireplace opening being so much reduced that an iron strap could be substituted. Plain and carved soapstone facings began to be used, followed by glazed Dutch tiles and various kinds of marble with plain surfaces and later with nicely chiseled Grecian frets. Toward the end of the century the mantelshelf proper came into general use, offering ready opportunity for elaboration, and thereafter the development of the mantel as the principal architectural feature of the room advanced apace.

The sentimental appeal of the open fire con-

tinued unabated. People of necessity lived close
to the hearthstone, for the fireplace still remained
the source of warmth for six months of the year
and therefore the very center of home life. But
builders began to realize that, in other rooms than
the kitchen, the fire is absent during warm weather,
and that while sentiment lies in the fire on the
hearth, permanent year-round beauty centers not
in the fireplace proper but in its architectural setting, the mantel or complete chimney piece. They
saw in the ensemble a thing of the utmost necessity
which could be rendered beautiful by architectural
treatment in wood with moldings, carving and other
decorations, and so devoted their best efforts to its
appropriate ornamentation with the result that
mantels and chimney pieces became the crowning
feature of the room, usually sounding the keynote
of the scheme for the other wood finish. And so
they remain to-day, for the charm of the open fire
will never cease, and the fireplace and its mantel
will ever appeal to the heart as well as the eye,
representing as it does the human and direct ideal
of homely comfort in the days of our great-grandfathers.

In America the development of mantels in modest
homes, and chimney pieces in more pretentious residences, naturally followed to a degree the prevailing mode in England. Early in the seventeenth
century when the Italian style was brought to

PLATE XCIV. — Detail of Chimneypiece, West Parlor, Pierce-Johonnot-Nichols House; Corner Section of the same.

PLATE XCV. — Chamber Mantel, " The Lindens ; " Mantel in the
Captain Edward Allen House, 125 Derby Street.

England by Inigo Jones, chimney pieces were of extremely simple design, often consisting only of the ordinary mantelpiece with classic architraves and shelf, the upper part of the chimney breast being paneled like the rest of the room. Toward the end of that century and for many decades following, the classic architraves were abandoned in favor of a much bolder bolection molding. The shelf was omitted and the paneling of the chimney breast took the form of two oblongs, the upper broader than the lower.

Such chimney pieces at their best are to be seen at "The Lindens", Danvers, erected in 1754, where the principal rooms have four paneled walls and most of the chambers one paneled wall, including the fireplace. The magnificent dark-painted chimney piece of the parlor was illustrated and commented upon in the preceding chapter. That in the dining room shows the pleasing qualities of this type in white-painted wood with fireplace facings and hearth of marble, or tiles of similar effect, with graceful brass andirons and handsome fender. As in the parlor the paneling of this room and its doors is excellently spaced and nicely worked.

The mantelshelf proper was too practical and attractive a thing to be long omitted, however, except possibly in the more formal rooms. In living rooms and chambers it furnished a place for clocks, candlesticks and other useful ornaments, and it appealed to the eye, not only because of its ornamental supports, but because of the homelike, livable appearance it gave to the room.

The Salem matrons of those days loved to display on these mantels their rare pieces of so-called "Lowestoft" ware, imported direct from China. Three jars and two beakers, all ten or twelve inches high, were usually set out symmetrically across the shelf with a pair of brass or silver-plated candlesticks between. Sometimes there were only two beakers and one jar, or the reverse, and in later years handsome whale-oil lamps often replaced the candlesticks. The "Lowestoft" ware of 1790 was mostly green and gilt, while that of about 1835 was decorated with colored butterfly patterns. There was also a period of blue and white, often with the addition of gilt.

In England architects of the eighteenth century returned to the Inigo Jones classic type; the shelf of former times was reinstated and the overmantel was developed into a single large and elaborately framed panel over the chimney breast. Sometimes this remained unadorned, but oftener displayed a family portrait, ornamental, gilt-framed mirror or more elaborate girandole.

A McIntire mantel of this period, based on Palladio's Ionic order with convex frieze, is the principal feature of the west parlor of the Pierce-Johonnot-Nichols house, on Federal Street. As in many

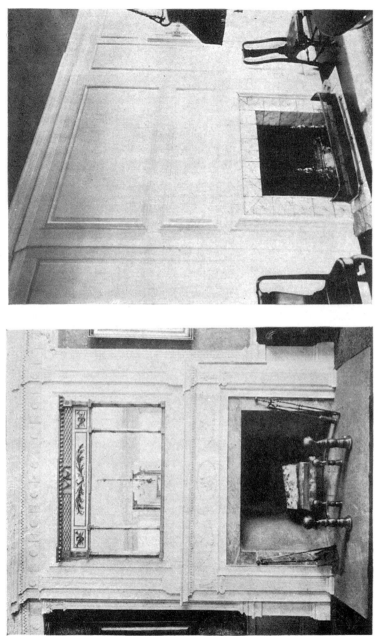

PLATE XCVI.— Adam Chimneypiece, East Parlor, Pierce-Johonnot-Nichols House; Dining Room Chimneypiece, "The Lindens," Danvers.

PLATE XCVII. — East Front Chamber Mantel, Pierce-Johonnot-Nichols House; Corner Section of the Same.

old houses of the time it forms part of one side of the room treated with wood paneling throughout. Decidedly substantial in character, it is essentially simple in conception and graceful in form and proportion. The moldings are especially interesting. The ovolo under the shelf corresponds to that in the cornice above the dentil course. While an interpretation of the classic egg and dart motive, it was employed without the customary bead and reel, and still further received the stamp of McIntire's personality by the small round borings at the base of the tongue. A related but dissimilar ovolo molding surrounds the broad panel of the overmantel, while the ogee moldings about the fireplace opening but distantly resemble any well-known classic motive, though restrained and effective. The beautiful brass hob grate mounted on soapstone compares favorably with any in America and its setting within a border of black and white tiles depicting Æsop's Fables is exceptional.

The hob grate was brought out in England during the latter half of the eighteenth century when coal replaced wood as a fuel and andirons were found unsuitable for burning the comparatively small lumps. Because of the abundance of fuel wood in America, however, relatively few hob grates were brought to this country until about 1830.

Many references to the work of Samuel McIntire occur in succeeding pages. A comprehensive chapter on Salem mantels inevitably reads like an eulogy of his achievements. The most skilled carver and resourceful designer of his time, the mantel provided the logical subject for his artistry. Its greatest development occurred during the period of his activities between 1782 and 1811 and most of the best examples in Salem have been authenticated as his craftsmanship. His designs range from the exceedingly simple to the highly ornate, often displaying daring originality and remarkable freedom in the use of the orders, yet they are never deficient in that chaste appearance, grace of line, and sense of proportion which characterized all his work.

Turning again to mantel design in general, toward the close of the eighteenth century all other designs were superseded by those of the brothers Adam, which were enriched with applied ornament of French putty cast in molds and sometimes copied from the carved wood decoration of old times, although oftener adapted in attenuated form from the stone detail of Roman architecture, notably Diocletian's palace at Spalato, in Dalmatia. McIntire and other American designers and architects elsewhere quickly came under the spell of their work, and much was executed in wood by the former in Salem that compares favorably with the achievements of Robert Adam.

Of these there is much to follow. First, however, it is interesting to record that in several Salem houses erected about the middle of the eighteenth century mantels more or less in the Adam manner have been placed against the original shelfless paneling about the fireplace. Their broad entablatures divide the lower panel over the chimney breast and form an overmantel of peculiar though obvious character, yet the resulting chimney piece is by no means displeasing. Two such mantels at "The Lindens", Danvers, were taken from the Salem residence of Honorable Nathan Read, a congressman and the inventor of a workable steamboat, when that house was razed in 1856 to make way for the building at Number 134 Essex Street, now the museum of the Essex Institute. The Read mansion had been designed by McIntire in 1790 and was well known as the birthplace of William Hickling Prescott, the historian, on May 4, 1796, and after 1799 as the home of Captain Joseph Peabody, a wealthy merchant in the Calcutta trade.

Rarely did McIntire's detail take such a light and fanciful character as in the more distinctive of the two mantels from the Read mansion shown by an accompanying illustration. The dentil course, with peculiarly hand-tooled members, was a favorite McIntire motive, and while the screw bead was occasionally employed elsewhere as a single motive, in this instance it provides a prominent repeated theme in the cornice, the architrave and the narrow, paneled pilasters. A broad Grecian fret of well-known pattern supplies the major portion of the architrave and sounds an unusual note in McIntire mantel design. Chief interest, however, centers in the applied work, not so much in the central panel, with its basket of fruit and flowers, as in the horns of plenty which serve as frieze spots at each side, and particularly the realistic grapevines and fruit which replace the conventional Adam garlands in the paneled pilasters. It will be noticed that these pilasters are carried up through the entire entablature, with characteristic projection of the shelf or cornice as well as frieze and architrave. While perhaps drawing rather too much attention to themselves, the Flemish tiles depicting historic scenes are of peculiar interest as antiques. Brass andirons and a fire set of especially graceful design complete a fireplace picture of rare attractiveness.

Another noteworthy mantel of this period is to be seen with paneling of an earlier date in the Captain Edward Allen house, Number 125 Derby Street, erected in 1770. Although executed by some local wood worker it is essentially an Adam design, exemplifying the exotic character of much of his work. While strongly under Roman and Italian influence Adam had the genius to mold and adapt classical models so as to create a new manner of superlative charm and distinction. With simple curvilinear forms, of which he preferred the oval, he evolved combinations of remarkable grace and variety.

PLATE C. — Mantel Detail, Hamilton Hall; Chamber Mantel Detail,
Derby-Crowninshield-Rogers House; Chamber Mantel Detail,
Derby-Crowninshield-Rogers House.

PLATE CI. — Mantel in a Chamber of the Cook-Oliver House;
Mantel in the West Chamber, Peabody-Silsbee House.

Mantels and Chimney Pieces

Flowing curves terminating the frieze, which is enriched with a profusion of applied ornament, including festooned garlands, horns of plenty and mythological figures, supply the chief distinction of the Allen mantel. The projection of the central panel, with corresponding treatment of the cornice, emphasizes the beautiful oval decoration, which, like the festooned decorations of the corona, the double-denticulated molding beneath and the fluted groups of the architraves are characteristic Adam details. As in the case of many old fireplaces this opening was at some later time closed that a Franklin stove or fireframe might be set up before the ornamental cast-iron frame that still remains.

One more instance of the chimney piece forming part of a paneled wall is particularly interesting. It is the recessed effect in the east front chamber of the Pierce-Johonnot-Nichols house, a room finished about 1800 in the Adam manner. Engaged columns support the frieze and cornice or shelf, the molded architraves casing the fireplace openings. The double denticulated molding much used by McIntire forms the most conspicuous part of the cornice, while the frieze is typically Adam, with a central panel of vertical flutings and garlands and flower baskets of applied work at each side. Flower-filled urns adorn the terminating frieze projections, which are emphasized by corresponding projections of the cornice. Over the chimney breast above the shelf a broad architrave, ornate with an applied border, forms a large oblong panel of pleasing proportions. In the restraint and nice selection of delicate decoration lie that charm which renders this one of the most admired mantels in New England.

Only in the principal chambers of large houses was the wall of the room where the fireplace occurred entirely paneled up. Elsewhere the treatment of the fireplace was very simple. The extreme treatment is shown in a third-floor chamber of the Pierce-Johonnot-Nichols house, which was finished soon after 1782 at a time when the mantelshelf was still being frequently omitted. Simple, molded architraves comprise the meager architectural features of this quaint fireplace which is notable for its shallow depth, narrow back and broad sides. The wooden turn-button at the top is used to fasten a blind in place, covering the entire opening during the summer when fires are not needed. Almost all good houses had these green summer blinds for fireplaces in every room about 1825, some of them being fitted in quite a complicated way to cover the grate openings. Black iron andirons, pleasing in design and proportion, an antique hand bellows and Windsor rocker complete a picture redolent of homely comfort and the spirit of long ago.

Most chamber fireplaces of the late eighteenth and early nineteenth centuries had mantels consisting of a complete entablature with the shelf forming part of the cornice and the whole supported by pilasters. Often of austere simplicity in respect to detail they were remarkably well proportioned and chaste in appearance, notably those by McIntire. One of his simplest and most effective mantels is that in the chamber over the dining room of the Cook-Oliver house, on Federal Street. Except for the dentil course of the cornice it depends entirely upon hand-planed moldings, including the paneled pilasters, yet by reason of nice proportion and careful workmanship it charms the eye as do few other equally modest mantels in Salem.

While on a larger and a trifle heavier scale with moldings differing somewhat, the mantels in Hamilton Hall, at the corner of Chestnut and Cambridge Streets, are very similar. It will be noticed, however, that the pilaster projections do not terminate the mantel at each side. They are mounted on broad, flat, vertical casings which extend the plain frieze and necessitate cornice extensions to correspond. Many of the more elaborate mantels by McIntire and others were constructed on this plan. The principal differences in the moldings occur in the cornice where a Tuscan cymatium in the latter mantel replaces one of the denticulated Doric order in the former; hand-tooled, vertical, fluted molding has been substituted for the usual dentil course and a vertical, reeded ovolo beneath it lends added weight. Both this and the foregoing mantel do

[195]

not depend upon the cymatium of the cornice to provide the shelf but have a supplementary shelf above it.

Two mantels in third-floor chambers of the Derby-Crowninshield-Rogers house on Essex Street are interesting examples of the use of figure work in the form of central bas-relief panels in composition applied to otherwise modest designs. The upper one of these in general effect recalls the Cook-Oliver mantel already referred to, and is a positive joy to look upon, so good are its proportions. Notable differences include the broader dentil course and heavier bed moldings, the absence of the supplementary shelf, and of cymatium projections over the pilasters, also the substitution of different though equivalent moldings in the architrave and pilasters. The lower mantel shows still further variation of the moldings and is enriched by the architraves about the fireplace opening, the reeded pilasters, the double denticulated cornice molding and the applied composition figures as frieze spots on the pilaster projections, which in this instance include the shelf. Despite the shameful treatment to which both of these mantels have been subjected by careless tenants since the house has been devoted to commercial purposes and the fireplaces have been closed for the use of stoves, their unaffected simplicity and fine sense of proportion appeal to every seeing eye, and were they cleaned and freshly painted

PLATE C. — Mantel Detail, Hamilton Hall; Chamber Mantel Detail,
Derby-Crowninshield-Rogers House; Chamber Mantel Detail,
Derby-Crowninshield-Rogers House.

PLATE CI. — Mantel in a Chamber of the Cook-Oliver House;
Mantel in the West Chamber, Peabody-Silsbee House.

would be counted among the most perfect of Mc-
Intire's work. Both of the bas-relief panels are
nicely modeled and the ensemble lacks little of the
daintiness and purity of Adam work in marble,
which in those days was almost prohibitive in price
in America.

Two other McIntire chamber mantels with reeded
pilasters form an interesting comparison to show
his versatility in design. The simpler of the two,
that in the chamber over the parlor of the Cook-
Oliver house, at once attracts attention for its great
breadth, indicating that the ornamental cast-iron
hobgrate was probably of later date, necessitating
partial closing of the original fireplace opening.
Many such were built into Colonial fireplaces when
coal began to supersede wood as a fuel for heating.
Aside from the pilasters virtually all fine-scale detail is confined to the cornice, in which he has de-
parted from conventional forms and relied upon
original ideas of his own with happy results. Above
a hand-tooled dentil course like that in a chamber
mantel at "The Lindens", already referred to,
he built up a unique substitute for cymatium and
corona of which a prominent hand-tooled rope
molding supplied the principal member. A straight,
square-edged board provided the shelf proper.

The mantel in the west chamber of the Peabody-
Silsbee house, Number 380 Essex Street, erected
in 1797, resembles the foregoing, but is richer, more

slender and shows greater refinement. Not only are the pilasters reeded, but a fine-scale, reeded belt supplies the capitals as well as the architrave of the entablature, while the same motive used in connection with a screw bead for the surbase of the dado unifies the architectural scheme of the entire room. A conventional cymatium and corona separated by a torus and fillet, the whole projecting above the pilasters, replace the rope and accompanying moldings of the foregoing mantel; the dentil course remains the same. The frieze is essentially Adam in decoration with graceful flanking urns and central basket of fruit and flowers in a sunken oval panel with beaded edge, all of composition applied.

Early in his career as a carver McIntire devoted considerable attention to sculpture in wood, a field in which he achieved several notable successes. Having embarked upon his professional career in 1782, the year George III announced his readiness to acknowledge the independence of the United States, it was natural that McIntire should have been inspired by those fine principles of liberty, justice and humanity for which the American people had fought with such determination and fortitude. His patriotic fervor prompted him to excel in carving that symbol of American ideals, the eagle, and to use it frequently in a variety of ways. Outdoors, as a sculpture in full relief, it found a place atop gateway arches, public buildings, cupolas and barns, while as a bas-relief it appeared as a decorative panel in the brick walls of public buildings and as a supplementary ornamental head above doorways. Indoors it was employed to adorn the frieze of mantels.

Two splendid instances of its use on a large scale to fill the central panel of the frieze still remain. One of these is to be seen at the Essex Institute, whither it was taken from the old Registry of Deeds at the corner of Broad and Summer streets, erected in 1807, when that building was taken down to make way for the former State Normal School. As a whole exceptionally well proportioned, this mantel displays only a modest amount of fine-scale detail. The dentil course provides a welcome foil for the other cornice moldings and one notes with pleasure that the reeded pilasters are reflected by reeded sections at regular intervals in the surbase. Delicate Adam urns in applied composition adorn the pilaster projections of the frieze, while a screw bead enriches the central panel. It will be noticed that the shelf projects over the central panel of the frieze as well as over the pilasters. The facings of the fireplace opening consist of blue and white tiles depicting Biblical quotations.

Reminiscent of this mantel a heavier and more elaborate one in the northwest parlor of the Hosmer-Waters house, Number 80 Washington Square, erected in 1795, is particularly interesting as exemplifying the use of a profusion of applied Adam detail, with the American eagle carved by McIntire himself for the central panel, which is raised but not molded. Exceptionally wide, the vertical casings on which the pilasters are mounted permit considerable extension of the cornice, frieze and architrave. Cymatium and corona are straight without any projections whatever and support a thin supplementary shelf with molded edge. The moldings throughout are properly of modest character because of the enrichment of the frieze and paneled pilasters with festoons, urns and straight-hanging garlands. Only the dentil course and the vertical fluted architrave bear hand-tooling, and that is of simple though effective character. A brass hob grate, very English in appearance, and set in slate, fills the original fireplace opening and is accompanied by a handsome fire set including a peculiar poker combining a pike and hook.

McIntire also carved the eagle on a shield as the central feature of a military group including swords, bugles, flags, cannon and balls, drum and the lictor's fasces of olden days. Such sculptured groups of wood in sunken oval frieze panels form the principal feature of McIntire's two most fanciful mantels. One is located in the front parlor of the Woman's Friend Society, Number 12 Elm Street, erected in 1800, the other in the Kimball house, Number 14 Pickman Street, erected in 1800. So similar yet so

PLATE CII. — Detail of Mantel in the Kimball House.

PLATE CIII. — Northwest Parlor Mantel, Hosmer-Townsend-
Waters House; Mantel from the old Registry of
Deeds Building.

different are they that comparison becomes interesting as showing the resourcefulness of their designer. Although considered over-ornate by many, none can but admire the intricate carving they display, for there is no applied work on either. Even the screw reeds of the columns and the screw bead of the cornices, the flowers and urns of the oval inserts as well as the central sculptured panels were carved out of wood. In both instances the projection of the fireplace into the room suggested carrying the mantel and shelf back around the corners. The fine-scale fluted pilasters were therefore supplemented by flanking columns to support the projecting corners and a second pair of pilasters around the corners like those in front. But the most unique feature of all lies in the dentil course with its widely spaced trumpet-like units, possibly suggested by the guttæ of the Doric order. Probably no designer before McIntire ever used such a decoration on a mantel, or inserted a band of wooden spheres into the edge of a shelf between two fillets as in the Kimball mantel.

In several instances McIntire employed this band of spheres to replace the dentil course of cornices. On a large scale it appears under the eaves of the Peabody-Silsbee house, while on a small scale it figures in the parlor mantel of the Home for Aged Women on Derby Street. Apart from the Composite feeling of the capitals and bases of the engaged columns, the detail adheres to no classic order. The columns are not fluted; the architrave rather than the frieze bears most of the ornament, and the cornice or shelf is a thing unto itself. Notwithstanding its unique traits and marked unconventionality this mantel is much admired. Both the sheaves of wheat on the pilaster projections of the frieze and the applied fruit groups in alternation with vertical reeded sections in the architrave symbolize the fullness of the harvest and present motives especially well suited to country house architecture.

In the rear parlor at the Woman's Friend Society is to be seen another unique mantel, featuring one of McIntire's sculptured military groups of wood, in this instance the sunken oval panel being edged with a tiny egg and dart composition motive which also provides the bed molding. Pairs of slender colonnettes support the complete entablature with corner projections extending around the sides, including the surmounting supplementary shelf. Here again a hand-tooled rope molding replaces the conventional ovolo, and a flat band with tiny triangular incisions simulating Doric guttæ provides a unique substitute for the dentil course. The sheaves of wheat are of wood nicely carved and glued to the sunken oval panels of the frieze projections. The ornamental hob grate of cast iron has a peculiar two-piece summer blind. This mantel came from the old residence of John Robinson, Number 2 Chestnut Street, built by John Stone in 1826 and now known as "The Studio."

Reminiscent of this mantel in its pairs of supporting colonnettes and corner projections of the shelf, that in the parlor of the Lindall-Barnard-Andrews house, Number 393 Essex Street, differs materially throughout the entablature. The latter mantel was designed and executed by McIntire in 1800. It is essentially Adam in its motives, with all the slender grace and refinement of detail that characterize genuine prototypes. Moreover it is particularly interesting for the fact that no composition work has been employed. All the enrichment of the frieze, including the central basket of fruit and flowers, the festoons and sheaves of wheat, is known to be McIntire's personal carving in wood applied with glue. Beneath the conventional cymatium and corona, which form the shelf proper, is to be seen a pleasingly ingenious modification of the dentil course, while the architrave with its screw bead and delicate vertical fluted groups in alternation with festoon borings provides the motive of the surbase, giving an Adam character to the dado which ties together the architectural features of the room. No small measure of the charming ensemble is due to the beautiful brass andirons and fire set, for both of which the urn, much favored by Adam, supplies the chief decoration.

[203]

A chimney piece in one of the chambers of the Lindall-Barnard-Andrews house is likewise of considerably later date than the house. Highly ornate, with a profusion of applied composition detail, including an enriched ovolo and vine fret along the edge of the shelf, it was probably not the work of McIntire, as it lacks his rare sense of proportion and good taste in the selection and use of ornament. It does not, for instance, stand favorable comparison with the accompanying corner section of a known McIntire mantel in a third-floor chamber of the old Derby-Crowninshield-Rogers mansion more ornate than the other two mantels on the same floor of this house already referred to. Paneled pilasters support a rather conventional entablature much like several previously alluded to. Simple, planed moldings predominate, the only departures being the double denticulated pattern of the cornice and the ogee enriched with Lesbian leaf composition edging the central panel of the frieze. All ornament is confined to the frieze and consists of favorite Adam decorative motives, such as urns, festooned garlands, oval medallions and a central bas-relief of figure work in an oval floral setting with scroll embellishments.

The finest Salem mantels done by McIntire in the Adam manner, exclusive of his chimney pieces, are generally regarded as those in the parlors of the David P. Waters house, Number 14 Cambridge Street,

PLATE CIV. — Parlor Mantel, Home for Aged Women; Front
Parlor Mantel, Woman's Friend Society.

PLATE CV. — Mantel in the Crowninshield-Devereux-Waters House; Parlor Mantel, Lindall-Barnard-Andrews House.

erected in 1805, and of the Crowninshield-Devereux-Waters house, Number 72 Washington Square East, also erected in 1805. The former is seen to be an elaboration of much that has already been considered, in response to the desire for richer effect, and gives opportunity for an instructive study in recombining conventional material. Generally speaking this mantel takes the form of that in the west chamber of the Peabody-Silsbee house. It has the same reeded pilasters and corresponding projection of the entire entablature, the same sunken oval panel with beaded edge and applied fruit and flower basket; also the same cymatium, corona and bed molding, in this instance employed with a supplementary surmounting square-edged shelf with projections like those of the cornice beneath. McIntire's favorite fret-like dentil course is here augmented by his well-known screw bead above it, replacing the plain fillet he often placed there. The sheaves of wheat on the frieze projections, also the architrave motive, recall the parlor mantel of the Home for Aged Women, although rosettes instead of tiny fruit baskets here alternate with the vertical reeded groups. The festooned garlands are like those of the east front chamber mantel in the Pierce-Johonnot-Nichols house, but the ornament in the middle above each consists of two tiny horns of plenty rather than a small fruit and flower basket. Repetition of various items of this mantel detail in the cornice and surbase of the room show how closely the entire architectural scheme was related. Three round-topped sections lend a quaint distinction to the summer blind.

When the chimney and fireplace construction projects into the room and a large mantel glass is hung over the chimney breast the resulting effect becomes virtually that of a chimney piece, especially when a heavy cornice is a feature of the room, as in the parlor of the Crowninshield-Devereux-Waters house. The mantel of this room displays great refinement in design and exceptional precision in workmanship, the dainty moldings being exquisitely carved and the applied-work festoons — urns, horns of plenty and straight-hanging garlands — of slender grace and unusually well drawn. Here again the cornice has been made heavier by an additional surmounting shelf with projections at the ends and molded at the edge with a torus between two fillets. A bead and reel separate the cymatium from the corona, beneath which in place of the usual dentil course occurs a nicely carved band of tiny vertical flutings between exceedingly fine-scale ovolo and ogee moldings. Groups of vertical flutings at regular intervals adorn the architraves about the fireplace opening and the same motive is used for the surbase of the dado. The slightly projecting central panel, a bead and reel oval within an oblong edged with a Lesbian leaf ogee, contains a group of musical instruments that is a positive gem without equal in Salem. Of attractive design, the brass andirons are perhaps a trifle heavy for so dainty a mantel, but the shovel and tongs are altogether charming.

To a somewhat lesser degree than a mantel mirror a scenic wall paper with prominent foreground objects sometimes gives the effect of a chimney piece to a fireplace construction that projects into the room. As a case in point may be mentioned the parlor of the Cook-Oliver house, on Federal Street. Here a famous old hand-blocked Zuber paper from Alsace depicts the panorama of Paris from the Seine a century ago, the colors being grays, greens, and black with touches of red and yellow, and all delightfully mellowed with age. A tree of striking shape and two buildings are spaced exactly right to emphasize the projection of the fireplace construction and to make the mantel seem a support for this scenic effect.

Like many other features of the house this mantel was designed and executed by McIntire in 1799 for the Elias Hasket Derby mansion, and removed to its present location after Mr. Derby's death. Delicate in design and superbly executed, few Salem mantels measure up to it despite its essentially simple character. Daintier moldings than the cymatium of the cornice with its tiny accompanying bead and the ovolo of the architrave, both enriched with acanthus leaf composition work, it would be difficult to conceive, while the quirked ogee molding about the fireplace opening displays an interesting pattern embodying a connected series of rosettes with a bead. The denticulated molding is nicely hand-tooled and consists of a square dentil and reed cross section in alternation, each dentil being vertical fluted and each reed cross section having a tiny drill hole in its center. A flat unadorned central panel with applied groups of musical instruments on the projections at each end provides the somewhat meager decoration of the frieze, while slender festooned garlands on the architrave lend an Adam character, as does the ingenious sole reliance upon the acanthus leaf ornamentation of the capitals of the two slender reeded colonnettes. The surbase of the dado displays a delicate incised guilloche consisting of two entwined bands or fillets, one a flat ribbon and the other made up of repeated round disks. It suggests a modification of the lozenge fret with segmental sides. By no means the least interesting feature of this fireplace is the handsome brass hob grate set in soapstone, the first of its kind ever placed in a Salem house and at the time considered a great extravagance.

Coming now to the true chimney piece, that by McIntire in the east parlor of the Pierce-Johonnot-Nichols house is generally regarded the finest in Salem. Done in the Adam manner it combines motives from the denticulated Doric, Ionic and

PLATE CVI. — Parlor Mantel and Scenic Wall Paper, Cook-Oliver House.

PLATE CVII. — Fireplace in the Crowninshield-Devereux-Waters House; Mantel in the David P. Waters Reception Room.

Corinthian orders with a skillful ingenuity that is altogether charming, despite all purist cries of anachronism. Generally speaking the mantel recalls others previously described, notably that in the David P. Waters parlor, but shows greater refinement in every detail, while the overmantel has been developed into a single large and elaborately framed panel over the chimney breast. By extending the cornice and frieze of the room around the chimney breast and carrying a pilaster effect from the shelf up through them, they have been made virtually a part of the chimney piece and a means to relate it closely to the architectural setting of the entire room. The hand-tooled moldings are refined and finished in workmanship, the applied composition detail delicate, graceful and exquisitely drawn. One notices the repeated use of McIntire's favorite double denticulated and vertical reeded ovolo moldings in the cornices of the room and mantel; yet while the form is preserved these have been varied in detail by the festoon motive in applied work on the lower corona and the shallow upper series of vertical cuttings in the lower dentil course. In fact, delightful variety combined with complete harmony throughout avoids monotony and preserves good taste.

Reeded pilasters with Ionic capitals support the frieze and cornice or shelf of the mantel, while paneled pilasters with charmingly slender applied work are employed for the overmantel, their acanthus leaf capitals in accord with the Corinthian capitals of the heavy flanking pilasters of the room. Nicely fluted architraves and marble facings about the fireplace opening lend a sense of refinement that is enhanced by handsome, heavy brass andirons and an accompanying fire set. The applied figures and other ornaments of the mantel frieze recall those of the Captain Edward Allen house, but are better drawn, and the garlands are more slender and elaborate. The central oval panel and the figures on the pilaster projections at each side are carved in wood; the garlands are composition. A beautiful vine pattern in applied composition adorns the architrave frame of the overmantel that surrounds a gilt Adam mantel glass of rare beauty. This pattern appears to be the same as that employed in the east front chamber mantel of this house already illustrated. Surmounting the entire construction, the handsome heavy cornice of the room, composed of hand-tooled moldings, repeats that of the mantel-shelf on a large scale, while the frieze with rosettes and vertical reeded groups in alternation on a flat ground is very effective. As a whole the effect is one of quiet elegance and graceful dignity.

CHAPTER XI

PUBLIC BUILDINGS

VARIED and interesting are the Colonial public buildings of Salem, especially if institutional homes, halls, societies, clubs, etc., be included under this broad classification.

Because of their spaciousness and large number of rooms, the three-story square houses of brick built during the early nineteenth century lend themselves admirably to adaptation as semi-public institutions, and several splendid old mansions have been so utilized. Thus in 1896 the Father Mathew Catholic Total Abstinence Society, organized in 1875, purchased the Tucker-Rice house at Number 129 Essex Street for its headquarters, and considerably remodeled it. This large three-story brick mansion with its roomy L was designed by Samuel McIntire and erected in 1800. Much of the handsome interior wood trim remains, but the splendid elliptical porch, one of the best proportioned in Salem, was removed to the garden of the Essex Institute for preservation, where it may now be seen with a contemporary three-piece door from the Rogers house on Essex Street and glasswork of attractive pattern.

At Number 12 Elm Street the Woman's Friend Society, a charitable institution organized in 1876, occupies two large brick dwellings of former days. The northern portion was donated by Captain John Bertram in 1879, and in 1889 the southern portion was purchased through the generosity of others interested in the work. Here the society conducts a home for girls at moderate rates, an employment bureau, a mission for the distribution of flowers and delicacies to the sick, and maintains a visiting nurse and a loan closet of hospital supplies, bedding, etc.

This building is an interesting example of the early Salem double house, of which there are several less notable examples. It consists of two end-to-the-street houses with doorways at each side and service wings in the rear standing back to back, as one might say, and to all outward appearance built as one house. A brick fire wall separated the two houses absolutely, however, until in 1889 openings were cut through the party wall so that what had formerly been numbered 12 and 14 Elm Street might be used as a single house. The interior wood trim is excellent, including mantels shown in Chapter IX and two good short hall stairways, one a "winder" and the other a broken-flight open newel staircase.

The Mack Industrial School, Number 17 Pickman Street, occupies a gray-painted, oblong, three-story brick house with two tall chimneys symmetrically located at each end and in general appearance some-

PLATE CVIII. — Woman's Friend Society, 12 Elm Street. Erected 1800; Tucker-Rice House, now the Father Mathew Society, 129 Essex Street. Erected 1800.

PLATE CIX. — Bertram Home for Aged Men, 114 Derby Street. Erected 1806-7; Mack Industrial School, 17 Pickman Street. Erected about 1800.

what reminiscent of the main part of the Mansfield-Bolles house, except for the projecting bands of brickwork at each floor level, as on the Gardner-White-Pingree house, and the flat stone lintels. Built as a private residence about 1800, this unpretentious but good dwelling was converted to use as a school for girls after the institution now occupying it had been founded in 1897 as a result of the bequest of Esther Mack. Instruction is given in needlework, dressmaking, cooking and other domestic sciences. A new door replaces the original, and while possessed of Colonial feeling can hardly be said to reflect the true spirit of Salem design.

A handsome three-story brick mansion at Number 114 Derby Street now serves as the Bertram Home for Aged Men, founded by Captain John Bertram in 1877. The house was erected in 1806–1807 for Captain Joseph Waters and evokes admiration for its pleasing fenestration with handsome keyed marble lintels and big pedimental doorway in the spirit of contemporaneous Philadelphia work. The side entrance holds considerable interest as an early example of the portico utilized as a veranda, in which the hipped portico roof is carried over the two-story "jut-by" of the L. The bay window on the street side is an unfortunate modern addition. For many years the west end of the house was the home of Judge Joseph G. Waters.

The substantial front portion of the building at

Number 180 Derby Street, erected in 1810 after designs by Samuel McIntire, and now the Home for Aged Women, was originally the residence of Benjamin W. Crowninshield, congressman and Secretary of the Navy under Presidents Madison and Monroe. When the latter toured New England in 1817, this house was placed at his disposal during the four days of his stay in Salem. At the banquet tendered to him there on July 9, Commodores Perry and Bainbridge, Generals Miller and Dearborn, Senator Silsbee, Lieutenant-Governor William Gray, Judge Story and other eminent men were present. Later the house became the residence of General James Miller during his term as Collector of the Port from 1825 to 1849. He, it will be recalled, was the hero of Lundy's Lane, and his was the famous reply "I'll try, sir," that was stamped on the buttons of his regiment by order of the government. In 1826 William C. Endicott, Secretary of War during Cleveland's first administration, was born here.

It was, however, through the generosity of a still later owner, Robert Brookhouse, a wealthy merchant prominent in the African trade, that the house was donated to the Association for the Relief of Aged and Destitute Women, organized in 1869 at the suggestion of Reverend Michael Carlton, city missionary. In 1896 the structure was enlarged considerably at an expense of $50,000, and in 1916 further extensive alterations were made.

Public Buildings

This hip-roofed mansion is almost devoid of ornamentation except for the marble lintels and sills of the windows and the Doric porch of the utmost simplicity and chaste appearance. It is eloquent in substantial comfort, however, and fulfills its present purpose admirably.

One of the most interesting of the private residences converted to public uses no longer remains. It was the former Salem Cadet Armory at Number 136 Essex Street, razed just prior to the erection of the present armory in 1908. The site includes land occupied in part by the house of Governor Simon Bradstreet, alluded to in Chapter I, which was built in 1640 by Emanuel Downing and torn down about 1750.

The armory of 1890 with its drill shed in the rear and to the left, as shown by the accompanying photograph, was erected in 1819–1821 by Captain Joseph Peabody, a merchant prominent in the Calcutta trade, for his eldest son, Joseph Augustus, and for many years was the home of his grandson, Colonel Francis Peabody. Among the first bow-fronted houses erected in Salem, it had the decked hip roof and belvedere characteristic of most residences of the time, the classic balustrade following the double-bowed contour of the eaves. The Ionic entrance porch appears to have been suggested by that of the Peabody-Silsbee house, but the door is three panels wide like most others of approximately the same date. It was the fenestration that gave individuality to the façade as much as the double-bow front. On the first floor three-piece sashes like those of the Gardner and Thompson houses were employed in front; on the second floor common twelve-paned, double-hung windows were used throughout, while on the top floor the foreshortened windows consisted of a lower six- and an upper three-paned sash. Square-headed mullion windows pierce the flat central wall spaces on each floor above the porch, the arrangement being a narrow window each side of one of normal width, slender Corinthian colonnettes supporting the lintels and adorning the mullions. The highly ornamental marble lintels appear to have been inspired by those of the Dodge-Shreve house, those of the first story being identical, of the third story similar, and of the second story a pleasing adaptation of the Adam festooned drapery nicely cut in stone. The lintels of the mullioned windows were especially attractive and the iron balustrades of the balconies at the first-floor windows and over the porch, simple and graceful in pattern, enriched the ensemble to a marked degree.

Perhaps the best known of the interior features of this house was the "banqueting hall" where Prince Arthur of England was entertained at dinner on the occasion of the funeral of George Peabody, the London banker, February 8, 1870. This spacious room was elaborately finished in intricately carved

PLATE CX. — The Assembly Hall, 138 Federal Street.   Erected 1782.

PLATE CXI. — Home for Aged Women, 180 Derby Street. Erected 1810; Former Salem Cadet Armory, 136 Essex Street. Erected 1819-1821. Razed 1908.

oak in the Gothic style of the Elizabethan period. At one end a stained-glass window consisting of four panels displayed representations of both sides of the Massachusetts seal, the seal of the city of Salem and the coat of arms of the Peabody family. At the other end a fireplace with Dutch jambs was surmounted by a heavy and elaborately carved chimney piece with niches for statuettes. Queen Victoria was the subject of the central figure, supported by mailed figures at each side, while a lion surmounted the whole with a guardsman on one side and a priest on the other. When the house was razed in 1908 the wood finish of this room was preserved and it now adorns one of the smaller halls in the Masonic Temple.

The stately three-story brick mansion at Number 29 Washington Square is now the home of the Salem Club. Built in 1818 for John Forrester, it was later enlarged and occupied for many years as the town residence of the late Colonel George Peabody, one of Salem's most successful merchants, particularly in the Russian trade, a fine musician and lover of art. Among his prized possessions which adorned the interior was one of Murillo's famous paintings of the "Immaculate Conception", valued at $100,000. The porch and doorway are much admired as among the most effective of the simple Corinthian entrances in Salem and display excellent glass and iron work.

The number of Salem institutions housed in old dwellings is indeed remarkable. Besides the seven instances already referred to, six more may be added, viz.: the Salem Public Library, Seaman's Orphan and Children's Friend Society, Knights of Columbus. Now and Then Association, Order of Elks and The Kernwood Country Club, although none of the buildings they occupy is of sufficient interest from the standpoint of Colonial architecture to call for illustrations in these pages. In striking contrast to this array, it is a singular fact that the old Assembly Hall, built expressly for public functions, long ago became a private residence. Although McIntire is known primarily as an architect of homes his versatility led him as early as 1782 to design this building at Number 138 Federal Street, the assembly house of the Federals. At once upon its erection it became one of the foremost social centers of the town and the scene of receptions, balls, banquets and other functions. Here Lafayette dined during his first triumphal tour in America in 1784, and here also Washington danced at a ball given in his honor in 1789. In 1795 the building was remodeled for dwelling purposes, Judge Samuel Putnam being among those who have since occupied it.

This hip-roofed house with its surmounting belvedere bespeaks attention chiefly for the elaboration of its flat-boarded façade with Ionic pilasters on the second story under the broad pediment, within which a pleasing semi-circular fanlight is located to admit light to the attic. Unlike the front, the side and rear walls of the house are clapboarded, a common custom of the time. The porch, probably of much later origin, claims special notice because of its festoons, ornamental scroll antefixes at the corners and heavy grapevine frieze, the leaves and fruit being life-size and carved out of wood in a masterly manner.

Regarding the old Courthouse of 1785, McIntire's second venture in designing public buildings, the *Massachusetts Magazine* for March, 1790, states:

"The Court Houſe in Salem, is a large, elegant building, and ſtands towards the end of a handsome ſpacious street. On the lower floor, on the eaſtern ſide is a range of offices, large and convenient; one of which is occupied by the Clerk of the Court of Common Pleas for the county of Eſſex, in which are kept all the records of the court: The other two are uſed as offices, for the Selectmen and aſſeſſors of the town of Salem. The remainder of the lower ſtory is a fine capacious area, for walking etc.

"The second ſtory is compoſed of a large court hall, with ſeats on every side, for the Judges, officers of the court, and for the auditors — ſaid to be the best conſtructed room, for the holding of courts, of any in the Commonwealth, and perhaps is not exceeded by any in the United States. In the ceiling is a handsome ventilator. Back of the Judges' ſeat is a Venetian window, highly finished in the Ionick order; which affords a beautiful proſpect of a fine river, extenſive well cultivated fields and groves; in addition

to which the paſſing and repaſſing of veſſels contin-
ually, in the river, makes a pleaſing variety. There
is alſo on this floor a convenient lobby for Jurors
etc. This houſe was begun in 1785, and completed
in 1786, at the joint expenſe of the county of Eſſex
and town of Salem. The plan of it was deſigned
by the ingenious Mr. Samuel M'Intire and executed
by that able architect, Mr. Daniel Bancroft, both of
Salem."

Felt, in his "Annals of Salem", amplifies this
description as follows :

"It was planned by Samuel McIntire, and built
under the direction of Daniel Bancroft, two ingenious
architects. It was two stories high, sixty-two feet long
and thirty-six and two-thirds feet broad. It was finished in 1786. Its cost was $7,145, paid, one moiety by
the town and the other by the county. Its walls were
of brick and its roof surmounted by á cupola. On
the front or southern end of it was a balustrade
opening into the second story, supported by a row of
Tuscan pillars. Under the balustrade were wide
stone steps, which could accommodate a large number
of persons and which led into a door of the lower
hall. On the east side of this hall were several offices
and the rest was left open for public assemblies and
the exercise of military companies. The part thus
occupied for the last purposes was too often ap-
propriated by unruly boys to their boisterous sports
and destructive propensities, until large bulls of

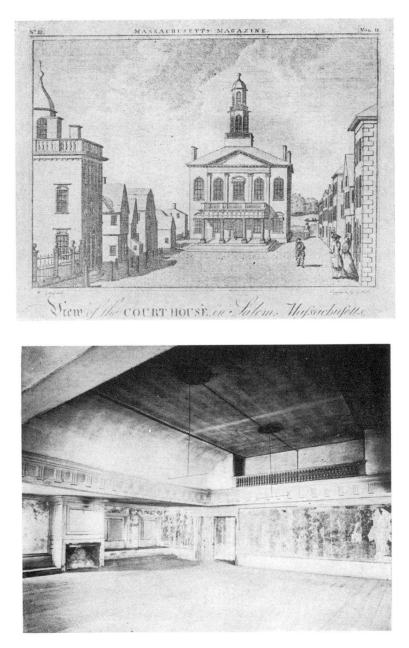

View of the COURT HOUSE in Salem, Massachusetts.

PLATE CXII. — The Old Courthouse of 1785.   From an Engraving in the Massachusetts Magazine of 1790; Interior of Washington Hall.   Erected 1792.   Razed 1898.

PLATE CXIII. — Hamilton Hall, Chestnut Street. Erected 1805; Fireplaces, Vaulted and Groined Ceiling, Hamilton Hall.

authority sounded in their ears and drove them from the premises."

The records at City Hall seem to indicate that the total cost of the Courthouse was considerably greater than Felt states. An additional appropriation of six thousand dollars and another of three thousand dollars are mentioned, and such a brick building must obviously have cost at least twenty thousand dollars even in those days.

This building, erected in 1785, was located in the middle of Washington Street, north end, about opposite the Tabernacle Church, as shown by several old steel engravings and a contemporary oil painting to be seen at the Essex Institute. There it stood until its removal was necessitated by the building of the railroad tunnel beneath; then the porch columns were taken to the Chase house, Number 21 Federal Street. From the balcony over the porch of the Courthouse George Washington was presented to the townspeople on the occasion of his visit, October 29, 1789. And as he stood bowing his acknowledgments to the acclaim of the populace, McIntire, seated at a window near by, studied the features of the first President minutely and made a sketch which formed the basis for his famous profile bas-relief, 38 × 56 inches and executed in wood, which for years adorned the architectural gateway at the western entrance of the Common and now hangs in the Essex Institute.

In 1792 Washington Hall, formerly at Number 101 Washington Street, was erected after plans by McIntire, and as the assembly hall of the Democrats became a prominent social center of the time. Dedicated on the anniversary of Washington's birthday, February 22, 1793, just previous to his second assumption of the presidency and amid great rejoicings over the success of the French Revolution, it was the scene of a notable banquet at which the Reverend William Bentley made the principal oration. This quaint hall, located on the third floor of the Stearns Building above stores and offices, presented a curious survival in the Doric style of the old-time English assembly room, with built-in seats along the walls, fireplace and a music gallery at one end. The balustrade of this gallery is preserved at the Essex Institute. In later days the hall became a theater, but being unsuited to present-day uses the entire building has been replaced by a modern structure.

Hamilton Hall, at the corner of Chestnut and Cambridge streets, also designed by McIntire, was erected in 1805 by the South Building Corporation, an association of wealthy men, as a place for assemblies and named for their much-admired friend Alexander Hamilton, who had visited Salem in 1800. Here Lafayette dined with three hundred guests on August 31, 1824, during his second triumphal American tour, when he was presented with $200,000 and a township of land by the government, in recognition of his service to the nation during the Revolution. Here, likewise, Commodore William Bainbridge, who succeeded Captain Isaac Hull as commander of the frigate *Constitution*, also Timothy Pickering, a politician with a record of public service equalled by few Americans, were accorded the full measure of Salem hospitality. In fact, ever since its erection, this building has remained the very heart of the city's social activities.

Exteriorly the structure boasts little adornment except its purely utilitarian features. The entrance porch at one end has been so remodeled as to make it difficult to judge with certainty regarding its original appearance. The sides, however, remain unchanged, except that the brickwork has been painted, and are pierced on the second and principal floor by five Palladian windows of simple character, somewhat recessed under a double arch of brick headers. A rectangular insert panel above each window displays a McIntire sculpture, that in the center being one of his well-known eagles, and the others consisting of the festooned drapery which he often used on a smaller scale to adorn doorways and mantels.

Dignified simplicity characterizes the interior treatment of the hall, with its groined ceiling and heavy cornice supported by fluted pilasters. Two fireplaces and a music balcony comprise the principal interior features and are distinguished by McIntire's careful attention to detail and proportion.

Unfortunately not a single church standing to-day represents old-time Salem. Of the several edifices of architectural merit, erected prior to 1818, notably the East Church on Essex Street between Hardy and Bentley streets, where the historian, Reverend William Bentley, preached for thirty-six years, and the South Church on the northeast corner of Cambridge Street, not one is left in anywhere near its original appearance. Only the South Church remained unaltered long enough to be photographed.

In this noble church, erected in 1804, McIntire manifested his versatility in design. The structure was of wood, 66 by 80 feet, with a graceful spire after the Wren manner 166 feet high, and cost $23,819.78, including the land. As in his other work McIntire employed the orders with considerable freedom. While generally speaking Ionic, with touches of Adam detail here and there, the cornice, frieze and flat pilasters of the bell deck were pure Doric. When completed, this church was considered one of McIntire's greatest achievements. The *North American Review* for October, 1836, contains the following appreciative description of it by James Gallier, architect:

"One of the best-proportioned steeples in our country is at Salem, in Massachusetts; the work of a native artist. The whole church is the best specimen of architecture in that city, notwithstanding the various efforts which have been made since its erection. We are not aware that it has any name; but the building will easily be recognized as the only church in Chestnut Street. The Ionic portico in front is uncommonly elegant, though simple and unpretending. Above this rises the steeple to the height of nearly a hundred and fifty feet. Its principal merit is beauty of proportion, which is not equalled in any steeple that we know of in the United States."

This Orthodox Congregational society originated as the result of a separation from the Tabernacle Church in 1774, under the leadership of Colonel Timothy Pickering. Until its church was erected the new society occupied an assembly hall that stood on adjoining land and in which many notable functions were held before the Revolution, among them a reception tendered to General Gage on the last King's Birthday celebrated in Massachusetts. It was from the bell deck of the old South Church that Captain Oliver Thayer watched the naval battle between the *Chesapeake* and the *Shannon* in June, 1813. Below this bell deck the base of the steeple, clapboarded like the building proper, had quoined corners after the manner of stone work. Within this steeple was housed an interesting piece of home-made mechanism, said to have been constructed by a Beverly blacksmith, possibly Samuel Luscomb, who also made the clock for the East Church. The clock in the South

Church was originally in the First Church at Essex and Washington streets, then removed to the Old North Church on North Street in 1826 and finally to the South Church ten years later. It had no face but struck the hour. An iron frame, a pendulum ten feet long and weights consisting of wooden boxes filled with stones were among the curious features of its works.

A large crystal chandelier imported in 1807 was a distinctive adornment of the interior. It had arms for thirty candles and is said to have cost a thousand dollars. For ninety-nine years this edifice continued to be one of Salem's most picturesque landmarks until destroyed by fire in 1903. Several of the hand-carved urns from the steeple are preserved at the Essex Institute.

During McIntire's active practice from 1782 to 1811 the people of Salem did not find it necessary or desirable to seek architectural talent for their important public buildings elsewhere. Upon McIntire's death in 1811, however, Bentley wrote in his diary that "no man is left to be consulted upon a new plan of execution beyond his bare practise", and in corroboration of this, Charles Bulfinch, the eminent Boston architect, designer of the Massachusetts State House in 1798 and architect of the National Capitol at Washington succeeding B. H. Latrobe in 1818, designed the Essex Bank in 1811 at Number 11 Central Street, now the home of the Salem Fraternity,

PLATE CXIV. — The Old South Church.   Erected 1804.
Burned 1903.

PLATE CXV. — The Market House, Derby Square.   Erected 1816;
The Salem Club, 29 Washington Square.   Erected 1818.

and the Almshouse on Salem Neck in 1816. These two buildings, the only ones designed by Bulfinch in Salem, and both erected after McIntire died, emphasize the loss his death meant to the community, especially as the efforts of Bulfinch in Salem do not bear favorable comparison with those of McIntire. The fraternity particularly is lacking in those qualities of simplicity, sincerity and refinement commonly attributed to Bulfinch's work, and deservedly in the case of the Massachusetts State House in Boston. Undoubtedly the best feature of the Fraternity, the wrought-iron balustrade of the entrance, is the equal of any similar work in the city. For eighty years this building was occupied by the First National Bank, and during its renovation for occupancy as the home of the Salem Fraternity the removal of a false ceiling in one of the lower rooms disclosed a beautiful stucco centerpiece in the original ceiling designed by Bulfinch.

The Salem Fraternity, the oldest boys' club in the country, was organized in 1869 to provide evening instruction and wholesome amusement for those who "being confined to their work during the day need recreation at the end of their labors." In addition to physical training and general education, there are classes devoted to many of the arts and crafts, a well-filled library and reading room.

In Market Square, extending through from Essex to Front Street, stands the Market House, erected in

1816, an interesting survival of the early custom of combining the public market with a hall for political meetings, which, like Faneuil Hall in Boston, continues to be used for its original purposes. A simple gable-roof structure, this substantial brick building is architecturally notable chiefly for its fenestration, which constitutes the only ornamentation aside from the pedimental treatment of the gable with cornice and segmental fanlight. The symmetrical arrangement of the round-headed windows and doors at once interests the appreciative eye, and the sash-bar division of the fanlights and second-story Palladian window accord with the best Colonial precedents. The market on the lower floor was opened November 25, 1816, and still continues to be leased for meat and provision stalls, while on Saturdays produce and provision carts line the square on Front Street. The second floor, furnished as the Town Hall, was first opened to the public July 8, 1817, on the occasion of a reception tendered to President Monroe that evening. Town meetings were held there until the incorporation of Salem as a city in 1836, and it has since been used for public gatherings.

Considerable historic interest attaches to the site of the Market House. At the outbreak of the Revolution it was the homestead of Colonel William Browne, Mandamus Councillor, and had been in his family for more than a century. Browne was a Tory, and proudly entertained Governor Thomas Gage and his staff when that autocratic official came to Salem on August 4, 1774, to dissolve the town meeting then in session. Gage's plan was frustrated, however, for Timothy Pickering, who had been summoned into their presence by the sheriff, kept the Governor in an "indecent passion" until the meeting had transacted its business and adjourned. Meanwhile an excited crowd filled Town House Square, troops had been ordered up from the garrison on Salem Neck and bloodshed was feared.

But during the next few years the Tories lost their grip upon government affairs, Browne's estate was confiscated and in 1784 was conveyed by the State to Elias Hasket Derby. The second edition of Felt's "Annals of Salem" contains a picture of it, reproduced on another page, and McIntire's own plans, showing the gradual development from preliminary drawings, may be seen at the Essex Institute. The grounds extended to the water's edge and were beautifully laid out and handsomely terraced. Famous throughout New England, the Derby gardens owed their beauty to the knowledge and good taste of George Heussler, an Alsatian, the first professional gardener in this vicinity. To the influence of his accomplishments at the town residence, and earlier at the farm of Elias Hasket Derby, must be attributed in large measure the attention which persons of wealth throughout Essex County gave to their gardens, and to him also must be given the credit for introducing many flowers and valuable fruits to America.

Derby had previously occupied the Pickman-Derby-Brookhouse estate, then located at the corner of Washington and Lynde streets where the new Masonic Temple now stands. Only a few months after moving from it into the new mansion, he died and the place was closed. No purchaser could be found for so luxurious an establishment, and so in 1804 the gateposts and much of the charming wood finish, including some of the best examples of McIntire's genius in design, were removed and built into the new residence then being erected under McIntire's direction at Number 142 Federal Street for Captain Samuel Cook and already referred to in Chapter IV. Later, in 1815, the Derby mansion was completely razed and the land on which it had stood was conveyed by the heirs to the town for use as a permanent public market, the area subsequently being named Derby Square in honor of its former distinguished owner. The present Market House was built at an expense of $12,000.

The old Latin Grammar and English High School, the most interesting of the early brick schoolhouses, still remains on Broad Street and is now known as the Oliver Primary School. Although the classic balustrade that formerly surmounted its hip roof has been removed, the original doorway has been bricked up and other exterior and interior changes made during the alterations of 1869, 1878 and 1884, enough remains in its pristine condition to be of architectural interest, while a lithograph made from a photograph by D. A. Clifford in 1856 shows the structure as it appeared while General Henry Kemble Oliver was principal and later during the six years that the late Honorable Joseph H. Choate prepared for Harvard College there. Completed in 1819, this building housed the Latin Grammar School until 1856 and the English High School from 1827 to 1858, when both, with the Girls' High School, were merged into the Salem Classical and High School and moved to a new building beside the old, the latter now being used for school administrative purposes.

This old two-story building is of interest chiefly for its brickwork, fenestration and the wood pilaster treatment of the upper story in the Ionic order above a projecting stone band about the entire structure at the second-floor level. The windows with plain stone lintels and sills stand in elliptical headed recessed panels, the sills reaching entirely across the recess from side to side, and the spaces below the upper windows being filled with a balustrade effect consisting of wooden pedestals at each end and half-round engaged balusters between. Altogether it is as quaint as any contemporary adaptation of the classic in brick construction to be found in New England.

Of all Salem public buildings erected a century or more ago none claims more interest in architecture or romance than the Custom House, Number 178

Derby Street, at the head of one of the two principal wharves during the period when Salem was at the zenith of its commercial prosperity. Previous to the erection of the present building in 1818–1819 the Custom House had been only a movable office following the collector from house to house wherever he might happen to live, and many were the famous men who held the offices of collector and surveyor. William Fairfax left the collectorship to go to Virginia, where he founded a family that intermarried with the Washingtons. William Hathorne, the ancestor of the romancer, is recorded as collecting a tonnage tax on gunpowder in 1667. Such names as Browne, Lynde, Bowditch, Veren, Palfray, Hiller and Lee are found on the roll, and it was upon the petition of James Cockle, then collector, for a warrant to search for smuggled molasses that James Otis made his historic plea against writs of assistance. A relic of this period of temporary custom houses is to be seen at the museum of the Essex Institute in the form of a large wooden eagle, carved by Samuel McIntire, that stood above the entrance of the building at Number 6 Central Street in 1805 while the office of the collector was located there.

But it is with Nathaniel Hawthorne and General James Miller, the hero of Lundy's Lane, that the present Custom House is chiefly associated. General Miller was Collector of the Port from 1835 to 1849, and in 1846 Hawthorne was appointed Surveyor of

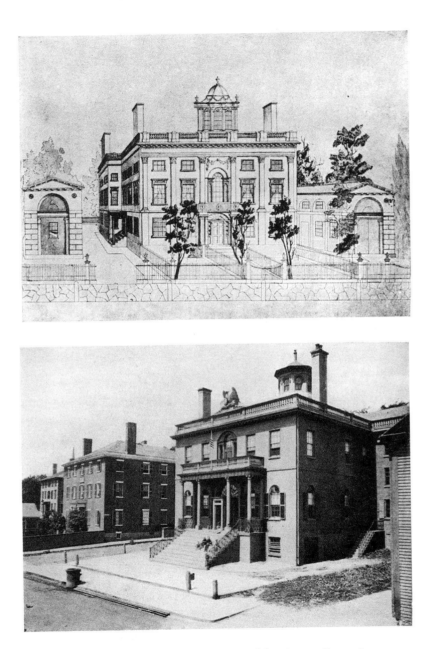

PLATE CXVI. — Elias Hasket Derby Mansion. Erected 1799.
Razed 1815; Salem Custom House, 178 Derby Street.
Erected 1818-1819.

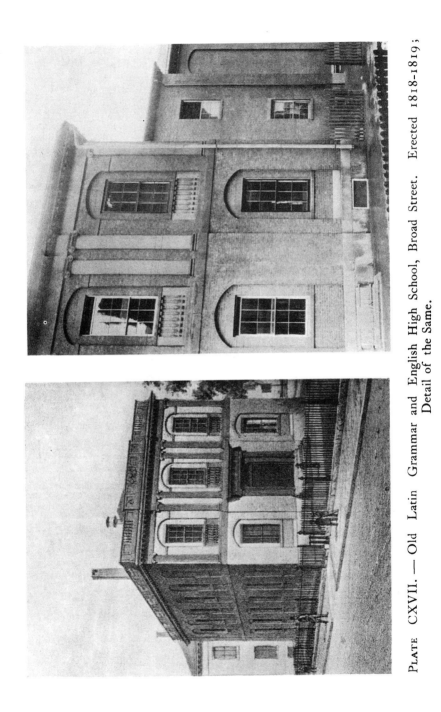

PLATE CXVII. — Old Latin Grammar and English High School, Broad Street. Erected 1818-1819; Detail of the Same.

Customs by the new Democratic administration, a position which he filled until the incoming Whig administration led to his dismissal in 1849. During this time he occupied the southwesterly front room on the first floor, and here in spare moments was evolved in part, at least, the plot for his immortal "Scarlet Letter." The stencil with which inspected goods were marked "N. Hawthorne, Surveyor" may still be seen there, while his quaint desk is still preserved at the Essex Institute. There was at one time a belief among unknown readers of Hawthorne's romance that the scarlet letter itself was discovered in a room at the rear of the collector's private office on the easterly side of the second floor. During Hawthorne's term of office and for several years afterwards this was an unfurnished room containing many old papers in boxes and barrels, yet it is probable that the discovery was a product of Hawthorne's vivid imagination. While several of the characters and scenes so graphically described in the sketch of the Custom House in the "Introduction to the Scarlet Letter" were indeed actual realities, the manuscript was as fictitious as Surveyor Pue's real connection with the tale. Certain it is that the old records were dispersed or consumed in the fire of October 5, 1774, which destroyed the building then serving as the Custom House, and it is doubtful if such an interesting historic document would have existed unknown in an accumulation of papers only forty-five years old. The cruel law described in the "Scarlet Letter" actually existed, however; an actual copy of it in antique print may be seen at the Essex Institute and it is a matter of record that this penalty was inflicted at Springfield, Massachusetts, on October 7, 1754, and that the law continued in force until February 17, 1785. Hawthorne had a way of giving his characters the names of real persons of the past and imputing to them acts and positions in life which were never theirs. Like Surveyor Pue, Doctor Swinnerton and many others, most of his names are to be found on the headstones of Charter Street Burial Ground, St. Peter's churchyard and other cemeteries. This for a time led readers to regard as fact many creations of his fancy. Tradition says that during his lifetime Hawthorne was inclined to encourage this tendency. For example, it is told that he assured an inquiring friend that he had the scarlet letter itself, but when urged to show it explained, "Well, I did have it, but one Sunday when my wife had gone to church, the children got hold of it and put it in the fire."

Returning now to the Custom House, it is interesting to recall that upon the site chosen by a committee of merchants had formerly stood the home of George Crowninshield, one of Salem's greatest ship-owners and the father of Benjamin Crowninshield, member of Congress and Secretary of the Navy, and of Jacob Crowninshield, also a congressman, but who declined an offer of the same cabinet position. The façade of the Crowninshield house was elaborated with pilasters, and as a weather vane on the cupola surmounting the hip roof stood the figure of a man with a spyglass held at arm's length, scanning the horizon for returning ships.

The present brick building was erected at a cost of $36,000, Perley Putnam and John Saunders being the contractors. But for its high flight of stone steps, wide, porch-like Ionic portico and broad doorway with a great semicircular fanlight it greatly resembles the hip-roofed residences about it and with which it accords so well. Both the handsome Palladian windows of the second story and the balustrade above the portico and at the eaves of the roof emphasize this relationship, while the large cupola with its flagstaff, the great eagle midway of the front roof balustrade and the round-topped windows of the lower floor help to distinguish it as a public building. But the foreign commerce of Salem has waned as that of Boston has grown, and on July 1, 1913, the Salem Custom House, so important in the early annals of American shipping, came under the direction of a deputy collector of the port of Boston.

CHAPTER XII

SALEM ARCHITECTURE TO-DAY

ON June 25, 1914, Salem was visited by a terrible conflagration that cost three lives, hastened the death of many of the ill and aged, destroyed eighteen hundred buildings, burned out fifteen thousand persons and caused a total loss of fifteen million dollars, yet happily claimed no residences or other buildings of exceptional historic interest or architectural merit. Then did the courageous spirit of old Salem reassert itself. Hardly had the ashes become cold before rebuilding was commenced and is still in progress. Five years after the disaster finds over three quarters of the burned district restored and every indication that the work of reconstruction will be virtually complete within another twelvemonth. Many of the detached dwellings are of fireproof construction, as are the other buildings of all sorts, and in every respect they are as a whole much better than the structures they replace. Slate, asbestos or other fire-resisting roof coverings are the rule.

It is a remarkable fact that this great fire ravaged the newer part of the city, leaving the better sections of the older part intact; and it is a matter of the

PLATE CXVIII. — George A. Morrill House, 2 Cedar Street;
House of Mrs. L. E. Noyes, 9 Roslyn Street.

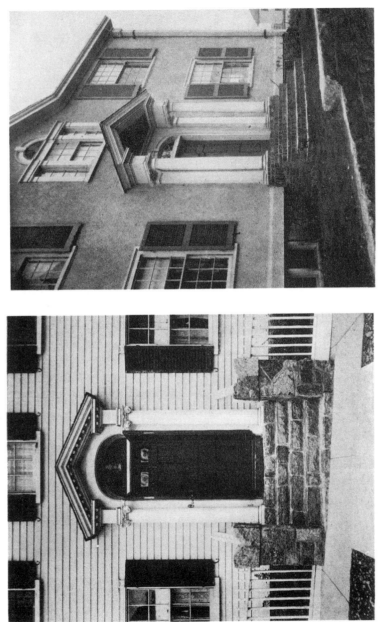

PLATE CXIX. — Doorway Detail, George A. Morrill House; Doorway Detail, T. Irving Fenno House, 3 Cedar Street.

utmost significance that most of the new buildings display Colonial motives and that nearly all of the residences of moment are purely Colonial in design. Not since 1818 and the advent of the illogical Greek revival have Colonial houses to any considerable number and worthy of the name been erected in Salem, and the present general reversion to them after an interval of a century indicates conclusively the power of persistence of the Colonial tradition. The aberrations of intervening years have been corrected by elimination ; the gap has been bridged, and architectural design again springs from the sound fundamentals of the past; home builders are collaborating with architects in the logical development of local prototypes so worthy of emulation. The continuity of the Colonial tradition has been re-established and it becomes evident as never before that the American style in architecture is, always has been and probably will continue to be Colonial.

In a city where all the best architecture is Colonial and much of it more than century-old, mature thought always convinces the discerning home builder that safety lies within the bounds of local traditions if one would have his new house live in accord with its older fellows. In the hands of a resourceful architect such a conservative course should insure a home of character and distinction, for in the adaptation of several motives of proved worth to individual needs and modern uses will come a new and varied ensemble sufficiently related to the past yet by no means conventional. And so it has been proved in this instance. In former years Salem architecture has been unique and especially valuable because of its several varied types and the opportunity afforded for ready comparison. Henceforth it will possess a wider interest by reason of its large and growing number of notable modern Colonial homes. As a source of building inspiration the Salem of to-day, consisting of an old and new city in juxtaposition, far outshines its former self as the architectural center of New England. Exigencies of space restrict the treatment of this modern Colonial architecture in these pages, but the few varied and especially noteworthy examples illustrated and described serve to show the ingenious manner in which architects find their inspiration bit by bit here and there, adapt it to their needs and often recombine it to serve new purposes.

In their search for a cottage prototype in Salem, architects of necessity went back to the days of the "codfish aristocrats" and selected the lean-to; for the gambrel-roof houses of Salem, unlike those of New York and New Jersey, are virtually three stories in height and furnish no precedents of distinctive yet modest character for direct adaptation. This type, although picturesque in mass and outline, is severe and almost colorless in façade and devoid of embellishment, but A. G. Richardson, the Boston architect residing in Salem, saw the possibilities it offered for elaboration and in designing the home of George A. Morrill, Number 2 Cedar Street, solved one of the most interesting problems of his career. The resulting house as it stands complete to-day represents virtually an exact copy of the Maria Goodhue house in Danvers, erected in 1690 and destroyed by fire in 1899. Its long roof-line, formed by the lean-to continuation at the same pitch, contributes a uniquely appropriate character to the modern architecture of Salem and was found to provide a very practical way of bringing a piazza in the rear and all service appurtenances under one roof, thereby saving expense and avoiding all leakage complications common to roofs considerably broken by gables or dormers.

The exterior embellishments savor of the practical for the most part and are better for it, including the doorway, blinds, lintels, fanlights in each gable, a cornice along the front under the eaves and a glazed piazza at the rear. No one who has seen the pedimental doorway of the Hodges-Webb-Meek house, Number 81 Essex Street, erected about 1800, will doubt the origin of that on the Morrill cottage. One notices the absence of side lights, so often a Salem feature, yet this simpler design accords well with the modest nature of the entire structure. In the translation, too, the fluted pilasters with their pleasing Ionic capitals have become round columns, always lighter in effect and more graceful. Square fluted columns without capitals, however, have been applied effectively to the glazed piazza at the rear.

Attractively spaced with molded panels, after the manner of several century-old examples near by, the door itself differs from them in the substitution of glass bull's-eyes for the two smaller upper panels. The double blind doors before it, with wire screen cloth on the inner side, so often seen on old Colonial houses, also vary slightly from the conventional type, as do likewise the window blinds in the omission of a middle cross rail. The idea may have been taken from an old Newburyport house or the William R. Colby house, Number 93 Federal Street, Salem. The hardware indicates careful selection and includes a charming brass knocker and thumb latch with a glass knob on the blind door outside. In the arch above hangs an old ship's lamp wired for electricity, a clever and useful reminder of the early days of Salem prosperity. One notices, too, the quaint, wrought-iron S blind fasteners; in fact, only an electric push-button betrays modernity. A characteristic fence with round, pointed pickets and simple rail and base between four stone posts completes a picture of genuine charm, even though one longs for steps of granite and gateposts of wood like those at the side or slightly heavier.

The well-proportioned windows contain twelve-paned sashes like most of those in Salem, lending

PLATE CXX. — House of Henry M. Bachelder, 204 Lafayette Street;
Semi-detached Houses, built by S. W. Phillips, Warren Street.

PLATE CXXI. — Doorway Detail, Francis A. Seamans House; Doorway Detail, B. Parker Babbidge House.

scale and picturesqueness to the façade. Their molded architrave casings follow conventional lines, but the lintels with their attractive corner blocks, although of wood, recall the hand-cut marble lintels so often seen on brick houses. And the way in which the second-story lintels engage the plate, which has gained the dignity of a cornice through its vertical fluted groups and surmounting bed molding, is strongly reminiscent of our earliest New England houses.

Another example of lean-to design is seen in the house of Mrs. L. E. Noyes, Number 9 Roslyn Street. In general mass reminiscent of Salem architecture of witchcraft days, the house as a whole is of composite rather than pure type. Motives characteristic of other localities, such as the Germantown penthouse hood, the Dutch porch, wide side settles and the Maryland farmhouse outside chimneys, have been freely employed, while the stucco construction, divisions of the window sashes, the long lean-to dormer and the glazed piazza in the rear are distinctly modern innovations. The ensemble is none the less picturesque and pleasing, and a credit to the architect and builder, A. J. MacDuff, of Everett, Massachusetts.

The end-to-the-street residence of T. Irving Fenno, Number 3 Cedar Street, also a stucco house, reflects Salem influences in its doorway and fenestration. The former, while considerably elaborated, recalls the

White-Lord doorway, Number 31 Washington Square North. Sufficient projection has been given to the open pediment to form a porch to shelter the waiting guest, and this is supported, not by engaged smooth columns, but by fluted columns and flat pilasters. One notices the omission of the blind doors, the substitution of a charming elliptical instead of round fanlight and the clever application of the fine-scale Doric triglyph and guttæ to the frieze ends. The simple, attractive Palladian window above this distinctive entrance accords with Salem practice, though adapted from other sources, while the broad thirty-paned windows, fifteen panes to the sash, were doubtless suggested to the architect, Louis Grangent, of Salem, by the "House of Seven Gables" and the sketch of the Philip English house at the Essex Institute.

The gambrel-roof period of Salem architecture has a worthy modern representative in the residence of Henry M. Bachelder, Number 204 Lafayette Street, Little and Brown, Boston, architects. It is notable chiefly for its pleasing mass and simplicity of detail. Substantial comfort and permanent construction were the aims rather than elaboration of motives. Dormers, cornice and windows correspond to those of several old houses near by, and the iron hand rails have the true Colonial feeling. The L, with its sun parlor on the lower floor, strikes a modern and unusual note, as do the three narrow windows on the third floor of the gable, and the inclosed entrance porch. The latter is exceptional in its engaged columns and flat-roofed wings, with high narrow sashes each side of the pediment. The door differs a trifle from several similar ones in Salem in the shorter proportion of the lower panels. The delightful interior woodwork includes two genuine McIntire fireplace mantels taken from the old building at Number 6 Central Street where the Custom House was located in 1805, and which was considerably remodeled a few years ago.

It is a hopeful sign of the times that the desire for real architectural merit in the home is now being expressed quite as insistently by prospective home builders of moderate means, and even tenants, as by those better situated financially. In meeting this demand landlords and architects have learned that the matter of small houses harmoniously treated on small plots constitutes a problem of the first magnitude, and the more they study it the more they come to appreciate the merits of the English semi-detached house with party walls on the side property lines, whether for rentable purposes or for the owner who feels the need of an income from part of his home property.

Not only is there economy in making one structural wall answer for two houses, but the very utmost is made of small building plots; appearances are improved immeasurably both in respect to the house itself and the grounds. No suburban property can be developed attractively with small detached houses on plots less than one hundred feet wide. On single forty-foot lots ugly, narrow houses resembling flats in floor plan must be adopted in order to leave the necessary space between them. Even two lots, totaling eighty feet in width, hardly permit anything better than a cubical eight-room house, with four rooms of nearly equal size on each floor, that seems clumsy in the extreme when of fireproof construction such as brick or concrete. To put as many rooms on the first as the second floor, or to build a one-story bungalow is expensive in respect to increased excavation, foundation and roof.

Conditions of this character presented themselves in replacing the famous Tontine Block, a group of splendid old dwellings erected in 1806, which stood at the corner of Warren and Flint streets in the path of the great fire. With commendable public spirit the owner, S. W. Phillips, undertook with the aid of William G. Rantoul, the Boston architect living in Salem, to restore the property with a group of modern dwellings in accord with its century-old neighbors, still intact. The task was to devise a plan which, within restricted limits, should provide every convenience and comfort required by the tenant of to-day, with the rooms so arranged as to insure plenty of sunlight and air, and thus overcome the usual objections to houses built in a block.

By joining three houses together under one roof,

PLATE CXXII. — Residence of Francis A. Seamans, 48 Chestnut
Street.   Erected 1910; Residence of B. Parker Babbidge,
14 Fairfield Street.

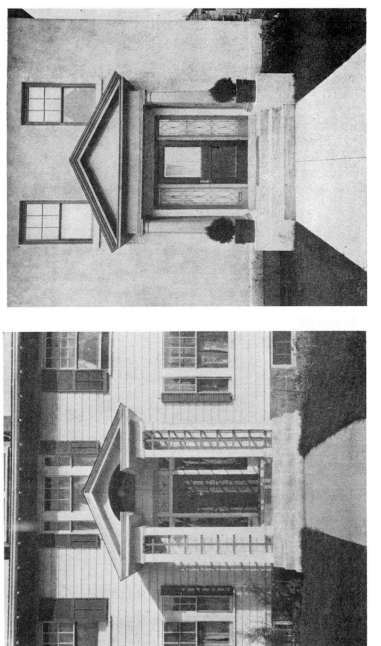

PLATE CXXIII. — George W. Fuller Doorway, 69 Summer Street; Alan Bouvé Doorway, 7 Fairfield Street.

yet separating them one from another by unpierced brick fire walls, Mr. Rantoul found it possible to design a dignified three-story structure, broad of roof, generally horizontal in effect, friendly with its site and harmonious in every proportion. It is at utter variance with any eight-room house on a single lot and is vastly superior ; it has, in other words, benefited by association with its neighbors. This applies not only to the appearance of the house itself but to its surroundings as well. There is a generous lawn stretching entirely across the front, opportunities for planting about the entrance at the ends, and three large service-yards in the rear instead of four painfully narrow spaces between three single houses and their neighbors. Brick walls at both ends and a solid wood fence at the rear insure to the entire grounds, except the front lawns, that privacy so desirable yet so often lacking in houses of this sort.

In the solution of his many complex problems Mr. Rantoul has achieved a notable success in creative adaptation, if such a term may be permitted. Not only has he preserved the spirit and general arrangement of the English semi-detached house, but in appearance he has given it a distinctly American character, its charm and beauty depending upon simple lines, pleasing proportions and the entire absence of useless ornament. Choosing as his principal motive the gambrel-roof house, all minor details were made to harmonize, and one who knows Salem architecture will have no difficulty in finding friendly prototypes for each with one exception. Broad, mullioned window-groups, such as those of the middle house, are much employed in England where the light is much of the time less intense than here. In the present instance they have only one outside wall.

Perhaps the most notable example of the modern gambrel-roof house of brick is the residence of Francis A. Seaman, Number 48 Chestnut Street, although not in the fire district and built shortly before the conflagration occurred. Its location on one of the finest streets of Colonial architecture in America, however, precluded the possibility of resorting to any other style. The house is a free adaptation of the Richard Derby house, on Derby Street, the oldest brick house still standing in Salem, and careful observation will disclose at once many details which correspond and several which differ. The paired chimneys at both ends of the older house have been omitted in the design of the new in accordance with the exigencies of the floor plan, and the newer doorway, while equivalent to the older in mass, varies considerably in detail. The recess of a sunken vestibule together with the projection of the Doric pediment supported by full, round, engaged columns constitutes an entrance porch. As a whole the effect more closely resembles that of the Pierce-Johonnot-Nichols entrance, on Federal Street, rather than the Derby doorway, although it has less projection, and low Roman rather than high Tuscan plinths have been used. The jambs of the older house, suggestive of cut marble blocks, have been retained and the door is similarly paneled, except that bull's-eye glasses replace the upper panels as a substitute for the horizontal top light. The simple wood fence reflects good Colonial spirit and altogether the house is a worthy companion of its older neighbor.

The Lancelot Gibson house, Number 6 Fairfield Street, although only two stories in height, otherwise well represents the square wood dwellings in vogue from about 1780 to 1810 with their hip roofs and surmounting belvederes. Like several early proto-types the façade is weatherboarded and has quoined corners, the other walls being clapboarded. Again the effect of an entrance porch has been obtained by recourse to a sunken vestibule with Doric pediment supported, in this instance, by columns of pure Grecian order. In the spacing of its panels the door brings to mind that of the Pierce-Johonnot-Nichols house, the moldings, however, having apparently been adapted from those of the Peabody-Silsbee door. One notices the pleasing effect of the paneled jambs spaced to correspond to the door. The doorway at Number 6 Downing Street probably suggested the narrow side lights. Shutters such as grace old Colonial houses elsewhere replace the customary Salem blinds, but the overhanging bay and the piazza having columns in accord with the entrance and a unique balustrade instance the resourcefulness of the architect, A. G. Richardson, of Salem.

The square brick houses of the last period of Colonial architecture in Salem have also furnished inspiration for recent two-story residences quite as attractive as their larger three-story predecessors, even if lacking a little of the grandeur lent by greater height. Among the handsomest of these may be mentioned the residence of B. Parker Babbidge, Number 14 Fairfield Street, an exceptional instance of intelligent Colonial adaptation. The ornamental detail in profusion indicates an appreciation of Salem's best motives. Beneath a hip roof surmounted by a balustraded belvedere, and pierced by dormers familiar to Salem, is seen a cornice with dentils hand-carved on their under sides and a ball molding distinctly reminiscent of the Peabody-Silsbee house. Both above and below, the balustrades appear to have emanated from the same source, the molded panels in the balustrade of the large glazed piazza, however, representing a pleasing innovation. The recessed doorway was obviously developed from that of the Ropes' Memorial by omitting the top lights, employing a finer scale pattern for the leaded glass of the side lights and refining the moldings of the similarly paneled door somewhat to correspond. In fenestration the Dodge-Shreve house, Number 29 Chestnut Street, was taken as the model. The windows, window frames and marble lintels correspond in pattern, and the beautiful Palladian window over the entrance displays only such minor variations as the flattening of the brick arch to elliptical form, the substitution of simpler spring blocks and keystone, and the use of leaded side lights like those of the doorway below. Blind shutters from other than local sources serve to fix this typically Salem dwelling as being of the twentieth century. Altogether no finer modern structure yet graces the rebuilt section of the city.

Across the street, the residence of George L. Hooper, Number 11 Fairfield Street, instances several well-designed and distinctly modern houses which, aside from minor details here and there, adhere to Salem precedent exteriorly only in the doorway. Here the architect, Robert Coit, of Boston, appears to have been influenced by the Barstow-West entrance porch, elaborating it by the addition of a surmounting balustrade about the second-floor bay above and broadening it from elliptical to nearly semicircular shape. The marble-capped brick buttresses of the steps, conforming to the floor of the porch, have been deemed sufficient without the charming iron work of the older entrance, while the door itself, generally speaking, conforms to the panel arrangement of the Pierce-Johonnot-Nichols door, the panels immediately above the thumb latch being of longer relative proportion in the later door.

Several picturesque new doorways in the rebuilt

section, especially entrance porches, cannot in any sense be regarded as Colonial, yet they exhibit unmistakable evidence of classic influence in their design and so live in accord with the pure architectural types about them. They are manifestations of the application of simple motives and minor bits of Colonial detail to the modest cottage architecture intended to appeal to the eye rather than the mind and to provide essential comforts and fulfill personal requirements rather than invite architectural classification. The doorway of the George W. Fuller house, Number 69 Summer Street, George H. Fanning, of Salem, architect, and the Alan Bouvé doorway, Number 7 Fairfield Street, merit study as denoting commendable tendencies of the present time.

Not only has the Colonial tradition established itself as the twentieth-century style in domestic architecture, but it has reasserted itself in public and semi-public work as well. To use a colloquialism, the Colonial style has in every sense "come back." And as indicated by the Francis A. Seaman house, already referred to, and the instances which follow, the beginnings of the coming reversion had already been made before the great fire occurred. This disaster did not, therefore, cause the reversion, but hastened it and made it more general.

As early as 1882 the desirability of perpetuating the Colonial spirit in public buildings was felt when

Plate CXXIV. — Lancelot Gibson House, 6 Fairfield Street; House of George L. Hooper, 11 Fairfield Street.

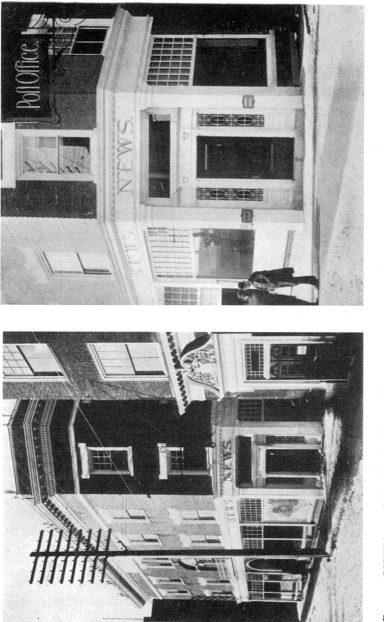

PLATE CXXV. — Peabody Building, Washington Street. Erected 1891-1892; Doorway Detail, Salem News Office, Peabody Building.

the block at Number 118 Washington Street was designed by Peabody and Stearns, of Boston, to house the Post Office on its lower floor. Generally Ionic in its ornamental detail, with capitals elaborated by an encarpus between the volutes, this brick structure represents a free interpretation of the order, yet is strongly reminiscent of much fine old work in Salem. The heavy balustrades, paneled pedestals and surmounting urns, also the entablature beneath are perhaps the best features, although the two doorways are also interesting.

It has been contended by some competent critics that an improvement would have been effected by the omission of the highly ornamented doorheads over both front entrances, consisting of a sort of broken pediment formed by two scrolls or curves of contrary flexure such as characterize the decorative contour of the classic console. However that may be, these high heads provide spaces for fine reproductions of the coat of arms of the United States and the seal of the City of Salem. The manner in which these pedimental heads tie into the entablature above is worthy of notice, although this practice does not find favor with many architects. The fenestration throughout is pleasing. The large lights of the lower sashes afford comfort in looking outdoors from within, while the many small square lights above lend a pleasing sense of scale. The windows of the lower story between the doorways represent a modernized adaptation of the

English bay, frequently a feature of the quaint shops of early days in America.

Next to the Post Office on Washington Street stands the Peabody Building, another brick structure in the Colonial spirit. It was designed by C. H. Blackall, of Boston, and erected in 1891 and 1892. Here, too, there is considerable freedom in the use of the orders, yet the ensemble possesses that indefinable grace and charm which McIntire often imparted by similar methods, and indeed, several prominent motives, such as the ball molding, will be recognized as having been employed by that master craftsman of Salem. While it might be said that generally speaking the building is denticulated Doric in character, as indicated by the main entrance, yet the continuations of the entablature along the second-floor level are Doric only in the guttæ of the architrave, the triglyphs of the frieze being omitted and the dentil course of the cornice being replaced by a cavetto jig-sawed to suggest a series of Gothic arches, the torus ordinarily used beneath it becoming in this instance a half sphere. The main cornice of the building is Corinthian with typical modillions, while the slender columns of the corner doorway and Palladian window above the main entrance have Ionic capitals and the urns in pairs on the roof balustrade suggest Adam influence. Both the marble lintels of the windows as a whole were obviously inspired by the façade of the Dodge-Shreve house, Number 29

Chestnut Street, while the fenestration throughout echoes pleasingly that of the Post Office beside it. Both the ornamental iron balcony and the semicircular leaded glass fanlight beneath are quite in accord with approved Salem motives, while a particularly effective feature of the main entrance is provided by the broad and heavy paneling in the reveal of the doorway which is carried up around the soffit of the arch. This building is the home of the *Salem Evening News* and the corner doorway to its office forms an interesting study in the effective adaptation of Colonial motives to modern commercial usage.

In 1906 the present building of the Salem Athenæum at Number 339 Essex Street, known as Plummer Hall, was erected to replace the first Plummer Hall of 1856, which the society had found unsuited to its needs and had sold to the Essex Institute for a museum. Plummer Hall had been built from a bequest of $30,000 in the name of her brother, Ernestus Augustus Plummer, by Miss Caroline Plummer, who also established the Plummer Farm School and the Plummer Professorship of Morals at Harvard University. One of the handsomest buildings in the city, in exterior appearance it is approximately a reproduction of the central part of "Homewood", that remarkable Baltimore residence, sometimes referred to as a Colonial bungalow, erected in 1803-1804 by Charles Carroll of Carrollton, a signer of the Declaration of Independence. "Home-wood" is now a part of Johns Hopkins University and offers a peculiarly suitable prototype for modern adaptation to public uses, either including the Georgian wings or omitting them as in the present Plummer Hall, designed by William G. Rantoul.

The Salem Athenæum is controlled by one hundred shareholders or proprietors, but a limited number of additional persons may avail themselves of its privileges by annual subscription. The library contains 30,000 volumes, including the old "Social Library" of 1780, and the "Philosophical Library" of 1781, founded on a collection of scientific works seized in the Irish Channel by Captain Hill, the privateersman.

The Police Station, Number 17 Central Street, erected in 1913, is situated among buildings of bygone days. While meeting the varied practical requirements of such a structure, the architect, John M. Gray, of Salem and Boston, has succeeded in imparting to it much of the spirit of old Salem brick-work. This important addition to Salem's municipal buildings is an excellent example of what can be accomplished by adhering to the spirit of our early architecture. The structure is of red brick with limestone trimmings and from the balustrade of the decked roof down to the ironwork of the doorways indicates an intimate knowledge of the best Salem precedents. At once distinctive and dignified, the

PLATE CXXVI. — Salem Masonic Temple, Washington and Lynde
Streets. Erected 1915-1916.

PLATE CXXVII. — The Salem Athenæum, 339 Essex Street.
Erected 1906; Salem Police Station, 17 Central Street.
Erected 1913.

façade is particularly happy in its fenestration. The ornamental fire balcony and panels with festooned drapery beneath the high round-headed windows are highly decorative, and the urns on the pedestals above the hooded entrances are pleasingly reminiscent of several delightful wooden gateposts. This is really three buildings in one as it houses the Police Department, Electrical Department and the First District Court of Essex County. Each department is entirely separate from the others and has its own entrances. The lower floor and basement are devoted to the Police Department. The Electrical Department is located in an L on the Charter Street side of the building, while the First District Court, the Civil and Juvenile Courts and their accompanying chambers occupy the second and third stories. The principal court room is on the front, where the high round-headed windows are seen, and is the equivalent of two stories in height, with the third story of the mezzanine type around it. Distinctly Colonial in character, the room is beautifully finished in mahogany with pure white vaulted ceilings and walls tinted a soft gray.

Of all the recent buildings in Salem, however, the Masonic Temple at the corner of Washington and Lynde streets, formerly the site of the Pickman-Derby-Brookhouse estate alluded to in Chapter IV, is the largest and most pretentious. Constructed of brick with limestone trimmings, it was erected in

1915 and 1916 at a cost of $250,000, Lester S. Couch, of the firm of Little and Brown, Boston, being the architect. While classic Renaissance rather than Colonial, no book devoted to the best Salem architecture would be complete which failed to include it. Moreover, it recalls old Salem work in several particulars; notably the adoption of the Corinthian order, which predominated in the local brick structures of a century ago, the application of the Grecian fret or double denticulated molding to the cornice, and the design of the ornamental iron fire balconies. Generally speaking, the façade is reminiscent of the Roman palaces of the sixteenth and seventeenth centuries as well as of the earlier Florentine palaces by reason of the first story of rusticated stone with three grouped arches at the main entrance and a surmounting continuous scroll band, and also because of the brick walling above, devoid of numerous pilasters and columns so common to the Renaissance architecture of Northern Italy. The projecting pediment supported by Corinthian columns three stories in height above the entrance, however, was a more frequent feature of the Renaissance in England. The fenestration is most interesting, the oval windows of the fourth story and the nearly square ones under the pediment recalling the round and square windows of Hampton Court, although differently employed in this instance. Adam influence is seen in the decorative stone panels between these

[256]

oval windows and in the garlands over them. Under
the pediment the stone casings of the windows, both
those with entablatures and segmental heads, are of
Italian character. Elsewhere simple gauged arches
with limestone keystones suffice, the only wooden
construction in any instance being the jamb linings
let into the reveals of the brickwork. Casement
sashes prevail on the fourth floor, with sliding
Georgian sashes on the second and third floors. Above
the heavy cornice rises a balustrade, but unlike the
usual classic type, it consists of a solid brick wall and
coping, with occasional projecting piers replacing
the customary pedestals.

Altogether it is a stately building of considerable
distinction and one of the finest Masonic edifices in
Massachusetts. Exteriorly it lives in accord with its
older Colonial neighbors, and interiorly its lodge
rooms are graced with excellent wood finish of appropriate character. Like the Police Station, it offers a
type worthy of emulation in future years.

May the complete success of these and a few other
less important recent efforts encourage the continued
use of Colonial motives in municipal and semi-public
work, so that the community as well as its citizens
individually may assist in perpetuating and develop-
ing a building heritage second to none in America,
and that henceforth, as up to 1818, Salem may have a
contemporaneous Colonial architecture in public as
well as domestic work.

INDEX

INDEX

A

ABBOT HOUSE, 130
Active, the, 6
Adam, the Brothers, 74; their influence, 81, 90, 181, 256; garlands a favorite motive of, 120; McIntire completely under spell of, 155; balance between plain surface and delicate ornament, 156; mantel design, 190, 203; frieze, 193; urns, 199; chimney piece, 204; festooned gardens, 208; festooned drapery, 216; mantel glass, 210
Adams, John, 43
Allen, Captain Edward, 170
Allen (Captain Edward) house, 65; interior of, 146, 147; corner china closet of, 164; stairway of, 169, 170; mantel of, 192, 193
Allen, Reverend James, 20
Allen, John Fiske, 101, 102
Allen-Osgood-Huntington houses, 101
Almshouse, Salem, 30
America, the, 6
Andirons, 153, 192, 194, 203, 207, 210
Andrew, John, 95
Andrew, John A., 95
Andrew-Safford house, 94–96; porch of, 128; centerpiece and cornice of, 149; interior doorway of, 163
Andrews, Daniel, 38–40

Andrews, Colonel Joseph, 104
"Annals of Salem." *See* FELT
Applied work, of the Read mansion, 192; of the Captain Edward Allen house, 193; of the Peabody-Silsbee house, 198; of mantel at Essex Institute, 199, 210
Archer, Samuel, 8
Arches, keyed round, 80; flattened, 94; elliptical, 165, 166, 181, 182
Architrave casings, 108, 139; of the house at 19 Chestnut Street, 68; of the Cook-Oliver house, 77; of the Bolles-Mansfield house, 88; of the house at 23 Summer Street, 114; the preferred form in modern colonial work, 136; of the Stephen W. Phillips house, 138; of the Pierce-Johonnot-Nichols house, 148; of the Crowninshield - Devereux - Waters house, 159
Archivolts, 182
Arthur, Prince, of England, 216
Asby, David, 88
Assembly Hall, Salem, 218, 219

B

BABBIDGE (B. PARKER) HOUSE, 248, 249
Babbidge-Crowninshield-Bowker house, 31; stairway of, 178
Bachelder (Henry M.) house, 242, 243

[261]

Index

Index

Index

Index

Index

preserved at, 131; fine old stairway at, 175; reconstruction of ancient kitchen at, 185; mantel with eagle at, 199; profile bas-relief of Washington at, 221; balustrade of gallery of Washington Hall at, 222; McIntire's plans of Browne's estate at, 229; wooden cage at, 232; Hawthorne's desk at, 233; copy of scarlet-letter law at, 234
"Evangeline", Longfellow, 15
Exterior wood trim, 47, 54

F

FAÇADE, of the Rea-Putnam-Fowler house, 18; of square three-story houses, 60; of the Simon Forrester house, 63; of the Crowninshield-Devereux-Waters house, 70; of the Gardner-White-Pingree house, 88, 89; of the house 12 Chestnut Street, 90; of the Pickman-Shreve-Little house and the Dodge-Shreve house, 92, 93; of the Andrew-Safford house, 96; of the Assembly Hall, 218; of the Masonic Temple, 256
Fairfax, William, 232
Fanlights, of the Pierce-Johnnot-Nichols house, 80, 117; of the Pickman-Shreve-Little house, 93; of the Hoffman-Simpson house, 100; development of, 108, 112; elliptical, of the Barstow-West house, 126; glazed, with elliptical arch, 165; segmental, in Market House, 228; of Fenno house, 242
Fanning, George H., 250
Farrington, Dr. G. P., 41

Fascia, 147, 162
Father Mathew Catholic Total Abstinence Society, 127, 211
Federal period of architecture in Salem, 64
"Federal Street", the tune, 76
Federal type of Colonial architecture, 62
Felt, quoted or cited, 52, 68, 101, 102, 109, 220, 229
Fence posts, 120
Fences, of the Ropes Memorial, 49; of the Briggs-Whipple house and the George M. Whipple house, 65, 66; of the Aaron Waite house, 67; of the Crowninshield-Devereux-Waters house, 71; of the Cook-Oliver house, 76; of the Pierce-Johnnot-Nichols house, 80, 117; of the Arthur W. West house, 91; of the Baldwin-Lyman house, 91, 125; of the Dodge-Shreve and the Pickman-Shreve-Little houses, 93; of the Mack and Stone houses, 97; of the Gardner-White-Pingree house, 127; of the George A. Morrill house, 240
Fenestration. See WINDOWS
Fenno (T. Irving) house, 241, 242
Festooned drapery, 62
Fields, James T., 83
Figure work, 196
Fire of 1914, at Salem, 236
Fireback, of the House of the Seven Gables, 13; of the Pickering house, 16; early, 184
Fireplace wall, 150, 151; symmetrical arrangement of, 152, 153
Fireplaces, in the General Israel Putnam house, 45, 46; location of, 52; early, 184; de-

[268]

Index

Index

Index

Index

of the Andrew-Safford house,
96; of the Hoffman-Simpson
house, 100; with seats, 109;
gable-roof inclosed, 109, 113,
114; Doric, on house at
23 Summer Street, 114; of
the Boardman house and
the Pierce-Johonnot-Nichols
house, 114, 115, 117; of
Whipple house, 115, 116; of
Stearns house, 117; of the
Cook-Oliver house, 119; of
the Kimball house, 122; of
the Peabody-Silsbee house,
122, 123; other similar, 123;
of the Gardner and Thompson
houses, 124; of the Salem
Club, 124; of the Baldwin-
Lyman house, 125; of the
Barstow-West house, 126; el-
liptical, 127; of the Tucker-
Rice house and the Gardner-
White-Pingree house, 127, 128,
211; of the Andrew-Safford
house, 128; of the Assembly
Hall, 219
Portico, 95; used as veranda,
213
Post Office, Salem, 251
Pownall, Governor, 58
Poynton (Thomas) house, 111,
112
Prescott, William Hickling, 10,
191
Prince, Dr. Jonathan, 29
Prince, Robert, 5, 6
Prince (Robert) farmhouse, 3, 5
Prince, Sarah, 5, 6
Privateers, 6
Public buildings, English, 2; of
Salem, 211-235
Putnam, Anne, 133
Putnam (Anne) house, 133
Putnam, Benjamin, 20
Putnam, Captain Edmund, 19
Putnam, Eleanor, 36

Putnam, Elias, 19
Putnam, General Israel, 28, 45,
46
Putnam (General Israel) birth-
place, doorway of, 116
Putnam (Jesse) house, 30, 134
Putnam, John, 20, 28, 45
Putnam, Joseph, 28, 45, 46
Putnam, Deacon Joseph, 30
Putnam, Lieutenant Thomas, 45
Putnam-Hanson house, 152
Puttenham family, 45

Q

QUOINED CORNER BOARDS, 53, 55,
60, 63, 67

R

RAFTERS, 42
Rantoul, William G., 68, 244,
254
Rantoul (William G.) house, 68,
69, 141
Rea, Bethia, 19
Rea, Daniel, 19
Rea-Putnam-Fowler house, 18,
26, 134
Read, Nathan, 10, 191
Read (Nathan) house, 11, 191
Recovery, the, 6
Redemptioners, 5
Reed, spiral, 160
Reeded ovolo, 157
Reedings, 160
Renaissance in England, 2
Returns on gable ends, 50
Revere, Paul, 17, 51
Revolution, American, 19, 46, 59,
62, 67, 79
Richardson, A. G., 238, 248
Robinson, John, 62, 88, 104
Rogers, John, 61
Rogers, Mrs. J. C., 150
Rogers, Richard S., 150

Index

[281]

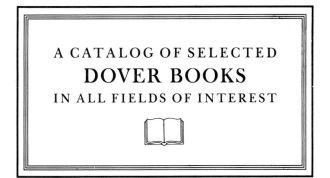

A CATALOG OF SELECTED
DOVER BOOKS
IN ALL FIELDS OF INTEREST

A CATALOG OF SELECTED DOVER
BOOKS IN ALL FIELDS OF INTEREST

CONCERNING THE SPIRITUAL IN ART, Wassily Kandinsky. Pioneering work by father of abstract art. Thoughts on color theory, nature of art. Analysis of earlier masters. 12 illustrations. 80pp. of text. 5⅜ x 8½. 23411-8 Pa. $4.95

ANIMALS: 1,419 Copyright-Free Illustrations of Mammals, Birds, Fish, Insects, etc., Jim Harter (ed.). Clear wood engravings present, in extremely lifelike poses, over 1,000 species of animals. One of the most extensive pictorial sourcebooks of its kind. Captions. Index. 284pp. 9 x 12. 23766-4 Pa. $14.95

CELTIC ART: The Methods of Construction, George Bain. Simple geometric techniques for making Celtic interlacements, spirals, Kells-type initials, animals, humans, etc. Over 500 illustrations. 160pp. 9 x 12. (USO) 22923-8 Pa. $9.95

AN ATLAS OF ANATOMY FOR ARTISTS, Fritz Schider. Most thorough reference work on art anatomy in the world. Hundreds of illustrations, including selections from works by Vesalius, Leonardo, Goya, Ingres, Michelangelo, others. 593 illustrations. 192pp. 7⅛ x 10¼. 20241-0 Pa. $9.95

CELTIC HAND STROKE-BY-STROKE (Irish Half-Uncial from "The Book of Kells"): An Arthur Baker Calligraphy Manual, Arthur Baker. Complete guide to creating each letter of the alphabet in distinctive Celtic manner. Covers hand position, strokes, pens, inks, paper, more. Illustrated. 48pp. 8¼ x 11. 24336-2 Pa. $3.95

EASY ORIGAMI, John Montroll. Charming collection of 32 projects (hat, cup, pelican, piano, swan, many more) specially designed for the novice origami hobbyist. Clearly illustrated easy-to-follow instructions insure that even beginning papercrafters will achieve successful results. 48pp. 8¼ x 11. 27298-2 Pa. $3.50

THE COMPLETE BOOK OF BIRDHOUSE CONSTRUCTION FOR WOOD-WORKERS, Scott D. Campbell. Detailed instructions, illustrations, tables. Also data on bird habitat and instinct patterns. Bibliography. 3 tables. 63 illustrations in 15 figures. 48pp. 5¼ x 8½. 24407-5 Pa. $2.50

BLOOMINGDALE'S ILLUSTRATED 1886 CATALOG: Fashions, Dry Goods and Housewares, Bloomingdale Brothers. Famed merchants' extremely rare catalog depicting about 1,700 products: clothing, housewares, firearms, dry goods, jewelry, more. Invaluable for dating, identifying vintage items. Also, copyright-free graphics for artists, designers. Co-published with Henry Ford Museum & Greenfield Village. 160pp. 8¼ x 11. 25780-0 Pa. $10.95

HISTORIC COSTUME IN PICTURES, Braun & Schneider. Over 1,450 costumed figures in clearly detailed engravings–from dawn of civilization to end of 19th century. Captions. Many folk costumes. 256pp. 8⅜ x 11¾. 23150-X Pa. $12.95

STICKLEY CRAFTSMAN FURNITURE CATALOGS, Gustav Stickley and L. & J. G. Stickley. Beautiful, functional furniture in two authentic catalogs from 1910. 594 illustrations, including 277 photos, show settles, rockers, armchairs, reclining chairs, bookcases, desks, tables. 183pp. 6½ x 9¼. 23838-5 Pa. $11.95

AMERICAN LOCOMOTIVES IN HISTORIC PHOTOGRAPHS: 1858 to 1949, Ron Ziel (ed.). A rare collection of 126 meticulously detailed official photographs, called "builder portraits," of American locomotives that majestically chronicle the rise of steam locomotive power in America. Introduction. Detailed captions. xi + 129pp. 9 x 12. 27393-8 Pa. $13.95

AMERICA'S LIGHTHOUSES: An Illustrated History, Francis Ross Holland, Jr. Delightfully written, profusely illustrated fact-filled survey of over 200 American lighthouses since 1716. History, anecdotes, technological advances, more. 240pp. 8 x 10¾. 25576-X Pa. $12.95

TOWARDS A NEW ARCHITECTURE, Le Corbusier. Pioneering manifesto by founder of "International School." Technical and aesthetic theories, views of industry, economics, relation of form to function, "mass-production split" and much more. Profusely illustrated. 320pp. 6⅛ x 9¼. (USO) 25023-7 Pa. $9.95

HOW THE OTHER HALF LIVES, Jacob Riis. Famous journalistic record, exposing poverty and degradation of New York slums around 1900, by major social reformer. 100 striking and influential photographs. 233pp. 10 x 7⅞. 22012-5 Pa. $11.95

FRUIT KEY AND TWIG KEY TO TREES AND SHRUBS, William M. Harlow. One of the handiest and most widely used identification aids. Fruit key covers 120 deciduous and evergreen species; twig key 160 deciduous species. Easily used. Over 300 photographs. 126pp. 5⅜ x 8½. 20511-8 Pa. $3.95

COMMON BIRD SONGS, Dr. Donald J. Borror. Songs of 60 most common U.S. birds: robins, sparrows, cardinals, bluejays, finches, more–arranged in order of increasing complexity. Up to 9 variations of songs of each species. Cassette and manual 99911-4 $8.95

ORCHIDS AS HOUSE PLANTS, Rebecca Tyson Northen. Grow cattleyas and many other kinds of orchids–in a window, in a case, or under artificial light. 63 illustrations. 148pp. 5⅜ x 8½. 23261-1 Pa. $5.95

MONSTER MAZES, Dave Phillips. Masterful mazes at four levels of difficulty. Avoid deadly perils and evil creatures to find magical treasures. Solutions for all 32 exciting illustrated puzzles. 48pp. 8¼ x 11. 26005-4 Pa. $2.95

MOZART'S DON GIOVANNI (DOVER OPERA LIBRETTO SERIES), Wolfgang Amadeus Mozart. Introduced and translated by Ellen H. Bleiler. Standard Italian libretto, with complete English translation. Convenient and thoroughly portable–an ideal companion for reading along with a recording or the performance itself. Introduction. List of characters. Plot summary. 121pp. 5¼ x 8½. 24944-1 Pa. $3.95

TECHNICAL MANUAL AND DICTIONARY OF CLASSICAL BALLET, Gail Grant. Defines, explains, comments on steps, movements, poses and concepts. 15-page pictorial section. Basic book for student, viewer. 127pp. 5⅜ x 8½. 21843-0 Pa. $4.95

BRASS INSTRUMENTS: Their History and Development, Anthony Baines. Authoritative, updated survey of the evolution of trumpets, trombones, bugles, cornets, French horns, tubas and other brass wind instruments. Over 140 illustrations and 48 music examples. Corrected and updated by author. New preface. Bibliography. 320pp. 5⅜ x 8½. 27574-4 Pa. $9.95

HOLLYWOOD GLAMOR PORTRAITS, John Kobal (ed.). 145 photos from 1926-49. Harlow, Gable, Bogart, Bacall; 94 stars in all. Full background on photographers, technical aspects. 160pp. 8⅜ x 11¼. 23352-9 Pa. $12.95

MAX AND MORITZ, Wilhelm Busch. Great humor classic in both German and English. Also 10 other works: "Cat and Mouse," "Plisch and Plumm," etc. 216pp. 5⅜ x 8½. 20181-3 Pa. $6.95

THE RAVEN AND OTHER FAVORITE POEMS, Edgar Allan Poe. Over 40 of the author's most memorable poems: "The Bells," "Ulalume," "Israfel," "To Helen," "The Conqueror Worm," "Eldorado," "Annabel Lee," many more. Alphabetic lists of titles and first lines. 64pp. 5³⁄₁₆ x 8¼. 26685-0 Pa. $1.00

PERSONAL MEMOIRS OF U. S. GRANT, Ulysses Simpson Grant. Intelligent, deeply moving firsthand account of Civil War campaigns, considered by many the finest military memoirs ever written. Includes letters, historic photographs, maps and more. 528pp. 6⅛ x 9¼. 28587-1 Pa. $12.95

AMULETS AND SUPERSTITIONS, E. A. Wallis Budge. Comprehensive discourse on origin, powers of amulets in many ancient cultures: Arab, Persian Babylonian, Assyrian, Egyptian, Gnostic, Hebrew, Phoenician, Syriac, etc. Covers cross, swastika, crucifix, seals, rings, stones, etc. 584pp. 5⅜ x 8½. 23573-4 Pa. $15.95

RUSSIAN STORIES/PYCCKNE PACCKA3bl: A Dual-Language Book, edited by Gleb Struve. Twelve tales by such masters as Chekhov, Tolstoy, Dostoevsky, Pushkin, others. Excellent word-for-word English translations on facing pages, plus teaching and study aids, Russian/English vocabulary, biographical/critical introductions, more. 416pp. 5⅜ x 8½. 26244-8 Pa. $9.95

PHILADELPHIA THEN AND NOW: 60 Sites Photographed in the Past and Present, Kenneth Finkel and Susan Oyama. Rare photographs of City Hall, Logan Square, Independence Hall, Betsy Ross House, other landmarks juxtaposed with contemporary views. Captures changing face of historic city. Introduction. Captions. 128pp. 8¼ x 11. 25790-8 Pa. $9.95

AIA ARCHITECTURAL GUIDE TO NASSAU AND SUFFOLK COUNTIES, LONG ISLAND, The American Institute of Architects, Long Island Chapter, and the Society for the Preservation of Long Island Antiquities. Comprehensive, well-researched and generously illustrated volume brings to life over three centuries of Long Island's great architectural heritage. More than 240 photographs with authoritative, extensively detailed captions. 176pp. 8¼ x 11. 26946-9 Pa. $14.95

NORTH AMERICAN INDIAN LIFE: Customs and Traditions of 23 Tribes, Elsie Clews Parsons (ed.). 27 fictionalized essays by noted anthropologists examine religion, customs, government, additional facets of life among the Winnebago, Crow, Zuni, Eskimo, other tribes. 480pp. 6⅛ x 9¼. 27377-6 Pa. $10.95

FRANK LLOYD WRIGHT'S HOLLYHOCK HOUSE, Donald Hoffmann. Lavishly illustrated, carefully documented study of one of Wright's most controversial residential designs. Over 120 photographs, floor plans, elevations, etc. Detailed perceptive text by noted Wright scholar. Index. 128pp. 9¼ x 10¾. 27133-1 Pa. $11.95

THE MALE AND FEMALE FIGURE IN MOTION: 60 Classic Photographic Sequences, Eadweard Muybridge. 60 true-action photographs of men and women walking, running, climbing, bending, turning, etc., reproduced from rare 19th-century masterpiece. vi + 121pp. 9 x 12. 24745-7 Pa. $10.95

1001 QUESTIONS ANSWERED ABOUT THE SEASHORE, N. J. Berrill and Jacquelyn Berrill. Queries answered about dolphins, sea snails, sponges, starfish, fishes, shore birds, many others. Covers appearance, breeding, growth, feeding, much more. 305pp. 5¼ x 8¼. 23366-9 Pa. $9.95

GUIDE TO OWL WATCHING IN NORTH AMERICA, Donald S. Heintzelman. Superb guide offers complete data and descriptions of 19 species: barn owl, screech owl, snowy owl, many more. Expert coverage of owl-watching equipment, conservation, migrations and invasions, etc. Guide to observing sites. 84 illustrations. xiii + 193pp. 5⅜ x 8½. 27344-X Pa. $8.95

MEDICINAL AND OTHER USES OF NORTH AMERICAN PLANTS: A Historical Survey with Special Reference to the Eastern Indian Tribes, Charlotte Erichsen-Brown. Chronological historical citations document 500 years of usage of plants, trees, shrubs native to eastern Canada, northeastern U.S. Also complete identifying information. 343 illustrations. 544pp. 6½ x 9¼. 25951-X Pa. $12.95

STORYBOOK MAZES, Dave Phillips. 23 stories and mazes on two-page spreads: Wizard of Oz, Treasure Island, Robin Hood, etc. Solutions. 64pp. 8¼ x 11. 23628-5 Pa. $2.95

NEGRO FOLK MUSIC, U.S.A., Harold Courlander. Noted folklorist's scholarly yet readable analysis of rich and varied musical tradition. Includes authentic versions of over 40 folk songs. Valuable bibliography and discography. xi + 324pp. 5⅜ x 8½. 27350-4 Pa. $9.95

MOVIE-STAR PORTRAITS OF THE FORTIES, John Kobal (ed.). 163 glamor, studio photos of 106 stars of the 1940s: Rita Hayworth, Ava Gardner, Marlon Brando, Clark Gable, many more. 176pp. 8⅜ x 11¼. 23546-7 Pa. $14.95

BENCHLEY LOST AND FOUND, Robert Benchley. Finest humor from early 30s, about pet peeves, child psychologists, post office and others. Mostly unavailable elsewhere. 73 illustrations by Peter Arno and others. 183pp. 5⅜ x 8½. 22410-4 Pa. $6.95

YEKL and THE IMPORTED BRIDEGROOM AND OTHER STORIES OF YIDDISH NEW YORK, Abraham Cahan. Film Hester Street based on Yekl (1896). Novel, other stories among first about Jewish immigrants on N.Y.'s East Side. 240pp. 5⅜ x 8½. 22427-9 Pa. $6.95

SELECTED POEMS, Walt Whitman. Generous sampling from *Leaves of Grass*. Twenty-four poems include "I Hear America Singing," "Song of the Open Road," "I Sing the Body Electric," "When Lilacs Last in the Dooryard Bloom'd," "O Captain! My Captain!"–all reprinted from an authoritative edition. Lists of titles and first lines. 128pp. 5$\frac{3}{16}$ x 8¼. 26878-0 Pa. $1.00

THE BEST TALES OF HOFFMANN, E. T. A. Hoffmann. 10 of Hoffmann's most important stories: "Nutcracker and the King of Mice," "The Golden Flowerpot," etc. 458pp. 5⅜ x 8½. 21793-0 Pa. $9.95

FROM FETISH TO GOD IN ANCIENT EGYPT, E. A. Wallis Budge. Rich detailed survey of Egyptian conception of "God" and gods, magic, cult of animals, Osiris, more. Also, superb English translations of hymns and legends. 240 illustrations. 545pp. 5⅜ x 8½. 25803-3 Pa. $13.95

FRENCH STORIES/CONTES FRANÇAIS: A Dual-Language Book, Wallace Fowlie. Ten stories by French masters, Voltaire to Camus: "Micromegas" by Voltaire; "The Atheist's Mass" by Balzac; "Minuet" by de Maupassant; "The Guest" by Camus, six more. Excellent English translations on facing pages. Also French-English vocabulary list, exercises, more. 352pp. 5⅜ x 8½. 26443-2 Pa. $9.95

CHICAGO AT THE TURN OF THE CENTURY IN PHOTOGRAPHS: 122 Historic Views from the Collections of the Chicago Historical Society, Larry A. Viskochil. Rare large-format prints offer detailed views of City Hall, State Street, the Loop, Hull House, Union Station, many other landmarks, circa 1904-1913. Introduction. Captions. Maps. 144pp. 9⅜ x 12¼. 24656-6 Pa. $12.95

OLD BROOKLYN IN EARLY PHOTOGRAPHS, 1865-1929, William Lee Younger. Luna Park, Gravesend race track, construction of Grand Army Plaza, moving of Hotel Brighton, etc. 157 previously unpublished photographs. 165pp. 8⅞ x 11¾. 23587-4 Pa. $13.95

THE MYTHS OF THE NORTH AMERICAN INDIANS, Lewis Spence. Rich anthology of the myths and legends of the Algonquins, Iroquois, Pawnees and Sioux, prefaced by an extensive historical and ethnological commentary. 36 illustrations. 480pp. 5⅜ x 8½. 25967-6 Pa. $10.95

AN ENCYCLOPEDIA OF BATTLES: Accounts of Over 1,560 Battles from 1479 B.C. to the Present, David Eggenberger. Essential details of every major battle in recorded history from the first battle of Megiddo in 1479 B.C. to Grenada in 1984. List of Battle Maps. New Appendix covering the years 1967-1984. Index. 99 illustrations. 544pp. 6½ x 9¼. 24913-1 Pa. $16.95

SAILING ALONE AROUND THE WORLD, Captain Joshua Slocum. First man to sail around the world, alone, in small boat. One of great feats of seamanship told in delightful manner. 67 illustrations. 294pp. 5⅜ x 8½. 20326-3 Pa. $6.95

ANARCHISM AND OTHER ESSAYS, Emma Goldman. Powerful, penetrating, prophetic essays on direct action, role of minorities, prison reform, puritan hypocrisy, violence, etc. 271pp. 5⅜ x 8½. 22484-8 Pa. $7.95

MYTHS OF THE HINDUS AND BUDDHISTS, Ananda K. Coomaraswamy and Sister Nivedita. Great stories of the epics; deeds of Krishna, Shiva, taken from puranas, Vedas, folk tales; etc. 32 illustrations. 400pp. 5⅜ x 8½. 21759-0 Pa. $12.95

BEYOND PSYCHOLOGY, Otto Rank. Fear of death, desire of immortality, nature of sexuality, social organization, creativity, according to Rankian system. 291pp. 5⅜ x 8½. 20485-5 Pa. $8.95

A THEOLOGICO-POLITICAL TREATISE, Benedict Spinoza. Also contains unfinished Political Treatise. Great classic on religious liberty, theory of government on common consent. R. Elwes translation. Total of 421pp. 5⅜ x 8½. 20249-6 Pa. $9.95

MY BONDAGE AND MY FREEDOM, Frederick Douglass. Born a slave, Douglass became outspoken force in antislavery movement. The best of Douglass' autobiographies. Graphic description of slave life. 464pp. 5⅜ x 8½. 22457-0 Pa. $8.95

FOLLOWING THE EQUATOR: A Journey Around the World, Mark Twain. Fascinating humorous account of 1897 voyage to Hawaii, Australia, India, New Zealand, etc. Ironic, bemused reports on peoples, customs, climate, flora and fauna, politics, much more. 197 illustrations. 720pp. 5⅜ x 8½. 26113-1 Pa. $15.95

THE PEOPLE CALLED SHAKERS, Edward D. Andrews. Definitive study of Shakers: origins, beliefs, practices, dances, social organization, furniture and crafts, etc. 33 illustrations. 351pp. 5⅜ x 8½. 21081-2 Pa. $8.95

THE MYTHS OF GREECE AND ROME, H. A. Guerber. A classic of mythology, generously illustrated, long prized for its simple, graphic, accurate retelling of the principal myths of Greece and Rome, and for its commentary on their origins and significance. With 64 illustrations by Michelangelo, Raphael, Titian, Rubens, Canova, Bernini and others. 480pp. 5⅜ x 8½. 27584-1 Pa. $9.95

PSYCHOLOGY OF MUSIC, Carl E. Seashore. Classic work discusses music as a medium from psychological viewpoint. Clear treatment of physical acoustics, auditory apparatus, sound perception, development of musical skills, nature of musical feeling, host of other topics. 88 figures. 408pp. 5⅜ x 8½. 21851-1 Pa. $11.95

THE PHILOSOPHY OF HISTORY, Georg W. Hegel. Great classic of Western thought develops concept that history is not chance but rational process, the evolution of freedom. 457pp. 5⅜ x 8½. 20112-0 Pa. $9.95

THE BOOK OF TEA, Kakuzo Okakura. Minor classic of the Orient: entertaining, charming explanation, interpretation of traditional Japanese culture in terms of tea ceremony. 94pp. 5⅜ x 8½. 20070-1 Pa. $3.95

LIFE IN ANCIENT EGYPT, Adolf Erman. Fullest, most thorough, detailed older account with much not in more recent books, domestic life, religion, magic, medicine, commerce, much more. Many illustrations reproduce tomb paintings, carvings, hieroglyphs, etc. 597pp. 5⅜ x 8½. 22632-8 Pa. $12.95

SUNDIALS, Their Theory and Construction, Albert Waugh. Far and away the best, most thorough coverage of ideas, mathematics concerned, types, construction, adjusting anywhere. Simple, nontechnical treatment allows even children to build several of these dials. Over 100 illustrations. 230pp. 5⅜ x 8½. 22947-5 Pa. $8.95

DYNAMICS OF FLUIDS IN POROUS MEDIA, Jacob Bear. For advanced students of ground water hydrology, soil mechanics and physics, drainage and irrigation engineering, and more. 335 illustrations. Exercises, with answers. 784pp. 6⅛ x 9¼. 65675-6 Pa. $19.95

SONGS OF EXPERIENCE: Facsimile Reproduction with 26 Plates in Full Color, William Blake. 26 full-color plates from a rare 1826 edition. Includes "TheTyger," "London," "Holy Thursday," and other poems. Printed text of poems. 48pp. 5¼ x 7. 24636-1 Pa. $4.95

OLD-TIME VIGNETTES IN FULL COLOR, Carol Belanger Grafton (ed.). Over 390 charming, often sentimental illustrations, selected from archives of Victorian graphics—pretty women posing, children playing, food, flowers, kittens and puppies, smiling cherubs, birds and butterflies, much more. All copyright-free. 48pp. 9¼ x 12¼. 27269-9 Pa. $7.95

PERSPECTIVE FOR ARTISTS, Rex Vicat Cole. Depth, perspective of sky and sea, shadows, much more, not usually covered. 391 diagrams, 81 reproductions of drawings and paintings. 279pp. 5⅜ x 8½. 22487-2 Pa. $7.95

DRAWING THE LIVING FIGURE, Joseph Sheppard. Innovative approach to artistic anatomy focuses on specifics of surface anatomy, rather than muscles and bones. Over 170 drawings of live models in front, back and side views, and in widely varying poses. Accompanying diagrams. 177 illustrations. Introduction. Index. 144pp. 8⅝ x11¼. 26723-7 Pa. $8.95

GOTHIC AND OLD ENGLISH ALPHABETS: 100 Complete Fonts, Dan X. Solo. Add power, elegance to posters, signs, other graphics with 100 stunning copyright-free alphabets: Blackstone, Dolbey, Germania, 97 more–including many lower-case, numerals, punctuation marks. 104pp. 8⅛ x 11. 24695-7 Pa. $8.95

HOW TO DO BEADWORK, Mary White. Fundamental book on craft from simple projects to five-bead chains and woven works. 106 illustrations. 142pp. 5⅜ x 8. 20697-1 Pa. $5.95

THE BOOK OF WOOD CARVING, Charles Marshall Sayers. Finest book for beginners discusses fundamentals and offers 34 designs. "Absolutely first rate . . . well thought out and well executed."–E. J. Tangerman. 118pp. 7¾ x 10⅝. 23654-4 Pa. $7.95

ILLUSTRATED CATALOG OF CIVIL WAR MILITARY GOODS: Union Army Weapons, Insignia, Uniform Accessories, and Other Equipment, Schuyler, Hartley, and Graham. Rare, profusely illustrated 1846 catalog includes Union Army uniform and dress regulations, arms and ammunition, coats, insignia, flags, swords, rifles, etc. 226 illustrations. 160pp. 9 x 12. 24939-5 Pa. $10.95

WOMEN'S FASHIONS OF THE EARLY 1900s: An Unabridged Republication of "New York Fashions, 1909," National Cloak & Suit Co. Rare catalog of mail-order fashions documents women's and children's clothing styles shortly after the turn of the century. Captions offer full descriptions, prices. Invaluable resource for fashion, costume historians. Approximately 725 illustrations. 128pp. 8⅜ x 11¼. 27276-1 Pa. $11.95

THE 1912 AND 1915 GUSTAV STICKLEY FURNITURE CATALOGS, Gustav Stickley. With over 200 detailed illustrations and descriptions, these two catalogs are essential reading and reference materials and identification guides for Stickley furniture. Captions cite materials, dimensions and prices. 112pp. 6½ x 9¼. 26676-1 Pa. $9.95

EARLY AMERICAN LOCOMOTIVES, John H. White, Jr. Finest locomotive engravings from early 19th century: historical (1804–74), main-line (after 1870), special, foreign, etc. 147 plates. 142pp. 11⅜ x 8¼. 22772-3 Pa. $10.95

THE TALL SHIPS OF TODAY IN PHOTOGRAPHS, Frank O. Braynard. Lavishly illustrated tribute to nearly 100 majestic contemporary sailing vessels: Amerigo Vespucci, Clearwater, Constitution, Eagle, Mayflower, Sea Cloud, Victory, many more. Authoritative captions provide statistics, background on each ship. 190 black-and-white photographs and illustrations. Introduction. 128pp. 8⅞ x 11¾. 27163-3 Pa. $14.95

EARLY NINETEENTH-CENTURY CRAFTS AND TRADES, Peter Stockham (ed.). Extremely rare 1807 volume describes to youngsters the crafts and trades of the day: brickmaker, weaver, dressmaker, bookbinder, ropemaker, saddler, many more. Quaint prose, charming illustrations for each craft. 20 black-and-white line illustrations. 192pp. 4⅝ x 6. 27293-1 Pa. $4.95

VICTORIAN FASHIONS AND COSTUMES FROM HARPER'S BAZAR, 1867–1898, Stella Blum (ed.). Day costumes, evening wear, sports clothes, shoes, hats, other accessories in over 1,000 detailed engravings. 320pp. 9⅜ x 12¼.
22990-4 Pa. $15.95

GUSTAV STICKLEY, THE CRAFTSMAN, Mary Ann Smith. Superb study surveys broad scope of Stickley's achievement, especially in architecture. Design philosophy, rise and fall of the Craftsman empire, descriptions and floor plans for many Craftsman houses, more. 86 black-and-white halftones. 31 line illustrations. Introduction 208pp. 6½ x 9¼. 27210-9 Pa. $9.95

THE LONG ISLAND RAIL ROAD IN EARLY PHOTOGRAPHS, Ron Ziel. Over 220 rare photos, informative text document origin (1844) and development of rail service on Long Island. Vintage views of early trains, locomotives, stations, passengers, crews, much more. Captions. 8⅞ x 11¾. 26301-0 Pa. $13.95

THE BOOK OF OLD SHIPS: From Egyptian Galleys to Clipper Ships, Henry B. Culver. Superb, authoritative history of sailing vessels, with 80 magnificent line illustrations. Galley, bark, caravel, longship, whaler, many more. Detailed, informative text on each vessel by noted naval historian. Introduction. 256pp. 5⅜ x 8½.
27332-6 Pa. $7.95

TEN BOOKS ON ARCHITECTURE, Vitruvius. The most important book ever written on architecture. Early Roman aesthetics, technology, classical orders, site selection, all other aspects. Morgan translation. 331pp. 5⅜ x 8½. 20645-9 Pa. $8.95

THE HUMAN FIGURE IN MOTION, Eadweard Muybridge. More than 4,500 stopped-action photos, in action series, showing undraped men, women, children jumping, lying down, throwing, sitting, wrestling, carrying, etc. 390pp. 7⅞ x 10⅝.
20204-6 Clothbd. $27.95

TREES OF THE EASTERN AND CENTRAL UNITED STATES AND CANADA, William M. Harlow. Best one-volume guide to 140 trees. Full descriptions, woodlore, range, etc. Over 600 illustrations. Handy size. 288pp. 4½ x 6⅜.
20395-6 Pa. $6.95

SONGS OF WESTERN BIRDS, Dr. Donald J. Borror. Complete song and call repertoire of 60 western species, including flycatchers, juncoes, cactus wrens, many more–includes fully illustrated booklet. Cassette and manual 99913-0 $8.95

GROWING AND USING HERBS AND SPICES, Milo Miloradovich. Versatile handbook provides all the information needed for cultivation and use of all the herbs and spices available in North America. 4 illustrations. Index. Glossary. 236pp. 5⅜ x 8½.
25058-X Pa. $7.95

BIG BOOK OF MAZES AND LABYRINTHS, Walter Shepherd. 50 mazes and labyrinths in all–classical, solid, ripple, and more–in one great volume. Perfect inexpensive puzzler for clever youngsters. Full solutions. 112pp. 8⅛ x 11.
22951-3 Pa. $4.95

PIANO TUNING, J. Cree Fischer. Clearest, best book for beginner, amateur. Simple repairs, raising dropped notes, tuning by easy method of flattened fifths. No previous skills needed. 4 illustrations. 201pp. 5⅜ x 8½. 23267-0 Pa. $6.95

A SOURCE BOOK IN THEATRICAL HISTORY, A. M. Nagler. Contemporary observers on acting, directing, make-up, costuming, stage props, machinery, scene design, from Ancient Greece to Chekhov. 611pp. 5⅜ x 8½. 20515-0 Pa. $12.95

THE COMPLETE NONSENSE OF EDWARD LEAR, Edward Lear. All nonsense limericks, zany alphabets, Owl and Pussycat, songs, nonsense botany, etc., illustrated by Lear. Total of 320pp. 5⅜ x 8½. (USO) 20167-8 Pa. $7.95

VICTORIAN PARLOUR POETRY: An Annotated Anthology, Michael R. Turner. 117 gems by Longfellow, Tennyson, Browning, many lesser-known poets. "The Village Blacksmith," "Curfew Must Not Ring Tonight," "Only a Baby Small," dozens more, often difficult to find elsewhere. Index of poets, titles, first lines. xxiii + 325pp. 5⅝ x 8¼. 27044-0 Pa. $8.95

DUBLINERS, James Joyce. Fifteen stories offer vivid, tightly focused observations of the lives of Dublin's poorer classes. At least one, "The Dead," is considered a masterpiece. Reprinted complete and unabridged from standard edition. 160pp. 5$\frac{3}{16}$ x 8¼. 26870-5 Pa. $1.00

THE HAUNTED MONASTERY and THE CHINESE MAZE MURDERS, Robert van Gulik. Two full novels by van Gulik, set in 7th-century China, continue adventures of Judge Dee and his companions. An evil Taoist monastery, seemingly supernatural events; overgrown topiary maze hides strange crimes. 27 illustrations. 328pp. 5⅜ x 8½. 23502-5 Pa. $8.95

THE BOOK OF THE SACRED MAGIC OF ABRAMELIN THE MAGE, translated by S. MacGregor Mathers. Medieval manuscript of ceremonial magic. Basic document in Aleister Crowley, Golden Dawn groups. 268pp. 5⅜ x 8½. 23211-5 Pa. $9.95

NEW RUSSIAN-ENGLISH AND ENGLISH-RUSSIAN DICTIONARY, M. A. O'Brien. This is a remarkably handy Russian dictionary, containing a surprising amount of information, including over 70,000 entries. 366pp. 4½ x 6⅛. 20208-9 Pa. $10.95

HISTORIC HOMES OF THE AMERICAN PRESIDENTS, Second, Revised Edition, Irvin Haas. A traveler's guide to American Presidential homes, most open to the public, depicting and describing homes occupied by every American President from George Washington to George Bush. With visiting hours, admission charges, travel routes. 175 photographs. Index. 160pp. 8¼ x 11. 26751-2 Pa. $11.95

NEW YORK IN THE FORTIES, Andreas Feininger. 162 brilliant photographs by the well-known photographer, formerly with *Life* magazine. Commuters, shoppers, Times Square at night, much else from city at its peak. Captions by John von Hartz. 181pp. 9¼ x 10¾. 23585-8 Pa. $13.95

INDIAN SIGN LANGUAGE, William Tomkins. Over 525 signs developed by Sioux and other tribes. Written instructions and diagrams. Also 290 pictographs. 111pp. 6⅛ x 9¼. 22029-X Pa. $3.95

ANATOMY: A Complete Guide for Artists, Joseph Sheppard. A master of figure drawing shows artists how to render human anatomy convincingly. Over 460 illustrations. 224pp. 8⅜ x 11¼. 27279-6 Pa. $11.95

MEDIEVAL CALLIGRAPHY: Its History and Technique, Marc Drogin. Spirited history, comprehensive instruction manual covers 13 styles (ca. 4th century thru 15th). Excellent photographs; directions for duplicating medieval techniques with modern tools. 224pp. 8⅜ x 11¼. 26142-5 Pa. $12.95

DRIED FLOWERS: How to Prepare Them, Sarah Whitlock and Martha Rankin. Complete instructions on how to use silica gel, meal and borax, perlite aggregate, sand and borax, glycerine and water to create attractive permanent flower arrangements. 12 illustrations. 32pp. 5⅜ x 8½. 21802-3 Pa. $1.00

EASY-TO-MAKE BIRD FEEDERS FOR WOODWORKERS, Scott D. Campbell. Detailed, simple-to-use guide for designing, constructing, caring for and using feeders. Text, illustrations for 12 classic and contemporary designs. 96pp. 5⅜ x 8½. 25847-5 Pa. $3.95

SCOTTISH WONDER TALES FROM MYTH AND LEGEND, Donald A. Mackenzie. 16 lively tales tell of giants rumbling down mountainsides, of a magic wand that turns stone pillars into warriors, of gods and goddesses, evil hags, powerful forces and more. 240pp. 5⅜ x 8½. 29677-6 Pa. $6.95

THE HISTORY OF UNDERCLOTHES, C. Willett Cunnington and Phyllis Cunnington. Fascinating, well-documented survey covering six centuries of English undergarments, enhanced with over 100 illustrations: 12th-century laced-up bodice, footed long drawers (1795), 19th-century bustles, l9th-century corsets for men, Victorian "bust improvers," much more. 272pp. 5⅜ x 8¼. 27124-2 Pa. $9.95

ARTS AND CRAFTS FURNITURE: The Complete Brooks Catalog of 1912, Brooks Manufacturing Co. Photos and detailed descriptions of more than 150 now very collectible furniture designs from the Arts and Crafts movement depict davenports, settees, buffets, desks, tables, chairs, bedsteads, dressers and more, all built of solid, quarter-sawed oak. Invaluable for students and enthusiasts of antiques, Americana and the decorative arts. 80pp. 6½ x 9¼. 27471-3 Pa. $8.95

HOW WE INVENTED THE AIRPLANE: An Illustrated History, Orville Wright. Fascinating firsthand account covers early experiments, construction of planes and motors, first flights, much more. Introduction and commentary by Fred C. Kelly. 76 photographs. 96pp. 8¼ x 11. 25662-6 Pa. $8.95

THE ARTS OF THE SAILOR: Knotting, Splicing and Ropework, Hervey Garrett Smith. Indispensable shipboard reference covers tools, basic knots and useful hitches; handsewing and canvas work, more. Over 100 illustrations. Delightful reading for sea lovers. 256pp. 5⅜ x 8½. 26440-8 Pa. $8.95

FRANK LLOYD WRIGHT'S FALLINGWATER: The House and Its History, Second, Revised Edition, Donald Hoffmann. A total revision—both in text and illustrations—of the standard document on Fallingwater, the boldest, most personal architectural statement of Wright's mature years, updated with valuable new material from the recently opened Frank Lloyd Wright Archives. "Fascinating"—*The New York Times*. 116 illustrations. 128pp. 9¼ x 10¾. 27430-6 Pa. $12.95

PHOTOGRAPHIC SKETCHBOOK OF THE CIVIL WAR, Alexander Gardner. 100 photos taken on field during the Civil War. Famous shots of Manassas Harper's Ferry, Lincoln, Richmond, slave pens, etc. 244pp. 10⅝ x 8¼. 22731-6 Pa. $10.95

FIVE ACRES AND INDEPENDENCE, Maurice G. Kains. Great back-to-the-land classic explains basics of self-sufficient farming. The one book to get. 95 illustrations. 397pp. 5⅜ x 8½. 20974-1 Pa. $7.95

SONGS OF EASTERN BIRDS, Dr. Donald J. Borror. Songs and calls of 60 species most common to eastern U.S.: warblers, woodpeckers, flycatchers, thrushes, larks, many more in high-quality recording. Cassette and manual 99912-2 $9.95

A MODERN HERBAL, Margaret Grieve. Much the fullest, most exact, most useful compilation of herbal material. Gigantic alphabetical encyclopedia, from aconite to zedoary, gives botanical information, medical properties, folklore, economic uses, much else. Indispensable to serious reader. 161 illustrations. 888pp. 6½ x 9¼. 2-vol. set. (USO) Vol. I: 22798-7 Pa. $9.95
Vol. II: 22799-5 Pa. $9.95

HIDDEN TREASURE MAZE BOOK, Dave Phillips. Solve 34 challenging mazes accompanied by heroic tales of adventure. Evil dragons, people-eating plants, blood-thirsty giants, many more dangerous adversaries lurk at every twist and turn. 34 mazes, stories, solutions. 48pp. 8¼ x 11. 24566-7 Pa. $2.95

LETTERS OF W. A. MOZART, Wolfgang A. Mozart. Remarkable letters show bawdy wit, humor, imagination, musical insights, contemporary musical world; includes some letters from Leopold Mozart. 276pp. 5⅜ x 8½. 22859-2 Pa. $7.95

BASIC PRINCIPLES OF CLASSICAL BALLET, Agrippina Vaganova. Great Russian theoretician, teacher explains methods for teaching classical ballet. 118 illustrations. 175pp. 5⅜ x 8½. 22036-2 Pa. $5.95

THE JUMPING FROG, Mark Twain. Revenge edition. The original story of The Celebrated Jumping Frog of Calaveras County, a hapless French translation, and Twain's hilarious "retranslation" from the French. 12 illustrations. 66pp. 5⅜ x 8½. 22686-7 Pa. $3.95

BEST REMEMBERED POEMS, Martin Gardner (ed.). The 126 poems in this superb collection of 19th- and 20th-century British and American verse range from Shelley's "To a Skylark" to the impassioned "Renascence" of Edna St. Vincent Millay and to Edward Lear's whimsical "The Owl and the Pussycat." 224pp. 5⅜ x 8½. 27165-X Pa. $5.95

COMPLETE SONNETS, William Shakespeare. Over 150 exquisite poems deal with love, friendship, the tyranny of time, beauty's evanescence, death and other themes in language of remarkable power, precision and beauty. Glossary of archaic terms. 80pp. 5$\frac{3}{16}$ x 8¼. 26686-9 Pa. $1.00

BODIES IN A BOOKSHOP, R. T. Campbell. Challenging mystery of blackmail and murder with ingenious plot and superbly drawn characters. In the best tradition of British suspense fiction. 192pp. 5⅜ x 8½. 24720-1 Pa. $6.95

THE WIT AND HUMOR OF OSCAR WILDE, Alvin Redman (ed.). More than 1,000 ripostes, paradoxes, wisecracks: Work is the curse of the drinking classes; I can resist everything except temptation; etc. 258pp. 5⅜ x 8½.   20602-5 Pa. $6.95

SHAKESPEARE LEXICON AND QUOTATION DICTIONARY, Alexander Schmidt. Full definitions, locations, shades of meaning in every word in plays and poems. More than 50,000 exact quotations. 1,485pp. 6½ x 9¼. 2-vol. set.
Vol. 1: 22726-X Pa. $17.95
Vol. 2: 22727-8 Pa. $17.95

SELECTED POEMS, Emily Dickinson. Over 100 best-known, best-loved poems by one of America's foremost poets, reprinted from authoritative early editions. No comparable edition at this price. Index of first lines. 64pp. 5³⁄₁₆ x 8¼.
26466-1 Pa. $1.00

CELEBRATED CASES OF JUDGE DEE (DEE GOONG AN), translated by Robert van Gulik. Authentic 18th-century Chinese detective novel; Dee and associates solve three interlocked cases. Led to van Gulik's own stories with same characters. Extensive introduction. 9 illustrations. 237pp. 5⅜ x 8½.   23337-5 Pa. $7.95

THE MALLEUS MALEFICARUM OF KRAMER AND SPRENGER, translated by Montague Summers. Full text of most important witchhunter's "bible," used by both Catholics and Protestants. 278pp. 6⅝ x 10.   22802-9 Pa. $12.95

SPANISH STORIES/CUENTOS ESPAÑOLES: A Dual-Language Book, Angel Flores (ed.). Unique format offers 13 great stories in Spanish by Cervantes, Borges, others. Faithful English translations on facing pages. 352pp. 5⅜ x 8½.
25399-6 Pa. $8.95

THE CHICAGO WORLD'S FAIR OF 1893: A Photographic Record, Stanley Appelbaum (ed.). 128 rare photos show 200 buildings, Beaux-Arts architecture, Midway, original Ferris Wheel, Edison's kinetoscope, more. Architectural emphasis; full text. 116pp. 8¼ x 11.   23990-X Pa. $9.95

OLD QUEENS, N.Y., IN EARLY PHOTOGRAPHS, Vincent F. Seyfried and William Asadorian. Over 160 rare photographs of Maspeth, Jamaica, Jackson Heights, and other areas. Vintage views of DeWitt Clinton mansion, 1939 World's Fair and more. Captions. 192pp. 8⅞ x 11.   26358-4 Pa. $12.95

CAPTURED BY THE INDIANS: 15 Firsthand Accounts, 1750-1870, Frederick Drimmer. Astounding true historical accounts of grisly torture, bloody conflicts, relentless pursuits, miraculous escapes and more, by people who lived to tell the tale. 384pp. 5⅜ x 8½.   24901-8 Pa. $8.95

THE WORLD'S GREAT SPEECHES, Lewis Copeland and Lawrence W. Lamm (eds.). Vast collection of 278 speeches of Greeks to 1970. Powerful and effective models; unique look at history. 842pp. 5⅜ x 8½.   20468-5 Pa. $14.95

THE BOOK OF THE SWORD, Sir Richard F. Burton. Great Victorian scholar/adventurer's eloquent, erudite history of the "queen of weapons"–from prehistory to early Roman Empire. Evolution and development of early swords, variations (sabre, broadsword, cutlass, scimitar, etc.), much more. 336pp. 6⅛ x 9¼.
25434-8 Pa. $9.95

THE INFLUENCE OF SEA POWER UPON HISTORY, 1660–1783, A. T. Mahan. Influential classic of naval history and tactics still used as text in war colleges. First paperback edition. 4 maps. 24 battle plans. 640pp. 5⅜ x 8½. 25509-3 Pa. $14.95

THE STORY OF THE TITANIC AS TOLD BY ITS SURVIVORS, Jack Winocour (ed.). What it was really like. Panic, despair, shocking inefficiency, and a little heroism. More thrilling than any fictional account. 26 illustrations. 320pp. 5⅜ x 8½. 20610-6 Pa. $8.95

FAIRY AND FOLK TALES OF THE IRISH PEASANTRY, William Butler Yeats (ed.). Treasury of 64 tales from the twilight world of Celtic myth and legend: "The Soul Cages," "The Kildare Pooka," "King O'Toole and his Goose," many more. Introduction and Notes by W. B. Yeats. 352pp. 5⅜ x 8½. 26941-8 Pa. $8.95

BUDDHIST MAHAYANA TEXTS, E. B. Cowell and Others (eds.). Superb, accurate translations of basic documents in Mahayana Buddhism, highly important in history of religions. The Buddha-karita of Asvaghosha, Larger Sukhavativyuha, more. 448pp. 5⅜ x 8½. 25552-2 Pa. $12.95

ONE TWO THREE . . . INFINITY: Facts and Speculations of Science, George Gamow. Great physicist's fascinating, readable overview of contemporary science: number theory, relativity, fourth dimension, entropy, genes, atomic structure, much more. 128 illustrations. Index. 352pp. 5⅜ x 8½. 25664-2 Pa. $8.95

ENGINEERING IN HISTORY, Richard Shelton Kirby, et al. Broad, nontechnical survey of history's major technological advances: birth of Greek science, industrial revolution, electricity and applied science, 20th-century automation, much more. 181 illustrations. ". . . excellent . . ."–*Isis.* Bibliography. vii + 530pp. 5⅜ x 8¼. 26412-2 Pa. $14.95

DALÍ ON MODERN ART: The Cuckolds of Antiquated Modern Art, Salvador Dalí. Influential painter skewers modern art and its practitioners. Outrageous evaluations of Picasso, Cézanne, Turner, more. 15 renderings of paintings discussed. 44 calligraphic decorations by Dalí. 96pp. 5⅜ x 8½. (USO) 29220-7 Pa. $4.95

ANTIQUE PLAYING CARDS: A Pictorial History, Henry René D'Allemagne. Over 900 elaborate, decorative images from rare playing cards (14th–20th centuries): Bacchus, death, dancing dogs, hunting scenes, royal coats of arms, players cheating, much more. 96pp. 9¼ x 12¼. 29265-7 Pa. $12.95

MAKING FURNITURE MASTERPIECES: 30 Projects with Measured Drawings, Franklin H. Gottshall. Step-by-step instructions, illustrations for constructing handsome, useful pieces, among them a Sheraton desk, Chippendale chair, Spanish desk, Queen Anne table and a William and Mary dressing mirror. 224pp. 8⅛ x 11¼. 29338-6 Pa. $13.95

THE FOSSIL BOOK: A Record of Prehistoric Life, Patricia V. Rich et al. Profusely illustrated definitive guide covers everything from single-celled organisms and dinosaurs to birds and mammals and the interplay between climate and man. Over 1,500 illustrations. 760pp. 7½ x 10⅛. 29371-8 Pa. $29.95

Prices subject to change without notice.

Available at your book dealer or write for free catalog to Dept. GI, Dover Publications, Inc., 31 East 2nd St., Mineola, N.Y. 11501. Dover publishes more than 500 books each year on science, elementary and advanced mathematics, biology, music, art, literary history, social sciences and other areas.